A CASE STUDY APPROACH TO HUMAN RESOURCES MANAGEMENT

A CASE STUDY APPROACH TO HUMAN RESOURCES MANAGEMENT

Dr. SORAB SADRI

Ph.D. (London) M.Sc. Econs. (LSE)
PGDBM (XLRI) PGDIR & W Hons. (XLRI)

Director
Alard Institute of Management Sciences
S. No. 50, Marunje, Near Infotech Park, Pune — 411 027.

Himalaya Publishing House

MUMBAI • NEW DELHI • NAGPUR • BENGALURU • HYDERABAD • CHENNAI • PUNE
LUCKNOW • AHMEDABAD • ERNAKULAM • BHUBANESWAR • INDORE • KOLKATA • GUWAHATI

First Edition : 2005
Reprint : 2005
Reprint : 2011
Reprint : 2013

Published by : Mrs. Meena Pandey for **Himalaya Publishing House Pvt. Ltd.,**
"Ramdoot", Dr. Bhalerao Marg, Girgaon, **Mumbai - 400 004.**
Phone: 022-23860170/23863863, Fax: 022-23877178
E-mail: himpub@vsnl.com; Website: www.himpub.com

Branch Offices :

New Delhi : "Pooja Apartments", 4-B, Murari Lal Street, Ansari Road, Darya Ganj, New Delhi - 110 002. Phone: 011-23270392, 23278631; Fax: 011-23256286

Nagpur : Kundanlal Chandak Industrial Estate, Ghat Road, Nagpur - 440 018. Phone: 0712-2738731, 3296733; Telefax: 0712-2721215

Bengaluru : No. 16/1 (Old 12/1), 1st Floor, Next to Hotel Highlands, Madhava Nagar, Race Course Road, Bengaluru - 560 001. Phone: 080-32919385; Telefax: 080-22286611

Hyderabad : No. 3-4-184, Lingampally, Besides Raghavendra Swamy Matham, Kachiguda, Hyderabad - 500 027. Phone: 040-27560041, 27550139; Mobile: 09390905282

Chennai : No. 8/2, Modley 2nd Street, Ground Floor, T. Nagar, Chennai - 600 017. Phone: 044-28144004/28144005; Mobile: 09345345051

Pune : First Floor, "Laksha" Apartment, No. 527, Mehunpura, Shaniwarpeth (Near Prabhat Theatre), Pune - 411 030. Phone: 020-24496323/24496333; Mobile: 09370579333

Lucknow : House No. 731, Sehkhupura Colony, Near B.D. Convent School, Lucknow -226024. Mobile : 09307501549

Ahmedabad : 114, "SHAIL", 1st Floor, Opp. Madhu Sudan House, C.G. Road, Navrang Pura, Ahmedabad - 380 009. Phone: 079-26560126; Mobile: 09377088847

Ernakulam : 39/104 A, Lakshmi Apartment, Karikkamuri Cross Rd., Ernakulam, Cochin - 622011, Kerala. Phone: 0484-2378012, 2378016; Mobile: 09344199799

Bhubaneswar : 5 Station Square, Bhubaneswar - 751 001 (Odisha). Phone: 0674-2532129, Mobile: 09338746007

Indore : Kesardeep Avenue Extension, 73, Narayan Bagh, Flat No. 302, IIIrd Floor, Near Humpty Dumpty School, Indore - 452 007 (M.P.). Mobile: 09301386468

Kolkata : 108/4, Beliaghata Main Road, Near ID Hospital, Opp. SBI Bank, Kolkata - 700 010, Phone: 033-32449649, Mobile: 09910440956

Guwahati : House No. 15, Behind Pragjyotish College, Near Sharma Printing Press, P.O. Bharalumukh, Guwahati - 781009, (Assam). Mobile: 09883055590, 09883055536

Printed at : Shri Krishna Offset Press, Delhi

Dedicated with love to
Vira and Sandhya

FOREWORD

It is my firm conviction that all academic pursuits in the twenty first century must be based on the tripod of teaching (pedagogy and androgogy), research (abstract and action) and consultancy (through interface with the corporate world and the larger civil society). This tripod must be sustained by a social conscience based on values, ethics and proper governance. Without this one cannot even approximate personal, organisational, and professional excellence. At the Dr. D. Y. Patil Pratishthan in Pune we have zealously pursued this path of progress by the sheer strength of conviction over the past decade and in the bargain approximated excellence.

As the saying goes, theory without practice is puerile and practice without theory is futile. The professor in this book has taken care to point out, there must be a symbiotic relationship between theory and practice and in B-Schools. I feel this realisation is very important. The student enters the portals of the academia as raw material and leaves it as a final product only to be absorbed for gainful employment by the ultimate customer in the civil society. This understanding of the conversion of theory to practice is often made possible through a proper use of the case study method. In his other works, Dr. Sorab Sadri has argued that once theory has been perfected reality will be unable to hold out. Hence, he has preceded these fifty cases with a brief introduction to the theory of Human Resources Management.

Many a time we make the error of thinking that there is a single best solution to any problem. Such a view is caused by our limited vision of reality and by the fact that at no time are all the facts available. However, the world must go on and time waits for nobody. We are forced to increasingly make decisions under conditions of relative uncertainty. Therefore, what is required is to think differently, innovatively and often even absurdly to find a solution. Case studies help us in doing so. The world is changing so fast that old views may no longer be relevant and new paradigms will have to be continually invented to enable us to thrive on the cutting edge of global competition. Let me give you an example. Once Osho asked the pupils as to how much of the open sky, he/she saw through the window from his/her chair in the classroom. Answers varied depending on the distance of the pupil's chair from the open classroom window. The great man then went on to explain that if the pupils wished to see more of the sky they must enlarge the window of their mind and remove the clouds of ignorance. That is precisely what these case studies have done for the student of management. That these case studies have been taken from real life situations makes them all the more relevant to the student. That more than a decade has passed by in the process of completing this task shows the seriousness and the dedication of the author (and his critic).

The author's style is lucid but the thoughts contained in the narration are profound, thereby making all of us at the Padmashree Dr D Y Patil Pratishthan truly proud that one of our senior academics has written this book. Having gone through the work myself, I strongly recommend that every student of management in India as well as the professional manager should take this collection of cases very seriously, since it would help them in taking decisions and improving their professional life. Anyone who wishes to become a teacher in human resources should certainly use this book gainfully in the classroom and anyone who wishes to write a management case study must learn from it.

Shree P. D. PATIL
Vice Chancellor
Dr. D. Y. Patil Vidyapeeth (deemed university)
Pune.

ACKNOWLEDGEMENT

Having completed writing the first case study befittingly on the Guru Purnima of 1993, I placed it at the feet of Pandit Ramji Upadyaya of Jamshedpur who at present is blissfully resting at the feet of his Devi in Her kingdom above. I completed writing the final version of the last case study in Pune on the Gudi Padva of 2005. That will give the readers some idea about the length of time that I took to complete this academic labour of love.

Twenty-four years of academic life coupled with fifteen years of work and consultancy experience in the world of industry was a big help. Corporate colleagues and friends across India who chose to remain anonymous are largely responsible for facilitating the research conducted over the years and developing every single one of these short case studies from real life scenarios. The experience in writing case studies on a TELCO sponsored consultancy assignment with colleagues like Arun Sinha and Peter Bonnerjee in Jamshedpur between 1993 and 1995 helped me a lot.

The credit for dovetailing, fine-tuning and validating cases presented in this volume, in the classroom and corporate training situations, across India, however, goes unreservedly to the co-author of my several works, Professor Jayashree Sadri, who is at present Visiting Faculty of Human Resources and Business Ethics at the Indira School of Management Studies Pune. In every instance, she obtained participant feedback and seriously acted upon it to improve upon the case content. Having done this diligently, she kept on advising me in amending, abridging and refining the text of these short case studies. She was the finest intellectual critic one could ever have. To that extent, she has an equal claim to the authorship of these case studies as I do. Participants in B-Schools and in Industry did their bit to help by being outspoken, creative, possessive of their views and sometimes even bizarre in their solutions when these cases were discussed in the classroom situation.

The idea of compiling these short case studies in a single volume goes to the publishers who single-mindedly pursued their project. Other friends in the persons of Professors Bijoy Guha, Sunil Mahajan, Sharukh N. Tara, Jayant Oke, Jai Shanker Tiwari, Vijay Page, D. K. Sinha and Dhan M. Madan offered valuable comments. Advocate Yasmin Tavaria, another scholar and good friend, helped to create conditions for the completion of this work in more ways than she perhaps realised. Institutional support from Wing Commander P. V. C. Patil (Retd.), Professor D. R. Karnure, and Dr. S. G. Tillu of the Dr. D. Y. Patil Pratishthan were singularly encouraging. Another friend, Ms. Bhurpreet Behll, painstakingly proof read the final manuscript in the Spring of 2005 to improve the syntax and help dot the i's and cross the t's while Ms. Anagha Sijapati helped with providing other administrative support.

Looking critically at the final product, and after discussing the matter at length with three learned friends, Dr. Madhav Tutakne, Dr. P. C. Shejwalkar and Dr. D. M. Pestonjee, I humbly opine that this compilation will be a valuable instrument in the hands of the postgraduate lecturer in HR and the corporate facilitator in Organisational Development. Case studies link theory to practice such that the distinction disappears. This is precisely why many Universities like the University of Pune have introduced a subject entitled *Case studies in HR* at the MBA level. I unreservedly extend my gratitude, with the usual disclaimers, to all these fine people who proactively made this published work possible.

13th April, 2005. **Dr. SORAB SADRI**

Acknowledgement

THE HISTORICAL DEVELOPMENT OF HRM

The full form of HRM is Human Resources Management. For the sake of convenience, we simply referred to the subject as HR and this is why we had entitled an earlier work as *Geometry of HR*. However, HRM is *not* the old Personnel Management in a new garb or old wine in a new bottle, (choose your idiom), as is commonly and mistakenly understood. This term, HRM, in fact, implies four things viz.

- Labour is an important resource that assists the organisation in meeting its goals. However, there are other resources too like land, capital, raw material, and technology.
- Management is a factor of production like land, labour, and capital. Its principal task is to insure that all available resources are optimally allocated and utilised so that the organisational goal is met.
- Since labour is a living entity, we must consider values, feelings, egos, beliefs, expectations and aspirations when dealing with labour.
- Organisations serve a business purpose as well as a social purpose, both of which have to be managed.

However, HRM does not exist in a vacuum. It exists within a given environment and adapts to the environment while influencing it in turn. This environment is organisational and social at the same time. HRM, above all else, is *People Management* and a specialised dimension within Applied Social Science. Hence, in understanding HRM one will have to borrow insights from Sociology, Political Science, Psychology, Anthropology, Economics, Mathematics and Philosophy to blend them into the practice of management science. For instance, the following aspects from each mother specialisation come into use in HRM.

Mother specialisation	**Learning and aspects borrowed**
Sociology	Group Dynamics
Political Science	Power
Psychology	Motivation
Philosophy	Social Responsibility
Anthropology	Customs and Traditions
Economics	Environmental Scanning
Mathematics	Manpower Planning

HRM of course was not always such a highbrow specialisation as it has come to be today. It began with basic economic exploitation of labour by capital, for profit through industry and business. This was followed by a rise of consciousness in stages and ended with the birth of the specialisation once again in stages.

The word management comes from the Italian word *managerie* meaning the art of handling horses. Hence, the origins of Management can be traced to the exploitation of labour. In fact, it was once described as the developed but gentle art of exploitation. History tells us that labour was managed even in the building of the pyramids in Egypt under King Remeses II and used as a resource in the slave galleys of the ships in Ancient Rome. However, before we trace the history of the growth of HRM as a subject specialisation within the realm of management, we must understand what Management in itself implies.

Management is the *science* of decision-making and the *art* of decision executing, as is usually applicable in a business or an industry.

Now let us examine how the process of Labour Consciousness rose and developed in stages between 1700 and 1950 and for this our argument will be placed on a world scale. Labour consciousness refers to the realisation of labour force of its own importance and its important historical role in the development of society.

- During the period 1650-1850 Europe witnessed unprecedented development in production of goods with the aid of technology. This is known as the Industrial Revolution and large-scale migration of labour in search of work from rural to urban areas was witnessed. By 1800 this movement had spread to the United States and soon the US was to overtake Europe at least in the production of automobiles and steel. Production aided by technology and innovation had become a byword of the times. Men, women and children worked long hours for meagre wages. Labour was a resource to be exploited and it was believed that wages should be just enough to keep body and soul together, since more money to workers meant more leisure and less output and so less profit.
- The period 1850-1910 saw a rise in labour power with the formation of trade unions, the six-day workweek, and the eight-hour workday. But the enforcement of labour laws was in the hands of the government and those who owned the industry also were in government, so labour always benefited either by default or through violent struggle.
- The same period witnessed a change in the thinking on economics and sociology. The theory of class struggle was put forward and urban society was divided into the haves and the have-nots. The first class was labour that owned nothing but worked to earn enough for living, and was called the *proletariat.* The second class, which represented the owners of industry to manage labour, was called the *bourgeoisie.* Rural society had also two social classes. Those who owned the fields were the farmers or the *landed bourgeoisie.* Those who did not own land but worked on the farms for a wage were called *peasants.* [The nobility or kings and the clergy or priests were kept out of this theory of class struggle not because they did not matter but because the bourgeoisie already represented their joint interests.]
- This was also the period of the expansion of colonialism. The trader and the monarch entered into a strategic alliance to plunder the world and amass wealth. Hence, the army and navy had a major role to play in promoting colonial trade through force.
- The industries of Europe also needed cheap raw material and this was taken from the colonies (tin, coal, iron ore, bauxite, copper, silver, gold, manganese, and mica). The industries of Europe wanted ready markets for their products and what could not be sold at home (due to poor quality or excess output) was sold to the colonies. Industries in the colonies were closed down by force and with the help of unscrupulous elements within the colonies who sought to personally benefit by this arrangement.
- Economists and Sociologists in the meanwhile started getting involved in the trade union movement and *the first real stage of growth of labour consciousness* was witnessed when

trade unions received recognition in England, Germany and France to be followed by recognition in the United States. Worker Power was born and with it was born the study of industrial relations. Sydney and Beatrice Webb wrote *Industrial Democracy*, in 1898 and that started academic inquiry and debate in high circles on the plight of labour. Labour welfare became a humanitarian and civilised issue to aspire for.

- The First World War started with the assassination of Archduke Ferdinand of Austria in 1914 and lasted until 1918. Armies of different countries that fought alongside of each other realised that labour exploitation was a universal phenomenon and something ought to be done about it. This was *the second stage in the growth of labour consciousness.*
- The fires of socialism began to ignite further as news spread about thousands that had died in the battlefields in what appeared to be a senseless war. But the war had also helped the industrialists to amass wealth who had to produce armaments of war, medicines for the wounded, ships for the sea and automobiles that could carry cannons. This was *the third stage in the growth of labour consciousness* with the active involvement of Political Scientists. The Pacifistic Movement, which was anti-war, grew and scholars from all disciplines wrote at length of the exploitation in society. From literature to science and from mathematics to sociology academicians began to support the cause of labour.
- Then came the Great October Revolution of 1917 and the Union of Soviet Socialist Republics was formed under the leadership of Vladimir Lenin and Leon Trotsky. Workers and peasants combined with the army and navy to grab power from the monarchists. Labour realised that it had the power to be free and this idea created a resounding impact on other cultures all over the civilised world. This was *the fourth stage of the growth of labour consciousness.*
- Countries in Europe that did not want the Soviet Revolution repeated in their own country started being a little liberal towards labour. The League of Nations was founded and it gave great importance to the dignity of man and the welfare of labour. This was *the fifth stage of the growth of labour consciousness*. Hence, labour benefited by default and welfare was an instrument used by the capitalist to prevent a violent overthrow by labour. Sociologists (Weber and Durkheim) and Anthropologists (Malinovsky) advocated an increase in welfare measures for the good of society.
- 1939-1945 marked the Second World War and the death of the League of Nations. The influence of Joseph Stalin (USSR) and Franklin Roosevelt (USA) was jointly responsible for the de-colonisation exercise to begin across Asia and Africa after the war ended. Combined with this were the defeat of Kuo Min Tang forces in China and the triumph of Mao Zedong after the Great Long March. The *domino theory* was propounded according to which one country after another would fall into the hands of the Communists like dominoes falling. This marked the *sixth stage in the growth of labour consciousness.* On one hand US presence in Asia and Africa tried to undo the rise of socialism, and on the other hand, countries like China and Cuba actively promoted socialistic revolutions.

Against the backdrop of these six stages of growth of labour consciousness, we will witness the birth of HRM. This birth also did not occur overnight and took place in stages, which we shall presently examine. Whereas we took the whole world as an arena for discussions on the growth of labour consciousness, we shall take the case of India alone to discuss the stages of birth as far as HRM is concerned.

But how did this subject come about and how did its character develop? For this we have to delve into the social and historical growth of what we call industrialised society. It will assist our understanding if we were to demarcate societal growth in stages and relate each stage to the role of both capital and labour within each of these stages. [The reader should be aware that one cannot discretely demarcate phases of growth that often overlap and with definite periodicity. However, one can attempt to indicate a general trend.]

The first known rural-urban migration took place centuries ago (4th Century AD) and since primitive industry was at the time either monopolised by skilled craftsmen and their guilds or owned by the monarch, reform took place spasmodically and quite infrequently. It was governed by the needs of the state e.g. war, famine, draught, trade links etc. This period lasted until about the late 1600 and early 1700. Developments that took place in India were similar to those that took place in parts of Europe, China, Russia and Turkey in content if not in form. This was because the ownership of industry was in the hands of the mercantile-trader that often thought and acted in the short term, was reluctant to plough back profits into the business and hoarded wealth. Labour was a commodity to be exploited, misused and discarded at will. Labour had no rights but a string of obligations and duties that could never be avoided. Treatment of capital was more decorous and respectful than the treatment of labour.

The technology led automation that had entered industry after the Industrial Revolution brought both capital and labour into direct and permanent contact for purposes of continued production. Such production was either: (a) In unique pieces where one of a kind was produced and the industry went on to make another product of another proportion but of the same kind (as in the case of ship building). (b) In batches or lots, when the mould, shape, size etc. of the product was kept uniform for that batch only (as in the case of utensils, toys, wheelbarrows etc,). (c) In mass production when the assembly line concept entered the scene and persons did just that much which was assigned to them and it contributed to the making of a final product (as in the case of the motorcar). In the case of (a) skilled craftsmen and their guilds continued to hold sway. In the case of (b) a certain amount of planning and designing was called for alongside of automation. In the case of (c) the worker was alienated from the final product and technology aided automation took over. This was during the 1800-1860 period and this is when a scientific concern for labour welfare first arose on a scale hitherto unknown. This was also when the 12 hour working day was the norm and the 16 hour working day as well as child labour was not uncommon. Because of the Second International Workingmen's Association meeting in Paris, an 8-hour working day was declared in the USA in 1889. Since then the International Labour Day is celebrated on May first all over the world. In USA and Canada it is celebrated on the first Monday of September. This technology driven industry came to India in late 1800s and saw results only in the first decade of 1900s.

Whereas the origins of the concern for labour's welfare had well begun by socialist writers who pre-dated the *Manifesto of the Communist Party* by Karl Marx and Frederick Engels in 1848, but it was only after their time that HRM as a subject began to take somewhat of an embryonic — nucleus form. The Industrial Revolution had created a supply of goods produced in the factories of Europe. To keep the supply going and maintain low costs, cheap raw materials were needed. Labour was paid just enough to stay alive because they thought that more money as wage would induce leisure and production would suffer. The goods that were being produced also had to be sold. So this role was filled up by the colonies that supplied dirt-cheap raw material like coal, iron ore, bauxite, copper, gold and even indented labour on the one hand and the nobility in the colonies bought European made goods on the other hand. This had three effects. (a) Colonialism served an economic function of supporting the industrial evolution. (b) Industry in the colonies could not compete with Europe because of military oppression and forced closures. (c) In the name of modernisation the colonial nobility, traders and other rich classes began to westernise and use goods produced in Europe. This was the point when concern for labour welfare joined hands with the nationalist-feudal cause and the people in the colonies began to unite under a common banner in India. (E.g. the strike at Buckingham and Carnatic Mills Strike under the leadership of Sorabji Shapurji Bengali in Madras and the strike at Bombay Mills Strike under the leadership of Ranadive). The trade union movement in the Indian colony had started but HRM had not. In Europe the Trade Union Movement remained in the form of Guilds and began to take serious roots. People like Wilfred Owen, Alexander Dumas and Charles Dickens wrote about the plight of labour but that was it. In India too, scholars like Rabindranath Tagore, Lala Lajpat Rai, Bankim Chandra Chattopadyay, Munshi Prem Chand and Mulk Raj Anand wrote eloquently about the poverty of the working class.

Then came the First World War (1914-18) and the Great October Revolution of 1917, which for the first time prompted labour to take control of industry in the Soviet Union. India as a British Colony has earlier supplied its army to fight alongside of the British in Mesopotamia, Sebastopol, and Constantinople. Now the Indian soldiers fought in France, Germany, Egypt and Eastern Europe. The Indian soldiers brought back with them ideas of socialist emancipation they had received from their comrades in the battlefield. England like the rest of Europe did not want this to happen in their country and so labour welfare became a serious concern for the political leadership in Germany (Bismarck), France (Clemencieu), Britain (Edward VII) and Italy (Mazzini). In India it was a palliative to prevent labour organisations being transformed into movements for seeking political freedom. This was the birth of HRM when concern for labour welfare became a part of state policy. The League of Nations was started and the Socialist Revolt in Germany was brutally crushed. At the same time Elton Mayo began work on Motivation Theory at the Hawthorne Plant of Chicago. Indian intellectuals read about all this and translated it back home in their speeches during the freedom struggle.

This was followed by the Second World War (1938-45) and since the League of Nations could not prevent war, it had died a natural death and with it seemed to have died the international concern for labour. But in 1945 thanks to President Roosevelt in USA and Premier Stalin in USSR, labour got a fresh lease of life and the de-colonisation process began two years thereafter. This is where the story of HRM in India actually begins.

The first phase immediately after independence, saw the rise of Labour Officers who were usually retired armed services personnel employed for four reasons: (a) Maintain discipline. (b) Prevent the formation of and break-up the leadership of trade unionism. (c) Handle Recruitment and Termination; and (d) Keep some form of attendance and personnel records. Between 1950 and 1957 (approx.) these Labour Officers controlled labour matters with a stern hand. With Industrial Policy Resolution of 1956 the need for educated Labour Officers rose and it is during the same period labour legislation became very important and many Labour Officers had to obtain Law Degrees to meet statutory obligations. During the 1960s Indian industrialisation got a fillip with the rise of the Public Sector especially in steel textiles, fertilisers, chemicals and automobile (2 wheeler and 4 wheeler) sectors. It was felt that to get more productivity wage incentives were needed and working conditions. Hence, four *more* functions were added *and this second phase of growth of HRM* saw the rise of qualified labour-welfare officers. (e) Managing canteens, latrines and crèches. (f) Filling and filing of returns to governmental agencies. (g) Record keeping for employed personnel.

Then came *the third phase* and the people management function was neatly divided into two by 1970; Personnel Officers who looked after industrial relations matters and dealt with the trade unions. Establishment Officers looked after personnel records, performance appraisals, and wage administration. The Personnel Officer and Establishment Officer complimented each other. In large companies like TISCO, TELCO, SAIL Factories, and Coal Corporation, one more function was added and Welfare Officers were appointed to look after the well being of employees and their families after working hours. Sports, housing, rehabilitating dependants of diseased workers, education in *bustees* were their main concern. The Personnel Officers, Welfare Officers, and Establishment Officers were usually similarly qualified, so job rotation was easy and they all reported to the Chief Personnel Manager. [Clerks who had become Establishment Officers by virtue of seniority were excluded from job rotation]. Some companies had Training and Development Sections but these invariably were not under the jurisdiction of the Chief Personnel Manager and remained an independent specialist activity concerned with *Skill Development*.

By 1976-77 only did *Behavioural Development* become a major concern and it was only by the beginning of the 1980s that people in this specialisation started speaking of *Attitudinal Development* as well. This marked *the fourth phase of growth of HRM* and workers training institutes began to spring up everywhere. Skill training was combined with behavioural training and scholars as Prof. K. S. Basu, Dr. Narayan Sheth, Dr. Subbiah Kannappan and Fr. E. H. McGrath held the fort.

In around 1985 *came the fifth phase of growth* of HRM when concern began to shift toward Human Resources Development to such an extent that the HRD function and the Personnel Function was clubbed under a common head. It became fashionable to call the person at the apex as the Chief of HRD and there was considerably confusion even amongst CEOs on whether HRD stood for Human Resources Department or Human Resources Development. Thinkers like Edgar Shein and Keith Davis had influenced thought, so this was also a time when several scholars spoke of HR as Human Relations rather than Human Resources. Consultants who entered the arena as trainers compounded this and their only real skill was the *gift of the gab*. They dished out outdated theories in outdated formats and added in a few gimmicks for good measure. Transparencies and handouts were not changed for years on end and very few of them had any personnel exposure to research in the field. Short case studies were copied from foreign books and merely the names and data were Indianised. These consultants built alliances with key people in organisations so that they kept being invited repeatedly irrespective of participant feedback or the utility of their programme. The gullible CEO who was a technical person either swallowed the bait or saw HRD as window dressing, to give his concern the modernised corporate image without his personal commitment. Japanese management methods became popular with Indian industry, as did Quality Assurance, Small Group Activity, Kanban, and Kaizen etc. that became a part of the management's common parlance.

In the late 1980s and early 1990s we saw the *sixth phase in the advent* of HRM when it was seen as a *Strategy*. This meant that HR interventions were used selectively as and when the CEO felt like it would aid the attaining of the company or top management objectives. The era of HR Strategy was indeed important since Neuro Linguistic Programmers and experts on Motivation and Stress became consultants who delivered results and were actually facilitators of change. Some well-known names were Professors Baldev Sharma, Dharani Sinha, Ishwar Dayal, Udai Pareek, T. V. Rao, Dinyar Pestonjee, T. K. Karunakaran, P. C. Anthony, Pritmam Singh, Rooshikumar Pandiya, Manohar Nadkarni, P. C. Shejwalkar, John C. Prabhu and Tehemton Dhabhar. It is, however, unfortunate that many self-styled NLP experts have done more harm than good to the organisations since unwitting HRD men erroneously sought their expertise to improve the attitudes and behaviours of people at the workplace.

By mid 1990s came *the seventh stage of growth* in HRM. The professionalisation of the HR function was no longer a matter of doubt. HRM consisted of several sub-specialisations viz. Industrial Relations, Training & Development, Information Systems, Personnel, and Manpower Planning. A fair bit of systems thinking had entered the HRM syllabus and industrial engineers who had entered the HR profession slowly began to be sidelined. Work-study and time study had gone out of fashion and even lost its usefulness in a fiercely competitive world where organisations had to be lean and mean.

During the seventh and eighth phases of growth, four phenomena attracted the attention of HR Managers: Small Group Activity, Business Process Re-engineering, Quality Management and Business Process Outsourcing. This had more to do with the economic compulsions of the environment than anything else.

In 1999 we saw the *eighth phase in the growth* of HRM with the advent of *Strategic HRM*, which meant that HR was not a selective management strategy, any more. The HR Expert was now a part of the Corporate Strategy Formulation and Strategy Implementation Team. He had graduated from the role of specialist to that of a super specialist and thence to the corporate leader. People who have led this movement were Dave Ulrich (USA), Sorab Sadri (India) and David Guest (UK). Knowledge management is no longer a buzzword and one had to keep running just to remain in the same place — so intense is the competition. Ethics, Governance, and Excellence enter our sphere of concern now.

This is where we find ourselves as a profession today and this is where we shall concentrate our inquiry during the coming weeks and months. HRM is no longer something that every manager can handle but it is certainly something every manager should know about and be involved in to the extent necessary. It is a specialisation that is best left to be handled by experts and novices as well as productivity-related technicians have been known to do more damage than benefit to the HRM profession.

Nevertheless, before we end this introduction to the textbook let us remind you that in any academic inquiry like the one we are going to embark upon, using the case study method, certain preconditions are usually laid down when we treat a subject especially at the postgraduate level. These pre-conditions for understanding the subject matter of Human Resources Management are:

- First, organisations must learn to thrive on the cutting edge of competition, for which good people management is important.
- Second, good people management helps the individual and the organisation to leverage their strengths and sideline their weaknesses.
- Third, all this can be sustained in the long run if all management is value based and is approached with a positive attitude.

- Fourth, there must be absolute clarity of vision, mission, goal and role if the intervention is to succeed.

However, there are four caveats also that must be kept in mind by those discussing these cases and those facilitating the discussions at all times.

- The employee is loyal only to his/her values. If his/her values are in harmony with those of the organisation, the employee will stay on. If they are at variance then the employee will either change his/her values or quit the organisation.
- It is the responsibility of the HR Manager to insure that corporate culture and work climate are congenial for the employees but this cannot be achieved unless top management support is ensured. Learning organisations invariably have a value centred work culture.
- Change is a part of life and has to be managed in such a way that the organisational objectives are achieved and in this process the least discomfort is caused to the employee. This is best enabled through a well-planned and well-managed training and development function.
- Above all else, if organisational excellence is to be seriously desired, then business ethics and corporate governance must harmoniously co-exist.

With this background in mind, the reader will be introduced to the method of using these short case studies to enhance learning and gain a deeper understanding of Human Resources Management.

ON USING THE CASE STUDY METHOD

Pedagogy in B-Schools can be divided into four types. (a) **The didactic type** where the professor comes to the podium and lectures in true classical style. There is a fair deal of oratory and seldom if ever are lectures read from a set of notes. The professor is completely a master of the subject on which he is propounding his/her thoughts. Questions are usually taken up at the end of the class and selectively so. (b) **The classroom interactive type** where the professor comes to class with no transparencies or notes but engages the lecture in a discussion mode and there is a great deal of use of the chalk and board. The professor is leading the class and hand holding it through a pre-planned learning process. There is some discussion but it is controlled. (c) **The presentations type** where the professor has prepared a power point presentation or have a set of transparencies, which he/she takes the class through. This presentation is on a particular topic and considerable homework has been done on the subject before the professor comes to class. (d) **The case study type** where learning is imparted with short case studies. This is also the point where androgogy replaces and joins hands with pedagogy and this is precisely what this compendium of short case studies attempts to help the facilitator of Human Resources Management with: to use androgogy to impart learning and reinforce the theory imparted through pedagogy.

Unfortunately, when the professor does not want to prepare a lecture and takes the easy route of discussion to kill time he/she sometimes uses short case studies. In addition, there is a fair degree of confusion on what a case study is and this is evident when students prepare case studies as a part of a competition or an assignment. The role of the facilitator is important and he must come well prepared otherwise students will open their mouths before engaging their brains into gear. Ideally the professor who writes the case must develop it as he goes along and gains student feedback year after year.

Case studies were known to be used by Cyrus II in ancient Iran to simulate war exercises, and during the Second Punic War, Cato the Elder used his case experience to famously proclaim ceterim censio Carthagenem ese delindami meaning "certainly I say, Carthage must be destroyed". In modern times, the first recorded use of case studies was at Harvard Law School in 1871 by Professor Christopher Langdell. One could define a case as a description of situation, consisting of a few pages of written description of an actual situation facing an organisation describing how the current position developed and what problem a key personality in the case is currently facing. Alternatively, one could posit that a case is a written or filmed description of an actual or imaginary situation, which the writer presents in some detail. One could also view a case study as an intensive or complete examination of a facet, an issue or perhaps the events of a geographic setting over a period of time.

Cases used in B-Schools can be categorised variously in terms of its form thus.

(a) Short case: a brief narration or illustration that serves to reinforce a general point of view through using practical relevance. The student can view reality through his/her own personal frame of reference as in values and beliefs. The length of such a case varies from one to five pages. These are used by facilitators in classroom situations for explaining the nuances of behavioural sciences and human resources management.

(b) Classic case: these are long studies giving detailed and factual accounts regarding maximum relevant material in the given context of the business situation. The student becomes an analyst who can spend up to a week studying and deciphering the nuances of the cases. The length of such a case can even extend up to sixty pages. These are usually used in strategy related subjects.

(c) **Technical case:** these describe a technique, process or system of analysis without taking account of the human factor. The student learns how to analyse and document given data to draw meaningful conclusions. These are usually used in finance and operations related subjects where calculations are called for and where a business or organisationally relevant problem has to be solved.

(d) **Complex cases:** these are usually complicated and aimed at bringing out deep rooted issues and are often a mix of individual, organisational and cultural forces that impinge upon industry and business. The coverage of such cases is wider than others and is used at the end of a postgraduate course when the student has already mastered several subject specialisations enabling a comprehensive analysis.

When cases are categorised in terms of content they could be either open ended or close ended in character. In the former instance participants have to find out the problem, exercise their minds and propose alternative solutions to one or more scenarios that may emerge. In the latter instance, the problem has been identified and a solution is sought given the assumptions and constraints.

Such a case either open ended or close ended can be of three kinds thus.

First, a **case history** details a series of events leading up to a conclusion. It is a researched body of work, which tells us a trend adopted in an organization or the contribution of a particular kind of leader. In a way, the presentation could be biographical. The learning derived is in terms of what happened and why it happened so.

Second is **a case analysis** that presents a set of data and either expects the student to analyse it or leads the students through the process of analysis. A good example is to be found in inter-sectoral growth in an economy, where the analyst sees trends and attempts to ascribe reasons for a particular success or failure of policy. Another good example can be found in market surveys that highlight consumer demand for a particular commodity in preference to another or as in financial data where a company's health is examined.

Third is a **case study** where an event, a set of events or policies is narrated in story form such that in analysing it the student imbibes a definite and pre-programmed learning. The facts are normally not massaged beyond recognition although the identities of the actors may be often concealed in the larger interest of society. Fake names and places are given but the facts are generally not tampered with. This is generally the case in HRM where the case study is used to impart a theory or a pre-determined learning.

Experts in Strategic HRM have treated the subject of ego at some length. At the risk of repetition let me reiterate that mankind's greatest enemy is his/her own self, his/her ego. Unmasking the ego can be very traumatic but its therapeutic value cannot be underestimated. The purpose of these short case studies is to help the student / participant / facilitator to unmask his/her ego and confront reality, or perceptions thereof. Even professors of management need to unmask their ego if they are to achieve real intellectual progress.

While the basis for writing the cases lay in our Indian experience, it *does not mean* that the problems are unique to either India or even to the Indian high-tech sector. Rather, they are relevant to all business and industry in the capitalist periphery that seeks to thrive in the 21st century. They are important for all HR facilitators and teachers of HR since it enables them to bridge the gap between perception and reality, in such a way that perception becomes the reality. This is where perception proves to be infinitely superior to description. In addition, in the **age of the intellect** and the predominant position occupied by the **knowledge worker,** HR intervention has become that much complex and inevitable. People who think of HR as a soft option are merely showing their own ignorance of objective social reality. Industries have a lot more in common, than they are credited for and so the appeal of these short case studies is to a wider audience.

Certain facets, we all know, are common to all such industries that depend on technology and the knowledge worker to propel their growth. Principal among these is selection of personnel, attrition levels and re-skilling of manpower. Trust, teamwork and transparency are the benchmarks against which effective project outcomes can be viewed. To some extent one could even, say that all these short case studies relate to the human aspects of project management. However, almost every activity is a separate project in the high tech sector. Hence, the term project management should be viewed in that light alone. In addition, this is the age of the knowledge worker whose loyalty is believed by many HR experts to belong to technology and nothing else. Hence, for them, HR intervention is the only way of creating a sense of belongingness and training where continuous upgrading of skills are needed, keeps attrition levels low.

Subsequent research by this author and Jayashree has unearthed two fallacies especially in the case of the knowledge worker. First, the term knowledge worker itself needs some understanding. Is cobbler, a tailor or a blacksmith not using his knowledge to work? Second, any skill contains an element of knowledge within it. Hence, how can we describe *only* the employee in high-tech industry as being a knowledge worker? After all, (we hope), the professors in classrooms teach on the basis of some knowledge and so can we not describe them as knowledge workers too? This comprises the first fallacy i.e. one of definition. The second fallacy arises out of a belief regarding employee loyalty. Throughout the works of this author, the contention remained that that the employee is loyal only to his/her own values. As long as individual values are in accord with organisational values, the employee will remain on the job. The moment these values differ the employee either changes the personal values or quits the organisation. That is why three types of organisations always have high attrition rates. (a) An organisation managed by a CEO with a *feudal-mercantilist-trader* mindset and having knowledge workers. (b) An organisation that is by the nature of its business operating in the short run i.e. on a project to project or assignment to assignment basis. Once the task is over the employees automatically leave the organisation. (c) An organisation that hires people on contracts rather than for long-term employment. Once the contract is over it may or may not be renewed. Free market capitalism and the withering away of the employee collectivity are solely to blame for this malaise. In all these three instances, the commitment of the employee is questionable and the belongingness need is negligible. This belongingness need is two edged: the employee acts as if he/she belongs to the organisation and that the organisation belongs to him/her. Hence, any organisation or any HRM intervention that fails to bring about this two edged belongingness fails to retain people.

Many CEOs do not invest in training as they point to high attrition rates and state that money spent on training is a waste. On the contrary, argue that it is always better to have a trained workforce who may leave for greener pastures than to try to compete globally with manpower on rolls that possess out-dated skills and expertise. Many a B-School has failed to make the grade since the Director, with one or more of the above-mentioned traits, runs it. Those who stay on do so because they have no other choice for some reason or the other. The number of part time lecturers who outnumber the full time ones in the non-premier institutes exposes the short sightedness of free market capitalism and its inability to create conditions to sustain a steady pursuit of knowledge.

Experience shows that most inter-personal problems in management are *ego based.* This often takes the form of *attitude based* and *behaviour based* being attached. The employee/subordinate is often said to have a problem managing his ego. This may not be true. When a senior manager tells an executive (reporting to him/her) that the executive has an attitude problem, many a time what the senior manager is actually saying is that *I need a yes man and you are not he*. Reading in between the lines of the message is a cultivated art in many ways and no training except that in the *school of hard knocks* can help.

However, there is little that cannot be understood with a little bit of healthy open-minded introspection and frank exchange of views. I shall, in these short case studies, attempt to *de-mystify management* and break that halo placed by the managerial ego and sustained in the name of managerial prerogatives. In so doing I shall try to lay bare the vital areas where Senior Level Management intervention can make a difference. But this cannot be done on the basis of either *historicism* or *empiricism.* It has to be based on the subjective perceptions of objective social reality. Objectivity like excellence can only be approximated and so to claim objectivity is in itself a subjective statement. This HR Managers must be well aware of since it is our experience that many of them tend to speak with an air of absolute certainty about things that they possess absolute ignorance. This must be avoided at all cost and one way of doing so is to understand what is perception? It is what reality seems like to the beholder. It is not a description as Soli Parukh reminds us. He uses the innate Kantian logic to rightly maintain that a description can never approximate reality since it is lacking in feeling.

To quote Parukh (1999):

> *Perception is the antithesis of knowledge. It is characterized by spontaneity, totality and discontinuity. It occurs when there is no escape from a challenge into ideals; when there is no interference with the fact one observes; when time is not used as a mechanism for postponement; and when adaptive techniques do not intervene between a challenge and one's response to it.*

These short case studies could similarly be envisioned as perceptions of what really occurred in reality. The background of this perception lies the unerring belief that no matter how technologically superior an organization or a technocrat is, he cannot afford to overlook either the human being behind the exterior of the employee or break the very rules he has laid down for others. In short every HR intervention must have a very humane face and the attitude towards all parties involve must be one of fairness, equity and propriety. The dignity of mankind as well as that of the organisation must always be respected.

- The concept of value (generation and contribution) is an integral part of Corporate Strategy.
- Human Resources Management cannot be divorced from the process of Business Policy formulation and execution.
- In the final analysis it is the Corporate Culture and the Ethics of the Managers, which will delineate the form, and content of the Behavioural Dynamics of the organization.
- The ultimate aim of Strategic HR intervention then would be to increase the satisfaction levels of the internal customer through a vibrant corporate culture and to leverage core

competencies for gaining advantage over other players. This has to be done in the global market such that corporate objectives are met without sacrificing core beliefs.

It is in keeping with these assumptions that the short case studies were specifically developed from real life situations. I opine that all value is created by Labour while Capital is man made aid to production. Investment is the process of capital creation and Business Policy aims to maximize returns on investment such that organizational goals are met. It uses HR to optimally allocate and utilize its manpower within the constraints of the immediate environment.

Hence, it would make a lot of sense to even approach an elective course on Business Policy from a *man management* angle. Students and teachers should not feel shy of being subjective well remembering that the very claim of being objective is a subjective perception.

As the ambit of competition is internationalised, the corporations, which will survive, are definitely those who have a value based business policy and a management strategy founded on ethics. Others will be consigned to the wayside along the great motorway of history. In most Management Schools students get a good grounding in Economics, Marketing and Finance with the result that teaching a full semester course would imply that the curriculum traverses such a path as has not been covered by either of the three mother disciplines, for fear of repetition. Hence, the approach from a position of *Man Management* is resorted to in this book. This is the basic *raison d'être* of this book is to predicate experience against the threshold of theory and give *man* his rightful place in business and industry. Philosophically speaking, *man* is the beginning and the end of all analysis; he is both the subject and the object of social inquiry. Hence, the present approach of making *man* the focus is further vindicated.

He, who knows not where he is going, cannot get lost. But at the same time, he cannot get anywhere in particular, except perhaps by serendipity. Corporate Strategy is therefore crucial to the future health of every organization. Unfortunately, it is side stepped in the interest of immediate returns and what we get is developmentless growth. It was further argued that like marketing or finance or any managerial function needs to be empowered and held accountable. Furthermore, all management actions not *only* have to be ethical but *also* perceived to be ethical by both the internal and the external customer.

Hence, the management of organizations in the next century has *per force* to be value based where the core values are without any apology purely ethical. And for this, a planned and proactive Management Strategy rooted in theory, and based on practice, is seen as being imperative. These are the core beliefs by which an organization stands by, is known for and act as a guide to managerial action.

The greatest danger to a logical mind comes from *uncertainties, not from risk.* This is because there is a theory for calculating risk but there is no way of understanding or calculating uncertainty. Similarly, the greatest danger to the smooth functioning of an organization comes from *external uncertainties*, which were referred to as the mutable nature of social reality and which are often caused by the market conditions.

Further, the danger to the smooth running of the organization comes from internal uncertainties, which are mostly caused by lack of *clarity* at the level of vision, mission, goal and role. In addition to the negative impact caused by uncertainty, it is the *definition* of the *problem* and the *premise*, which goes a long way in removing uncertainty by bringing about clarity. Once a situation is properly defined, the limitations are known and the variables affecting its behaviour have been identified, it ceases to be uncertain and therefore poses little danger to the logical mind. It is almost a truism that even with the best of systems, reality continues to remain opaque and decisions are made under conditions of relative uncertainty. The art and the science of management, in the main, are geared towards removing the cobwebs and reducing the level of uncertainty. HR plays a positive, proactive and facilitating role in this activity by laying down employee friendly policies, and ensuring their compliance without losing sight of the fact that organizational objectives have to be met.

In this new age of globalised competition four aspects have assumed enormous importance and must never be lost sight of. These are Corporate Governance, Total Quality Management, Core Competency and Business Ethics. This is brought out clearly in all high level discussions involving Strategic HR.

Some terms need to be clearly defined at the outset so that there is no ambiguity among the discussants of these short case studies. Readers are cautioned against getting confused since the lines drawn are very thin and the distinctions are often academic in nature while being quite blurred in reality. Nevertheless, they need to be defined, if for nothing else, then at least in the name of academic clarity, which being a pedagogical imperative also enables the strategy to be properly communicated through the organization's systems and sub-systems.

Vision: Every entrepreneur has a dream, which his creativity helps to actualise. The vision in this case is nothing but a dream of what the future holds for the company and where the company sees itself in *n* year's time. This is the light at the end of the tunnel towards which the company/organization will move.

Mission: Organizations exist within a given society and are a part of it. But there are some functions, which the organizations perform in keeping with the vision. The mission statement defines the role, which the organization wishes to play within society. To that extent, it brings about synergy between the needs and activities of the organization and those of the society giving the former a sort of *locus standi*.

Purpose; The mission statement has an external orientation. What the organization desires to achieve internally in line with the corporate vision is called purpose. This is born out of organizational values that represent the personal beliefs and convictions that underlie choice decisions.

Objective: It is an open-ended attribute, which attempts to denote a future state or business outcome. This is indicative of action to be taken and are stated in general terms. Usually this is a long run attribute.

Goal: It is a short run and close-ended attribute, which is expressed, in specific terms within the dimensions of quantity, quality, time and cost. An objective is actualised through goals.

Target: What a goal is to an organization, a target is to a function or a team or an individual within it. Performance is bench marked against targets and every time a target is achieved it has to be re-set or re-formulated. An organizational goal is broken into specific targets.

Role: It denotes the range and kind of activity, which is functionally expected of an incumbent because of his particular status, is the organizational structure. Role is always in relation to a stated or un-stated goal and the expectations that arise therefrom. Hence, a role could be both overt as well as covert.

Policy: Policy can be seen, as a guide to action required to be taken to attain a goal. In a way policies are value-based contingent decisions, which guide managers and organizations about what to do or what not to do, when faced with a dilemma.

Strategy: We derive the word from the Greek *strategos* meaning general-ship. Strategies are a means to an end and are best seen as a set of decision-making rules meant to guide organizational behaviour. They lead managers and organizations to definite action. It can be seen as an overall plan of action, which is to be implemented if a target has to be achieved or a goal is to be realized.

Tactics: Whereas a strategy can consist of one or more tactics, it is possible that the distinctions here are extremely foggy. Several tactics can make up a composite strategy just as several battles go into making a war.

Corporate Planning: It is but a term used to denote a formal, systematic and comprehensive appraisal of the constraints and assumptions, which go into making strategies to achieve a desired organizational goal. It is usually undertaken either by or at the behest of top management. It involves an apex view of the entire planning process in a systematic, logical and sequential manner.

Actual Costs: These are costs actually incurred in the pursuit of business. They can be *fixed* by which is implied that they do not vary with increase or decrease in output or they can be *variable,* in that they vary with changes in output. Rènt and salaries are a fixed cost. Raw material used and wages are a variable cost. When the manager talks of maintaining his eye on *the bottom line,* he implies that short run actual costs should be held in check. That is good business sense so long as he does not turn a blind eye to long run opportunities due to a myopic vision.

Opportunity Cost: This can best be understood as the cost of an opportunity foregone because of a particular decision taken. For instance, a marketing manager may have 1000 leads of which only 80 could be converted into an account due to one reason or the other. The profits that would have accrued to the company had the other 920 leads been successfully converted are an opportunity cost. Strategic managers always keep an eye on long run opportunity costs because it is the power to envision or accurately perceive what the future state of affairs may be like, helps him to plan realistically and beat the competitors.

Infrastructure: Technically speaking, infrastructure refers to the economic relationship between the four factors of production: land, labour, capital and organization. Hence, when an economist speaks of infrastructure he speaks of the industrial base required for growth. In management parlance, infrastructure refers to the body that will deliver the goods. E.g. if a company has to undertake expansion they find it necessary to have the infrastructure in place. This means that people (labour), machinery and materials (capital) as well as buildings (land) must be in place so that desired objectives may be met. For instance, a company cannot launch a global marketing campaign by merely having one man placed in New York, one in Lagos, one in Hamburg and the other in Sydney to liase with potential clients and keep in touch with customers. It needs an entire network upon which marketing growth can be based. That is the infrastructure.

Superstructure: In pure economic terms superstructure refers to the socio-cultural and political relationships based on the economic relationships between factors of production. Hence, when an economist speaks of superstructure, he speaks of law and bureaucracy that make governance possible. In management parlance, superstructure refers to the systems, procedures and polices that are needed to obtain the promised deliverables. Systems ensure conformity to acceptable norms and can be a very potent basis for objectivity in managerial action.

Growth: In economics this stands for an annual increase in per capita income or net national product. Hence, it is a mere statistical indicator that does not *ipso facto* imply progress. In management terms, growth is said to exist when either one or more economic variables registered an increase annually. This variable could be positive such as profit and net bloc (fixed assets less depreciation) or it could be negative such as costs and inventory. Growth does not necessarily imply a change in the corporate mind set since many a feudal-mercantilist-trader has made it big in the world of business. Man then becomes just another resource to be exploited and the de-humanization of wage labour is the inevitable result.

Development: In economics this stands for a holistic and total improvement in the quality of life. More particularly, it stands for an increase in *per capita* productivity without a commensurating fall in the *aggregate level of employment*. This means, that the number of *exercisable choices* available to the average citizen increases. If a company is seen as a body corporate or as a legal entity, the logic can as well be applied in the case of a company. This is a sure test barometer for the measurement progress. Development *ipso facto* implies a positive change in the corporate mind set so that both the internal customer (employee) and the external customer (client) is satisfied while making sure that organizational objectives are met.

Tender Mindedness: I have borrowed this term from Van Dusen Kennedy. It signifies *high-mindedness not sufficiently conditioned by intellect*. For instance, companies speak of a *momentum of progress* that they can only hope to achieve, if all goes well. However, investment in both infrastructure and superstructure is found to be wanting. Hence, this remains a pious wish. In scientific terms, *momentum* is equal to *velocity* multiplied by *mass*. Velocity in this case is brought about by the corporate mindset but an absence or inadequacy of both infrastructure and superstructure prevents the existence of the required mass. Hence, the desired momentum is not achieved. And the management is seen as being tender minded.

While writing these short case studies, from real life data in the fast track industries, one belief was reinforced. Just as metaphysics is not easily understood and the ritual of religion is something, which the majority are more comfortable with, so too, the majority of managers are comfortable, when others do their thinking for them. However, they wish to retain their power so they feel themselves so indispensable that they continue to wear that false halo. Using an analogy, some could argue that God had to make the Devil to ensure His perpetual employment and importance. In the same manner, managers create problems only to solve them, feel good about it and retain their importance. They try to play God.

Leaders are not necessarily managers and *vice versa*. The former envisions and leads, the latter follows and obeys. However, like a good leader, a good manager is one whose team functions as efficiently as in his absence as it did in his presence. Conscious management through positive and proactive strategic HR interventions must aim at creating such a climate through out the organization, such that problems are not intentionally created only to be solved and the mediocrity take credit theretofore.

Taking the example cited above further, let us say that the Bible erred when it claimed that man was made in the image of God. Rather this Immensity that engulfs us, this *magna mater*, is too vast, complicated and profound for our puny brains to understand. The mind-body genome of man is grossly inadequate and can never comprehend this nature that surrounds us. So man makes God in his own image: a forgiving God, an angry God, a fearful God, a loving God, a beautiful God, and so on. This is because we see what we want to see, hear what we want to hear and willingly block out that which is unpalatable. So is true of our perception of all reality.

Given below, are fifty short case studies culled from real life scenarios in the industrial environment and meant for imparting classroom learning only. Their purpose is academic and meant to generate debate so that the level of social consciousness of participants is elevated. Names and other data have been suitably camouflaged so as to retain the organization's anonymity. Any resemblance to persons and institutions living, dying or dead is purely accidental and certainly unintended. Apologies in advance are tendered, should any person or institution be inadvertently hurt or offended.

The case study approach to learning has been quite contentious. Some management trainers replace prepared lectures by giving out short case studies for discussion to fill in the time. In such instances, the case study degenerates into story telling sessions. There are some again who use short case studies to reinforce a message. In such instances the case study becomes a parable or a homily. This is what teachers who appeal to the sentiment and the heart are more comfortable in doing. However, pontificating is not necessarily an intellectual or academic exercise and must be eschewed. Here the intention of the cases is to bring out learning through the discussion. The discussants would have arrived at a solution or an outcome, which they will *own,* and therefore, be committed to. This outcome will lead to a theory and form the basis of action at any point where value is being added to the product or the process chain.

There is a great need to insert an important *mia culpa* here. *There can be no single correct solution to any case study since social reality is mutable in nature and the human mind is difficult to comprehend.* What you, as serious students of the managerial science should do is to place yourself in the shoes of the executive and then take an informed decision. Having taken the decision, execute it. In addition, having executed the decision, see that your superiors, your peers and your subordinates *accept* it. You are all participants who, as responsible managers, are expected to read the cases and come prepared for a full-fledged discussion in class. The facilitator/teacher is advised not to take up more than one case study *per* day. Each session should ideally begin with a strong theoretical input, and then followed by the case study so the learning will thus be re-enforced through case discussions. Hints, questions and issues given at the end of the case are at best tautological and should *never* be taken very seriously, since in doing so innovation and creativity will be sacrificed and the purpose of learning itself will be defeated.

Theory must emanate from the discussion and *not* precede it. Some tips for discussion have been given at the end of each case, but as managers and technocrats (both those in waiting and those in position), you cannot be expected to restrict your intellect to these points. These tips are more meant for the facilitator who has to make sure that the discussion does not go out of control. Let the spirit wander, let the mind charter new territories and let not the constraints of conventional wisdom fetter your thoughts: *cast off the fetish of society.*

Unlike what some fundamentalists, spiritualists and normative thinkers would wish to argue it is fairly certain that reality cannot be seen in clear black and white terms. It is a vast grey area with shades in between. How you behave within that vast grey area depends on how well an executive you are and what where your values lie. But merely attending a training program, as some management theorists are wont to argue cannot facilitate change and bring about development. A conscious effort to change and having an open mind often works wonders.

Learning does not end with classroom interaction. Nay, it begins there. A useful book that I shall recommend that every middle level manager read is Gerry Johnson and Keran Scholes (1997) *Exploring Corporate Strategy: Text and Cases* (Prentice Hall). Another good book, which fellow professionals will learn from and that has recently entered, the Indian market is Lyle M Spencer Jr (1995): *Re-engineering Human Resources* (John Wiley). If the reader just wishes to have a compendium of Indian short case studies based on value based policy then I recommend the collection *Business Ethics: Concepts and Cases* (Tata McGraw Hill 1998). To glean an understanding of the ethical dilemma and managerial responses to it, readers and students of management as well as senior executives should consider reading *The Theory and Practice of Managerial Ethics* (JAICO Pub. 1999). A good compendium, which every student of man management must have, is *Geometry of HR,* which was brought out by Himalaya Publishing House in 2002. On the issues on Business Ethics, Corporate Governance and Business Excellence the book *A Starfish in a Sea of Sharks* (2005) contained another noteworthy collection.

These are the basic working tools that every Senior Manager should have in his personal library. Here I have given a selection of short case studies in an attempt to link theory to practice and make the understanding of the subject that much easier. The underlying theme of these cases can be stated as *value based human resource management strategy*. The focus of attention is high growth sectors in a globally competitive environment. Some points around which discussions can generally centre are given below. These are not merely *beliefs* but definite and actualised lessons culled from experiential learning and action research that went into the writing of these cases, which reflect some particular aspects of objective social reality in the high growth industry of India between 1994 and 2000. Every single case highlights one or two intended aspects of Strategic Human Resources. I have not stated these and left it to the creativity of the facilitator to treat the case as he wishes.

At the risk and expense of being called normative, the following pieces of advice are worth handing down to all managers during executive development programs wherein these cases could be used.

- Never forget the human being behind the mind-body genome of the employee. Respect the person in every man, for he is ultimately an aspect of that great Immensity.
- The primary product is *people driven* and the loyalty of knowledge workers is seemingly to technology. However, technology is a unique commodity that we buy without seeing. For, if we see it we need not buy it. Hence, it is absurd to have loyalty to a commodity. Loyalty can only be to one's values.
- There must be *absolute clarity* of vision, mission, goal and role.
- Managers must *learn* to walk their talk, think holistically and act locally.
- Decisions are best taken democratically but enforced autocratically.
- Trust and faith relationships hold the key to synergy and growth.
- Managers who contradict themselves or are inconsistent in their decision-making are poor leaders and not trusted by those down the line.
- Transparency in decision-making is crucial to building faith and trust.
- Communication must *freely* take place in all directions, truthfully and politely. There must be sufficient maturity to take and receive criticism provided it is well meant.
- One must avoid using criticism to re-enforce one's presumed superiority or to *retain* control.
- Empowerment must accompany accountability: they are not mutually exclusive,

- Managers must learn to be *constructively unreasonable* so that breakthrough is possible.
- Managers must not only act *ethically* but also others must see them as acting so.
- Values and Ethics can be imbibed but never imposed.
- One cannot afford to forget opportunity costs due to a preoccupation with actual costs although one cannot overlook actual costs in themselves.
- Even the basic concepts of Human Resource Management are being re-engineered.
- Many HR and especially Training and Arbitration functions are being outsourced and the right choice of HRD consultants can make or break a company. Negotiation skills assume importance and purchasing needs to be added to the current MBA syllabus.
- Quality must be *built into* the system and procedures must be streamlined and followed scrupulously.
- Do not delegate authority upwards and always take positive charge of the situation. (Your superior may not be as efficient as you think or he poses to be).
- Under no circumstances must one resort to either apple-polishing or petty politicking. These are contemptible and below managerial dignity.
- If someone speaks ill of others in front of you and in their absence watch him well. He will most likely be doing that to you too. He may mean well, but he is a slave of habit.
- Always commit to deliver and deliver as committed without compromising your values. It helps to ask yourself: does your action *add value*?
- Bullying, passing the buck, taking undue credit, harassment, fudging facts, whistle blowing, discrimination etc., are signs of mediocrity, insecurity and general managerial immaturity. [Once the fear of the bully is taken out from the mind of the victim, the bully loses his power.]

The present era is typified by a change process heralded by the concurrent collapse (of old beliefs and structures), on one hand, and a quantum change (in technology and its outcomes), on the other. Developing a value based corporate culture is the need of the hour. Achieving this through strategic HR interventions is hardly likely to happen without a proper understanding of the basic beliefs, values and ethics along which the business of the organization is conducted. Neither ethics nor corporate governance can be thrust upon an organization nor administered to its employees by HR. What Strategic HR does is to help create an environment in which ethics and corporate governance can blossom within an organization. Yes, ethics can be imbibed and this happens when those around you are ethical and when these values are within you. Strategic HR merely clears the smog to enable one to see reality more clearly.

Recalling what the late and erudite Justice Bakhtavar Lentin once said: a non-conformist conscience is the harbinger of change and a necessary component of the HR Manager's psyche. One cannot and should not dismiss this. This non-conformist behaviour comes from an inner belief, a value system that stands against the tide of accepted public opinion. Possessing this quality is what makes the difference between chalk and cheese, the leader and the follower, the creative-innovator and the mediocrat-bureaucrat. What makes a leader walk his talk, blaze a trail or lead from the front by example? Does this come from within the person or is it caused by some externality? Is the decision-maker acting in a rational, mechanical robotic manner each time a dilemma is confronted? Does he depend on his sixth sense or his intuition? Or does he fall back on some inherent values and beliefs? Is he supposed to be sufficiently "angry" or "uncomfortable" to want change?

Would the rational decision-maker follow the Sadri-Jayashree (1995) five-step model elaborated here at length or adopt the Kitson and Campbell (1966) five step methodology used by management students? Alternatively, would the teacher and the taught take the oft-trodden path and restrict their analysis to SWOT (strength, weakness, opportunities and threats)?

The second analytical structure mentioned above, is well known to all academics that use the case study method of imparting learning seriously. However, the Kitson and Campbell model is more apt for cases in finance, marketing and production management while the Sadri and Jayashree Model is more suited for cases in Human Resources Management, Organisational Development and Diagnosis. The case study approach ideally links theory to practice so that knowledge creation and learning result from it. Hence, a case is never static. As it is used increasingly, varied feedbacks are received and the author acts on some of these feedbacks to enrich the case and make the discussion based learning that much intellectually interesting.

The students should be aware that the choice of the model is highly subjective and depends on the facilitator's preference.

The Kitson and Campbell methodology consists of the following steps:

(a) Identify the problem

(b) Generate alternate solutions

(c) Evaluate alternatives using the cost-benefit analysis

(d) Select the solution

(e) Implement the chosen solution.

If the decision-maker will depend on his subjectivity instead, then what is the ideological basis of his decision? For some managers it is fashionable to say they are non-ideological. Little do they realize that in so saying they are making an ideological statement! Anyone who has been in a decision making position long enough will vouchsafe for the fact that more than 90% of decisions are based on the subjective perception of an objective social reality. This subjectivity takes us into a discussion on ethics that is something that can make or break and organization.

The Sadri and Jayashree *Five Ds of HR Intervention* make a unique instrument to analyse cases. The HR Specialist cannot lose this fact either, since he is involved in decision-making and decision executing all the time. To recap the 5 Ds:

1. **Diagnosis** of the Organization before deciding whether HR intervention is required.
2. **Definition** of the problem and the ambit of enquiry so that the parameters of the solution are bounded and the constraints are taken into account.
3. **Designing** a solution which will address the issues germane to the organization and which spring from the diagnosis.
4. **Development** of the strategy so that it synchronizes with organizational requirements as well the environmental constraints.
5. **Delivering** the results by implementing the strategy and activating the process of HR intervention so that desired goals be met.

What makes the second methodology superior to the first one is the inclusion of the *sixth or hidden D* that stands for **data and documentation.** We Indians are particularly poor on this aspect, as many an organisation has found out on eve of any accreditation exercise. Perhaps the fact that adequate data and documentation was not preserved is the reason why in our present day the knowledge of Ayurveda, Vastushastra, and Vedic Mathematics is so dependent on beliefs rather than on science.

Research and experience shows that good leadership comes from within the individual's self. It comes from a sense of self-esteem and an inherent belief in oneself. The strength of conviction can move mountains and make giants out of dwarfs. All great leaders have this common trait even when their ideologies or *modus operandi* differs. What made great corporate leaders to stand out like beacon lights were their high self-esteem, strong sense of values, respect for mankind and an inherent humility. Values are imbibed and can rarely be imposed on anyone, as any scholar will agree.

In analysing these short cases within a limited time allocated for it, the individual or group taking on the task will (hopefully) undergo an intellectual and emotional involvement, that will prepare them to face similar situations in real life as when the manager in waiting is metamorphosed into a manager in action. In all cases the participant is encouraged to think outside the euphemistic box, free the spirit and be constructively unreasonable to borrow the phrase of George Bernard Shaw. The fact that many students will not have the administrative experience and will lack the ability to comprehend the complexity and start looking for the non-existent one best solution to the issues will be easily overcome when the horizons of imagination are extended and fetish of structured reason is cast aside.

When analysing these short cases the participants should bear in mind the four fallacies of positive social science which this author has always avoided and rather depended on objectivity and bounded rationality to understand the situation. These fallacies, which participants must avoid, are explained below.

- *The fallacy of composition*: When what is true for a part is taken to be true of the whole as well. One cannot forget that the whole is more than the sum of its parts and has its own identity and characteristic as well.
- *The fallacy of accident:* When what is true for a whole is taken to be true for the part as well. When we speak of characteristics of the whole certain generalities and averages are used. This is not necessarily the case when we speak of a particular part.
- *Post hoc sed non-proctor hoc:* When we assume that an occurrence after the event was because of the event. Sequencing of occurrences is usually random in real life and we cannot ascribe motive or reason to something merely because one occurrence followed another.
- *Correlation does not amount to causation*: Just because two variables are related statistically to each other, it does not follow that one causes the other.

One sure shot way to make a mark and leave your footsteps on the sands of time is to stand by certain values and ethics come what may, and, rely heavily on good governance practices if excellence is to be approximated. This is neither simple nor easy. Nevertheless, it is strongly recommended.

Especially HR experts must remember at all times this famous tenet borrowed from Karl Marx: *Man is the beginning and the end of all analysis; he is both the subject and the object of all inquiry*. (Here the word *man* is gender neutral and refers to mankind). Anybody who respects himself will surely respect others. In addition, if anyone wants to be respected, he/she must begin by respecting the other. Trust, faith, transparency, honesty, respect and love are virtues that must be cherished and they are always reciprocal. For instance, one cannot expect to be trusted by others if one does not give others the trust that is due to them. The influence of the internal as well as the external environment cannot be assumed away or under estimated. This is because, in the end, to quote Fredrick Engels, *Every man, like every country, makes his own destiny; but he makes it under certain specific conditions over which he has little control.*

To end this homily it would be always better for participants to use statistics judiciously and not read too much meaning into them. In short, do not look for reason when reason need not exist. A healthy mistrust for statistical inferences is safe. George Bernard Shaw, the first Director of the London School of Economics and Political Science had once thus remarked: *Statistics is like a blind man looking for a black cat in a dark room that does not exist.*

SOME POINTS TO REMEMBER

The Facilitator's Obligations:

- The facilitator ensures that channels of communication are open and there is no inhibition on the part of the participants to speak their minds freely. Anything that would impinge creativity is removed.
- He/she acts as a guide, integrator and moderator of the discussion amongst the participants. He/she merely insures that deviance is prevented and convergence of ideas and cohesiveness of logic is made possible.
- The facilitator asks questions throws an idea here and there so that any glut in the discussion is not prolonged and when deadlocks occur, he/she ensures that tension is relieved.
- He/she ensures that discussion is kept at an objective level and no personalised criticism of people or views is allowed.
- He/she clarifies and summarises the discussion and relates it to theory so that learning takes place.
- The facilitator encourages those who are silent to speak up and those who are too noisy to calm down. To that extent, he/she plays a moderating and encouraging role.

What the Participants Should Do:

- They must read the case thoroughly and usually two readings are minimal. Avoid giving immediate reactions based on part reading of the case.
- Look for clarity when identifying the problem remembering that the real problem is seldom the apparent one.
- Analyse the facts as objectively, dispassionately and logically as possible. Never skip the diagnosis since that can prove fatal to the argument.
- Be as creative as they can since the most outlandish solutions are sometimes the best. However, while holding your own ground, always be ready to listen to others and mend your views.
- Conduct a SWOT analysis and list down all the assumptions and constraints before beginning the argument.
- Use the Pareto paradigm to distinguish between the vital few and the trivial many issues thrown up by the case.
- Detail the methodology and the process while addressing the issues and base this on the imbibed theoretical understanding of the subject.
- Never stop at positing the solution. After all there is no one-best solution to any case and every solution must be actualised based on a theory of the subject. The participant must state how the solution will be actualised.

DOZEN HATS OF THE HUMAN RESOURCES OFFICER

In the course of analysing the case studies given in this volume the reader will be forced to don the garb of a Human Resources expert. In order to enable him/her to do so effectively, it must be clarified that the HR Officer often wears a number of hats, i.e. fulfils a number of roles. The authority of the HR Officer emanates from people management policies and programmes of the organisation. The advantage of these policies and programmes and the acceptance of the HR Officer's specialised knowledge enhance this authority. However, the role of the HR Officer is multi-faceted and in fact he/she wears a dozen hats viz.

- **The Advisory Hat:** He/she advises the line management in all matters relating to people management so that motivational levels are kept high so that stress levels are reduced and productivity is increased.
- **The Conscience Keeping Hat:** The humanitarian aspect of management, ethics and governance fall within his/her purview of responsibilities. Management is informed about its ethical obligations towards the internal customer (employee), the external customer (client) and the society at large.
- **The Counselling Hat:** In the course of work the employee faces a host of problems many of which are not job related. These may be related to issues of health, finance, housing, or social mores. The task of ameliorating these problems and giving wise counsel falls to the lot of the HR Officer.
- **The Mediating Hat:** During inter union and intra union rivalries and during employer-employee conflicts the HR Officer mediates to diffuse the situation and insure that conflict does not escalate.
- **The Representative Hat:** In front of the larger civil society the HR Officer represents the humane face of the capitalist and during grievance handling sessions he/she acts as the employees' voice to convince the employer to demonstrate equity and social justice especially in non-unionised organisations.
- **The Record Keeping Hat:** In matters of time keeping, wage and salary administration, statutory compliance and personal records, the HR Officer acts as a maintainer of records.
- **The Statutory Hat:** Under a plethora of labour legislations the HR Officer has to insure that statutory compliance takes place. In addition he/she has to deal with matters in Labour Courts, Industrial Tribunals and National Tribunals. Hence, his/her knowledge of labour law must be up to date.
- **The Welfare Hat:** Under the provisions of the Factories Act the HR Officer (personnel officer) performs a welfare function looking after canteens, latrines, crèches, hospitals, consumer co-operative societies etc. His/her employment is quite secure.
- **The Problem Solving Hat:** In case of disputes as well as issues involving human resources in any way, the HR Officer is expected to deal with the situation at hand and solve the problems arising thereto from.
- **The Change Agent Hat:** The HR Officer is the initiator, catalyst and manager of all change processes within the organisation and this is because there is an inherent resistance to all change and it is his/her task to marginalize this resistance.

- **The Decision Making Hat:** As a part of the strategic management team, he is a part of the decision-making process formulating policies and procedures to facilitate the decision.
- **The Decision Executing Hat:** Once the decision is made, it has to be carried out and enforced to meet the best interests of the organisation. It is the task of the HR Officer to facilitate this process simply because most decisions involve a human angle.

In analysing these cases the participant must select which hat is most appropriate for the occasion and remember that the HR Officer has to juggle several hats at the same time in real life.

CONTENTS

SECTION THREE

SHORT CASE STUDIES IN HUMAN RESOURCE PLANNING

SECTION FOUR

SHORT CASE STUDIES IN CORPORATE CULTURE

SECTION FIVE

SHORT CASE STUDIES IN INDUSTRIAL RELATIONS

SECTION ONE

SHORT CASE STUDIES IN STRATEGIC HRM

CASE 1

ASSOCIATE STAINLESS STEEL LIMITED

Associate Stainless Steel limited is a Rs. 200 crore company, which is located in Jabalpur. It has a total manpower strength of 8500 of which 100 are Senior Managers, 300 are Managers and 600 are Junior Managers/ First Line Supervisors.

You, (Mr. C. R. Narayanan), are the Divisional Manager in the steel plant unit consisting of a forge and a foundry. Both these departments form one unit and there are five other such units in the company such as the rolling mills, the blast furnace and steel melting shop, the general engineering division (which includes maintenance), quality control and inspection, commercial division which consists of the support functions. This means that you are a very senior line executive. You have a Masters Degree in Mechanical Engineering from IIT (Powai) and a Masters Degree in Industrial Engineering from NITIE (Mumbai). Hence many issues relating to HR are marked to you and you assist the General Manager in manpower planning. However, you have a flair for technology and consider HR a soft option which always occupies a secondary position in your scheme of things.

Each unit is a separate profit centre but all the five units commonly share the support functions, which fall under the commercial division. The commercial division consists of finance, personnel, electronic data processing, training and development, corporate communication and marketing and sales. Within materials management comes the production planning and control function. The personnel function is not involved in manpower planning since that is the General Manager's job. It is involved mainly in industrial relations and welfare related tasks. Training and development function consists of two engineers acting as liaison officers who arrange trainers from outside to impart mainly technical training to employees, who gets trained in what function is determined by the Departmental Head and there is no fixed training budget.

There is one senior representative from the commercial function, who along with a small team, works for each of the four production units. For the foundry and forge a Manager, Dr. R. B. Sharma, who is a very efficient, 35 year old, soft spoken, sincere, and hard working engineer with a flair for computerised systems control, heads this function. Employees of his Section are very pleased with him and he generally commands respect among his subordinates and peers.

However, Dr. Sharma's performance depends on the co-operation given to him by Mr. Ulhas Naik the Senior Manager (Production) and Mr. Fred Suarez, the Senior Manager (Materials). The Maintenance Function comes under the purview of Mr. Naik's section and the Stores Function falls under the purview of Dr. Sharma's section. And it is the Stores Control Function that is letting Dr. Sharma down.

The annual target realization exercise has just been concluded for the year. You have made certain discrete inquiries about the reason for the poor performance of Dr. Sharma although the foundry and forge, as a unit has done well. Independently, both Mr. Naik and Mr. Suarez speak highly of Dr. Sharma both as a performer and as a manager. However, both Mr. Naik and Mr. Suarez are in their mid 50s who have risen up from the ranks and do not have anything more than a plain Bachelor's Degree. They feel that if Dr. Sharma is permitted to succeed, management may soon promote him and they may have to report to the young man. This, they secretly wish to avoid but are too decent to make it obvious.

Individually both Mr. Naik and Mr. Suarez are very capable managers who have held on to their commitments and attained their individual KRAs all along. But, there is also a long-standing rivalry between the two at the personal and at a professional level. Hence, they do not co-operate with each other, to the extent that is expected. As a result of this especially, the Commercial Section is not being able to support unit targets and perform as per the organization's expectations of it. Requisitions to the stores are not given in time and stated clearly. Hence, Dr. Sharma is at a loss to support the profit making functions.

You are sitting in your room after a lunch break and are about to go over the regular but important divisional reports to be sent by you to the General Manager of the Steel plant. Just then Dr. Sharma, who is usually a calm and dignified person, storms into your office and starts to blabber in an agitated voice. You calm him down, order two cups of tea and glean the facts from him. After an hour long meeting you are convinced that Dr. Sharma has performed poorly since he is the unwitting victim of circumstances that lie beyond his control and it is clear that you have to intervene in the matter.

What will you do? This is clearly a Strategic HR problem and top management expects you to handle it.

HINT:

Desired Discussion:

To counsel two senior executives such that personal disagreement no matter how constructive should not be allowed to adversely effect the performance of the organization or any part thereof. That the overall organizational effectiveness takes precedence over individual or sectional effectiveness is not a matter of debate. Senior managers must learn to think and act in overall organizational terms rather than in narrow sectional terms.

Desired Message:

(a) Three sections working in close proximity should have synergy, which comes from the realization that all sections belong to the same unit and cannot work independently of each other. (b) It is the principal task of Mr. Narayanan to see that there is a commonality of purpose and that all 3 units work in tandem. (c) Inter unit communication appears to be ineffective, since there is a perceived threat from Dr. Sharma's success.Each of these must be addressed and solved.

Desired Solution:

Mr. Narayanan calls in Mr. Naik and Mr. Suarez separately to see what their problems are Mr. Narayanan assures them that even if Dr. Sharma at some point were to be promoted, they are not threatened, as they are valued employees. Mr. Narayanan calls in all 3 for a joint meeting to discuss the unit performance.

Desired Strategy:

(a) Get Messrs. Naik, Suarez and Sharma to state their targets for the next year. (b) Targets must be quantified and qualified as well as cost and time bound. (c) All 3 must agree to the targets set by them as a team, and be committed to achieving them.

Desired Action:

Discuss — Communicate — Thrash it out. Take decisions democratically to ensure commitment. Implement decisions autocratically to ensure compliance. Never point fingers if a team is to be built. Unit goals supersede sectional/ individual goals.

Desired Learning:

Not all managements are alive to the need for Strategic HR. So the development of top management mindset takes time. To begin with, never have a line manager look after HR functions. Always have personnel (HRA), industrial relations, manpower planning, and training functions under a trained expert who does not have to report to a line manager.

❑❑❑

CASE 2

INTERNATIONAL TELECOMMUNICATIONS

International Telecommunications is a part of the medium size company located in Borivali, Mumbai. It is a family owned company that went in for a public issue of shares in 1995. The Software Support Function in the Telecom Company consists of a highly dedicated team of young persons who are not really software professionals but who have learnt the science individually in the school of hard knocks. A very prestigious Government of India project in the area of fax store and forward has been given to your Company by the MTNL. Software to run the proposed program has to be developed in-house and then alone can the project be executed. This is one of the terms in the MTNL contract.

The software team has already spent three months and not come up with any meaningful results. They have been working night and day on the job. Then suddenly in May 1997 they have come up with a program, which has been tried and tested for quality as well as for accuracy and reliability. The MTNL project has been saved in the nick of time. A euphonious project manager has directly recommended that the software team be given an incentive by way of an annual increment thrice that of the other good performers. Top management has agreed to the recommendation. The team has been issued congratulatory letters but the actual increment has not been given yet.

You are the HRD Manager who was not a party to this decision and subsequently you find out that: (i) There was only one dedicated and competent person in that team and the others were only busy playing second fiddle to him. (ii) The competent person in the team privately does not like to be equated to other non-performers in his team and resents getting the same quantum of increment. (iii) Giving this team a special annual increment would de-motivate other teams and other departments since it comes across as if the Company rewards those who come up with immediately discernible results and not those who may have silently contributed to the overall performance of the company.

You have reason to believe that Top Management had not been given the complete picture, not so much by intent but by default, when approval for special increment had been sought. What will you do?

HINT:

Desired Discussion:

How to award incentives and remunerate employees in teams for performance so that motivation levels is kept up? Should such recommendations be made without prior HR intervention and involvement? Clearly, if the HR has to have any meaningful contribution to make then its interventions must have executive approval and the Department must be empowered to act. Incentives are usually valued in monetary terms but there are a lot of non-monetary incentives such as a good climate the ability to take decisions and job enrichment.

The question is what should be the ideal mix of monetary and non-monetary incentives? Is there an optimal mix possible? Who besides the HR expert can decide on this issue?

Desired Message:

Anything, which has concern with human resources, needs HR involvement from the start to the finish.

HR must vet all recommendations in the light of

- Equity and parity·
- Reward for performance·
- Motivate a team without de-motivating other teams.
- Neither of the above was done in this case.

Desired Solution:

Make sure that the silent (behind the scenes) workers are also recognized and rewarded. Sincere and efficient workers seldom toot their own trumpet. They leave it to results to speak for themselves, as their ego will not permit them to shout from rooftops about what they have achieved. Call in the high performer and tell him that he was a part of a team so he must not be separated in getting a reward. However, a note will be made in his file so that when the time comes he will be rewarded appropriately. And this must be actually followed through at the correct time. Inform top management and the project manager not to make recommendations in respect of personnel without HR involvement.

Desired Strategy:

Make sure that such competent people are made Team Leaders so that additional rewards are made easy to give.

Clarify that performance is rewarded by pay rise but for promotion, ability as well as performance is considered.

Be totally transparent so that room for doubt is greatly reduced. This will help keep teams motivated.

Remind people that motivational plans and programs will flop unless the person is self-motivated and has a sense of belonging to the company.

❑❑❑

CASE 3

INDIA TEXTILES (PVT.) LTD.

After graduating from VJTI as a Mechanical Engineer you were gifted a legacy by a rich relative in his will. So you decided to become an entrepreneur. Approaching a co-operative bank you started a small Textile Company in Bhiwandi, which employs 400 persons, and became its CEO. When other textile mills were closing down you started exports and minted your money between 1980 and 1990. The year now is 1995. Messrs. Meat Parwick has just approved the ISO 9001 certification for the company. The Company has a Senior Manager, Human Resources Management under who are Manager Training and Development and Manager (Personnel). You look after production, Commercial and HR departments yourself well knowing that your expertise lies in technology and in striking commercial deals.

There is a highly efficient Senior Human Resources Manager who reports to you. The Manager (Personnel) and Manager (Training) report to him. He is trustworthy and transparent. He is incapable of playing organizational politics and the employees respect him a lot. But he is known to speak his mind and put his money where his mouth is.

The Manager (Training) is a young graduate from TISS and this is his first job. His training skills are excellent and he has successfully undertaken a number of HRD interventions. He has computerized the personnel records and streamlined policies under the guidance of his boss. The pay for performance scheme introduced by him as well as the Suggestion Box Scheme was very successful. Unfortunately, he is a man of few words, has a very self-effacing attitude, and not very ambitious.

The Manager (Personnel) is a middle-aged ex-army man who had joined the company as a Security Officer ten years ago. He was promoted five years ago and transferred to the Personnel Department. He is loud mouthed, arrogant and has little finesse at the personal level. But at the public level he is an excellent PR man who has kept the labour authorities and the state bureaucracy pleased as a result of which the company has had no problems in respect of statutory compliance under labour law. The Trade Unions too have stopped showing off their muscle ever since he took charge of the Industrial Relations function. However, he has no formal qualification in Human Resources Management, he is not interested in training, cannot write or speak good English and does not really come across as a corporate executive in his manner and bearing. But in his task of maintaining external liaison and strike free industrial relations, he is very effective.

Due to a fall in export orders your company has started recording losses and all HR initiatives like training were halted on the advice of Manager Personnel. The Senior Manager, Human Resources Management has resigned and while going had stated that unless the company starts taking HR seriously it will face acute problems in future. He has accused you of paying lip service to HR and for indulging in double-speak. He also accused you of paying Manager Personnel the same salary as you did to him even when it was he who the Manager (Personnel) reported to. He added that this was because you were weak and did not want to upset both your managers so you had equated their pay but changed reporting relationships. You are so miffed that you have withheld his last salary. The Manager (Personnel) who the employees do not respect has started lobbying for promotion. He has let it be known that if an external candidate is recruited he will make life miserable for the person and the company would suffer. You also know that if you do not promote him the liaison built with the external authorities may be jeopardized. You also suspect that if he is made to supervise the work of Manager (Training) the young graduate from TISS would quit because they do not see eye to eye on many matters, and their style of functioning is very different. Besides, if you do promote him, you are aware that the image of the company might suffer and internal customer satisfaction might no longer be the same.

How will you deal with the situation?

HINT:

Desired Discussion:

How do you tell an executive that he has reached a level beyond which he cannot rise and that the organization needs will be served best by not promoting him? If this option (of promoting him) were to be removed, how do you continue to keep up his motivational level? Perhaps, job enrichment as a method of motivation along with constant challenges through job rotation holds the key.

Desired Message:

(a) Promotion is not automatic.

(b) Promotion is only one way to recognize talent.

(c) People work generally for two things: money and recognition.

Desired Solution:

Reward the Manager (Personnel) and upgrade him (if) you can increase his job description to include other tasks like overseeing security in which he has had experience.

Reward the Manager (Training) and upgrade him (if) you can increase his job description to include other tasks like firming up a Training Calendar and actually taking sessions himself.

These awards must come after the job descriptions have been enlarged and the new targets have been met. [In the case of software or any other professionals there will be a job profile rather than a job description]

Desired Strategy:

Make it clear that each of them is a valued member of the organization and has a future provided conscious efforts to be made towards self-improvement.

Do not hire an outsider for at least 3-4 months during which period both men have had a chance to prove themselves.

Absolute clarity of the CEOs thinking on the subject must be communicated and no room for blackmail must be given.

Immediately appoint an Assistant to Manager (Personnel) ostensibly to help him but actually to cushion the shock should he leave. Do the same for Manager (Training) so that there is always a buffer available and the project is not in jeopardy of anyone quits.

Desired Action:

If you pay peanuts you will get monkeys.

Avoid increasing pay after resignation has been tendered.

HR intervention must ensure recognition before it is too late to do so.

Remember that once an employee thinks of leaving and begins to look for a job you have already lost him.

❑❑❑

CASE 4

BANGALORE SOFTWARE TECHNOLOGIES

You are a Marketing Specialist from Lancaster University who has just been recruited to serve in India from abroad. You are to head a small-scale industrial unit in the software industry set up by Non Resident Indians some years ago. The story of the company is typically one of from rags to riches variety. At the top level the original team had loyally stayed on and grown with the company. The erstwhile CEO who had brought them with him, when he left a British Multinational to start this venture with NRI funds swore by their loyalty and individual excellence. And in the past they had delivered the goods. Now the CEO has left due to a more challenging (and financially rewarding) assignment in the Middle East, which came out of the blue and you have stepped into his shoes at short notice. You are new to the environment but you sense that something is not quite right.

As the new CEO of the small but growing computer software company in Bangalore, you decide to employ a Business Policy Analyst to study the company and give you a confidential report. Three months later you get the report only to discover that a large chunk of the market in Southern India is not being exploited. As a result of this, your company has lost out on possible profits and the possibility of increasing its market share. This is because of a variety of reasons principally among which are the following three: (i) Managers are concerned with immediate short run actual costs and profits rather than long run opportunity costs. (ii) Managers do not maintain records of clients they have serviced so that follow up cannot be done and further customers cannot be tapped. (iii) There is an unusually high rate of turnover among software professionals so that continuity of personnel dedicated to specific projects cannot be ensured.

When you pose the problem in a meeting with the Senior Managers of the Company you are informed that your fears are unfounded because: (a) The net profits have risen by average rate of 150% per annum since 1993. (b) The company shares are after all doing very well in the National Stock Exchange. (c) The attrition rate is an industry wide phenomenon and since every person wants to do development tasks as against software maintenance tasks, there is an in-built frustration in the profession anyway. (d) The company may not be a bad paymaster but the engineers recruited from Institutes of higher learning have grandiose ambitions that the market forces cannot allow the company to fulfil within the present financial constraints. (e) There is more demand than supply so why should you bother about marketing the company aggressively?

You realize, by dint of your exposure to international business, that this is a typical trading firm syndrome and that the senior managers are either unprepared to face up to or unwilling to meet the challenges of globalised market competition.

How will you go about changing the mindset of the men at the top? Should you even attempt to do so? If the men at the top resist change in themselves what moral right do they have to enforce it on others?

You decide to call in an HR expert from IIM (Bangalore) who after studying the situation suggested that the mindsets of senior managers needs to be changed first of all. You do not have time to moot a prolonged HR intervention as suggested by the expert. So you decide to handle the matter yourself. Consequently, you book a hotel in Ooty and take the senior managers over for weekend of brainstorming and a free for all discussion on issues germane to the organization's future. You invite the HR Expert from IIM (Bangalore) to accompany you as an external - impartial facilitator. He declines the offer and suggests that you keep it an internal affair first.

What will be the message you would like to convey to the managers and in what direction should the brainstorming exercise move? Why?

HINT:

Firstly, share the findings of the HR expert freely with everyone in the weekend retreat and sit back. Maintain that since it is a collective problem so a collective solution must emerge. Try to be a patient listener and let the managers do the talking. A leader will automatically emerge to enable facilitation. The aim is to get the senior managers to take decisions about change in attitudes democratically even if it takes time to do so and then to pursue these decisions with zeal since the senior managers themselves own the ideas.

Desired Discussion:

Should Senior Executives not realize that records of projects to be documented, that investment in the product market (through building a marketing network) and investment in people (through training programs) are organizational imperatives? Should executives stop considering short run actual costs and start looking at long run opportunity costs instead? The support systems need to be fine-tuned to suit organizational aims and put in place so that vital time is not lost in building the infrastructure each time a new project comes in hand. But is it worth the cost?

Desired Message:

In an era of liberalized markets, privatised ownership and globalised competition, executives must be prepared to grab every opportunity that comes along. If not, they will be surely overtaken. Every project must be documented, and client contact must be maintained even after the project is over, this is the job of marketing.

Desired Strategy:

Persons remain in a company for compensation, career enrichment and growth. If every one is addressed well and clearly, attrition can be contained. Career enrichment is the best option open to Management for retaining any professional. So job rotation as well as technological update/ training must be high on the agenda of a CEO. This will ensure a continued competitive edge and the desire to be technically updated will contain attrition among professionals.

Desired Solution:

Never get in an outsider unless the problem first has already been posed internally. This means that a major brain storming of top-level executives must be the first step of the CEO.

Solutions must be seen to come out of the senior managers even if the CEO already decides them. He should make it seem as if it was their idea. This will ensure commitment.

Do you need top quality technocrats/ technicians for mediocre quality tasks? Why not hire persons from second-rate institutes who can be groomed to grow with the organization?

Training professionals when they are relatively unoccupied saves idle time and keeps the professionals motivated enough to stay on.

There is a cost of attrition. Therefore, why not think in terms of long run opportunity costs instead of being bogged down by short run actual cost considerations?

❑❑❑

CASE 5

BANERJEE AND CHATTERJEE CONSTRUCTIONS

Banerjee and Chatterjee Constructions is a reputable and large civil engineering company in Kolkata with an annual turnover of Rs. 500 crores and involved in developing specific projects has gone in for business process re-engineering in 1993. The whole operation has been divided into eight Focus Groups that are evolving into independent profit centres. Each profit centre will have its own sales cell, accounts cell, administrative cell and planning cell. Of course there are some corporate functions like HRD, finance, marketing, strategic planning and environmental management, which service the needs of each of these eight Focus Groups. The Focus Group concept has by and large worked very well.

The Chief of each Focus Group acts as a mini CEO and is extremely powerful. Due to a healthy rivalry for a greater slice of the total corporate profit, each Focus Group is competing with one another in containing costs. As a result of this, training is seen as a cost, which will be incurred only when the market/client needs so require. Otherwise the thinking is that why should the company train an employee if there is little guarantee that he will stay on anyway. Marketing is another function that is paid lip service to and the Focus Group Chief actually goes out and gets the customer himself. Each Focus Group exists independently of the rest and there is little interaction between them except on matters of common business interests. Hence, the organization in terms of people and process has grown but not really developed.

As an economist who graduated in Industrial Relations from XLRI and who is now looking after the HR function, you have made a private analysis, which now stands vindicated. When the business cycle was on an upswing, profits were not diverted into people and process development activities with the result that when the recession came, the company had no funds for these kind of activities, which remained under-developed. With the liberalization, privatisation and globalisation, of the Indian economy the company has to have the required competitive edge to battle foreign capital intruding into the national market. This it seriously lacks and is losing out to competition. It is conceivable that a Korean firm may make a bid to take over your company unless you had the financial muscle to offset its threat, since the economy has now opened its doors to direct private foreign investment. The company needs the inflow of capital badly but cannot raise it nor can it withstand foreign competition in terms of quality of output and meeting client's required delivery schedules.

Traditionally HR has been treated, as a support function not directly involved in managerial strategy formulation. There was clearly a Catch 22 type of situation looming large on the horizon and as the HR Chief you are at your wits end on what to do. Your Managing Director now realizes that HR ought to be part of corporate policy formulation and looks upon you to provide a strategy for survival. He has asked you to come up with an action plan and present it at the next Key Managers Meeting. You have 10 working days in hand.

How will you react and why?

HINT:

You are advised to look at issues from the point of Strategic HR and not just develop HR Strategy as has been stated in the brief given to you.

Desired Discussion:

Should foreign take-over be permitted and how can it be prevented? What is the company's area of core competence and can this be exploited positively for creating sustained growth?

Desired Learning:

In any industry such as infotech, biotech and architecture, the human brainpower is crucial. This has to be nurtured and updated to retain an edge in the competitive market.

In a federal organizational structure, the onus lies heavily on the corporate level functions, to maintain a unified force, give direction and monitor progress. This will ensure constancy and enable the Company to make use of its full potential.

Corporate Marketing, Corporate Finance, Corporate HR, and Corporate Planning need to play a proactive interventionist role and not a policing role.

Effective Marketing and HR hold the key to the growth of a corporate culture.

Corporate Governance is indispensable in this day and age. Therefore, this function must be developed in the organization.

Desired Message:

Training is not a cost but an investment that an organization makes in the growth of its people so that the individual performance is enhanced and collective growth is made possible. Training persons to suit immediate organizational needs is myopic. If training is to be need based then when a new project comes along where new skills are needed, the organization cannot take advantage of the opportunity, as the desired skills are just not there. The attitude that one should not train persons unless they are sure to retain the employees is self-defeating. Research shows that many young persons leave organizations simply because in-house training has not helped them to keep up their knowledge and skill levels at par with the accepted technological modernity in the industry. Moreover, it is better to train a person and allow him to leave than to pull on with an organization where men have had little or no new training since their employment.

❑❑❑

CASE 6

RAJU'S GARAGE

Raju was a motor mechanic who worked for TELCO Pune and had to return home to take care of his family when his father died. Not being able to maintain the family without a steady income he used the land with a 10,000 square foot area to start the only business he knew: the repair of trucks. This was in 1970 and Raju soon became well known among the truckers who plied the Mumbai-Pune Highway. There was a small tea Stall attached to the garage where the truckers could get a bite to eat and rest a while. Even today there is a small garage in Navi Mumbai named Raju's Garage, which specializes in repairing broken down trucks, and four wheelers on the national highway ever since it began. Raju's son who had passed his B.Sc., unlike his father who had no formal education whatsoever, took over in 1980 and gave the garage a new decor by concreting the floor and building a proper tea stall which even served dhaba (wayside inn) food.

However, since 1993 the development of the Mahape-Turbhe-Thane-Belapur industrial belt led to an inordinate growth in the business of this garage. It developed into a small workshop to meet the growing demand with facilities for servicing, maintenance and painting vehicles in 1995. A year later it also obtained a permit to trade in second hand vehicles, which thrived with the growth of Navi Mumbai. To this was added a small restaurant (Raju's Hotel) and in 1997 a petrol pump was due to be added to the business.

Annual sales turnover in 1980 was Rs. 1 lakh but in 1993 it had risen to Rs. 250 lakhs. By 1996 Raju's Garage was a roaring business and the proprietor had started a machine shop with 5 lathe machines and 3 milling machine employing 20 persons. His business was set up so as to service the needs of small-scale industries in the region, which may off load work on contract. From a mechanic, he became a trader and now he is an industrialist. Raju had purchased a Mercedes Benz car and his life style was nothing but opulent. The net profit figures were not very impressive though. Raju barely made Rs. 10 lakhs per annum after paying back the banks and the other creditors. It was not adequate to support his life style but the regular sales turnover had helped pay his bills. The Bank Manager advised him to professionalise his business and have a second in command who could help streamline functions. However, Raju was insecure so he consciously refrained from taking on an assistant who would be able to professionalise his business. Instead, he continued to say openly that he was a professional himself so his business was professional too. He, seldom if ever, shared his views about the business with his assistants saying that they would not understand his ideas anyway.

In 1999, Raju made a deal with Wadia and Co., who had a dubious business reputation and dealt in imported motorcars and parts. This gave Raju an avenue to enlarge his business interests and with it his income. The relationship with Wadia and Co., began on a good note and there was bon homey.

In the meanwhile, Navi Mumbai itself went through a bad patch and development was stemmed. There were many reasons for it and some of these were as follows: The area was notorious for malaria carrying mosquitoes and people hesitated to move into the flats that they had invested in.

When the police began to wage an unending war on the underworld in Mumbai, the lesser-known criminals shifted base to Navi Mumbai making the residents quite insecure. The opening up of the economy clipped the wings of Wadia and Co. Accordingly, the price of imported motor parts were hiked. This affected Raju's clientele who now began to replace imported car parts with the Indian ones. The State Housing Scheme unfortunately flopped when construction defects were found to be glaring and there were fewer takers as news spread. In sum the infrastructure expected by Raju in the initial years of his venture failed to materialize in the immediate environment of his business.

With the recession setting in at the end of 1997, Raju was in deeper trouble. The second hand car business was not earning much revenue since most people went in for new cars where bank finance was available. Raju's Hotel no longer attracted the clientele it once did since better hotels had sprung up. Industry in the area too was not doing do well so contract jobs were no longer available. To add to this, Raju had to pay back to the bankers Rs. 25 lakhs, which he had borrowed when things were looking up for his business.

A mile away from Raju's Garage was Modern Motors set up by two graduates from IIT (Mumbai) who had obtained MMS Degrees from the University of Mumbai. After a preliminary but methodical survey they decided to compete with Raju's Garage. They took one year to study the market, carve out a niche and through a conscious strategy developed that niche'. For them it was vital to have a plan first and then develop that plan. Identifying their customer was of great importance to them. Their aim was to give such high quality service that customers turned into clients. Accordingly, they bought land, took a bank loan and started the garage with Rs. 5 lakh venture capital. Within 5 years they had built a showroom and sold Maruti Cars for which they had obtained a small franchise. They even had a tie up with a bank to finance loans to persons who would purchase a car from them. However, they made one thing sure. Everyone who mattered was fully involved in the decision making process and held accountable for deliverables. Today Modern Motors was still in the automobile business, had not ventured into horizontal integration, but in spite of the recession were still doing well. From selling new cars, they had begun to sell second hand cars now and their garage had a steady clientele from the various industries, which had entered contracts for vehicle maintenance with them. Net business growth at steady rate of 50% per annum had been retained. The scenario at Raju's Garage was just the opposite and the year is 2004.

What had strategically gone wrong for Raju? After all, both the businesses were identical in many ways and operated within the same environment. Using Raju's example develop strategic HR practices for a small sales and service organization.

HINT:

Desired Discussion:

(a) Who is the customer? What does he desire? What will delight him?

(b) Should organizational growth be consolidated before another spurt of development takes place?

(c) Is there not a crying need to develop an overall Corporate Vision and Mission irrespective of the size of business? Should that Vision and Mission not be translated into Goal and Role Clarity?

(d) Should this Clarity not come out of Transparency and Communication?

Desired Message:

Whenever the growth of business is contingent entirely upon externalities rather than on managerial entrepreneurial skills, the company would usually have benefited by default, just because it happened to be at the right place at the right time. Growth is then not planned nor is the company prepared to face up to downturns. This was not a learning organization, if the analogy can be used. Above all, whenever a tie up is envisaged the credibility and soundness of the proposed business partner must be thoroughly investigated.

Desired Strategy:

- Have a definite vision, which is written down and clear to all.
- From this vision must spring a definite mission.
- Out of the mission comes direction, role and goal clarity.
- Plan the work accordingly and then meticulously work the plan. Develop transparency and a chain of command.

Desired Caution:

Unless you know where you are going you will not get lost. But not knowing where to go will make you over commit yourself and take unnecessary risks. In projects similarly, one tends to over commit unless one knows one's capabilities and also is aware of the other's expectations.

Desired Action

Besides having a vision, a mission, role and goal clarity, a company needs to have a steady clientele, which can come only by investing in marketing. By investing we do not imply employing a titular figurehead but actually having a dedicated team to harness and exploit market potential. Raju had failed to realize this moot point. Many organizations have fallen by the wayside due to a similar managerial mindset.

Remember that small companies cannot afford an exclusive HR function. But that does not mean that HR issues do not arise or that they are unimportant. In such cases strategic HR must be built into corporate policy.

❑❑❑

CASE 7

M. N. KASTOORI LIMITED

M. N. Kastoori Limited was an Indian based multinational, which operated in the Middle East and West Africa as a Construction Engineering Company in a major way since 1980. It had the distinction of building two international airports, three palaces for Sheikhs and five major highways linking the capitals of ECOWAS countries. The Kastoori Group also had trading firms that supplied construction material like cement, mild steel rods, sand, paint and so forth.

As a conscious policy it had bifurcated its operations into geographical areas by forming one company in each region. Each such company had a different name, a different business policy team and a very different managerial style but followed certain broad guidelines set up by the Corporate Office in Mumbai. Although each such company had its own Vision Statement, Mission Statement, and Quality Policy, it stated on its letterhead that it was a part of the M. N. Kastoori Group of Companies. It is of course possible for a company looking after Africa, for instance, to bid for a contract in Middle East, if it felt it had the expertise required. Such was the level of autonomy that prevailed.

The Corporate Office has an HR Wing, a Marketing Wing and a Strategic Planning Wing, which theoretically supported the Group Companies, but in practice the companies were very autonomous. The CEO of each company was either a hard core construction engineer or an architect who had either joined the company soon after passing out of college or had a long innings with the company. They were the team of old faithful soldiers who had always stood by their General (Mr. M. N. Kastoori who was now in his eighties). However, they were non-conformist in the sense that proper systems and procedures for administering projects were never developed and each project was handled uniquely.

In early 1996 a very prestigious UN sponsored development project in Latin America invited tenders for taking up the re-building of a small country that had been devastated by a prolonged civil war. As it happened three of the ten Companies whose bids were short listed belonged to the M. N. Kastoori Group and were invited to make presentations before a team of international experts in Santiago later that year. One Group Company was unaware that the other was invited nor that they had bid for the same tender.

When the representatives landed up in Santiago it was then that they knew that they belonged to the same group. No investment in manpower was made, nor was adequate planning done since the CEO was convinced that once the project was finalised companies would deliver the goods. None was awarded the contract and through an influential local resident Indian, they decided to find out more. The three Group Company representatives managed to informally obtain the UN Team's opinion on what went wrong. They learnt that the reason none of them had got the eventual contract was partly because each of them had a separate way of computing their quoted price, each had a different parameter and none could convince the UN Team that it had a realistic HR intervention policy at their base which took care of internal customer satisfaction. The most powerful objection was if the three Companies in the same Group did not know how the others were bidding, they had no internal co-ordination and could not be expected to have good co-ordination where a major reconstruction project involving several major Companies would be involved.

On their return the result of the feedback was placed before the Corporate Office Strategic Management Team.

Suppose you were as an HR expert were to Head the Corporate Strategic Management Team for the M. N. Kastoori Group what would you do?

HINT:

A team leader is an enabler, communicator, facilitator and visionary all rolled into one. He has to take his team along with him and lead from the front. E.g. he cannot speak of changing managerial mindsets unless he demonstrates that he is willing to change himself too.

Desired Discussion:

When several business units within one corporate umbrella compete for the same client and give price bids, which are different from each other, the image suffers. Things get worse when these are computed differently and when one is not aware of the existence and submission of the other's bid, the corporate image in the market takes a beating from which it is hard to recover. Is a corporate image really important?

Desired Learning:

- A federal organizational set-up is very productive so long as there is transparency and communication between the various units.
- Hard core technocrats tend to overlook corporate interventions due to their pre-occupation with the tasks at hand. This is not abnormal. But this is undesirable.
- When a system for project management is non-existent then bench marking of progress is not easy not is it viable to monitor progress and take corrective action.
- Investment in infrastructure after the contract is obtained is possible only if the contract provides for a lead-time for work to begin. If not, all personnel and systems must be on line waiting the awarding of the contract so that work may begin at once.
- It is vital that when Companies within a Group bid, they should do so through a single channel; marketing or a liaison office. A single window policy is always safe so long as the window is subjected to monitoring and its practices are subjected to benchmarking against others in the market.
- Always aim high and yet be realistic about taking risks. Risks can be statistically calculated but uncertainties cannot.

Desired Action:

Call for a meeting and brainstorm issues fully before you lay down guidelines, which are followed uniformly for:

- Assessing infrastructure — requirements.
- Project administration — (PERT-CPM Charts).
- Fall back positions in event of non-conformity with the project guidelines.
- Costing of projects and estimation of lag times.
- Procedures for constant charting and monitoring of projects.
- Lay down rules by which a CEO making a bid does so through a Corporate Marketing Office so that only one bid goes. This may be dispensed with if all procedures are uniform and policy permits various companies to compete for a single bid.
- If companies in a group are geographically divided then they should confine to their territory.
- Overlapping territories, duties, responsibilities and accountabilities are the sure shot methods to embrace failure.

Desired Policy:

It is fatal for any project management to proceed without a definite plan which is cost bound, time bound and can be monitored.

Quality must be in-built into the process at all costs if international competition is the target.

❑❑❑

CASE 8

INDIA PHARMACEUTICALS

India Pharmaceuticals was a small firm that had grown remarkably well in the face of competition from the other giants in the field. However, you as the General Manager were hell bent on making as much money for the CEO before the year 2005 A.D. when GATT imperatives on patents would be promulgated. This was the message you gave to the sales manager who in turn conveyed it to his young sales force and along with the HRD Manager you devised an incentive scheme, which linked rewards to sales revenue.

The sales force took up the challenge and in their enthusiasm to earn greater revenue fought zealously to guard their turf but thought nothing of cutting corners and encroaching on their colleague's market segment. To add to all this, delivery contracts with hospitals were signed with fluid specifications so the customer in the midst of the contract often altered conditions. Also, commitments were made only to gain immediate benefits with little concern for retaining the clientele in the long run. As a result, quality of product as well as service suffered. Claims of products were not supported by scientific evidence as well as market performance. So the credibility of the sales pitch was in doubt. Salesmen found newer ways to sell their products and outdo each other. Many a time separate teams approached the same client from the same company making a separate sales pitch.

What had started as healthy competition in 1990 had degenerated into an undeclared cold war between factions and sales teams. Sales persons became more and more ruthless and trust relations at the customer level plummeted to an all time low. The market image too was fast losing its erstwhile glitter as customer complaints rose. In their zeal to do better than the rest, Sales persons did not share information and resources were not being used for the overall good of the organization. The General Manager was very concerned with what was happening and rightly realized that organizational aims and market goodwill were being overlooked for the sake of short run revenue. He took up the matter with the CEO and it was decided that the General Manager calls a "general meeting" and along with the HR Manager starts laying down the do's and don'ts of sales practices.

You agree to the CEO's suggestion and tell the HR Manager that the meeting is scheduled for the Friday and today is Monday. The HR Manager insists that the Sales Manager be asked to call the meeting instead and invite you, the General Manager, and the HR Manager to attend. Therein, he says that decisions should be taken democratically but enforced autocratically. This is not in consonance with what you and the CEO had agreed. It was a time-honoured practice that corporate decisions were taken at the top and at the lower levels people met to democratically decide how to implement them.

What will your strategic response be and why?

HINT:

Desired Discussion:

Should contracts not be watertight so that mid-course alterations are not possible? Should there not be an in-built clause for quality as well as non-compliance penalty? At what point does competition no longer remain healthy?

Desired Learning:

When there exists general insecurity leading up to an environment of mistrust, a situation where subordinates vie with one another for meeting the company sales targets and end up stabbing each other in the back, what the Unit Head has do is to create a climate of faith. Profits, no doubt, are a necessary condition of business but cannot become the principal aim of the company. To remedy the situation, he should act in a manner where ethical conduct is emphasized. He will have to walk his talk and lead from the front while making sure that decisions taken are accepted and implemented.

Desired Solution:

- Most organizational problems can be set right once systems and procedures are perfected and followed. This is also true for inter-personal relations as well as sales.
- Many unit heads subconsciously prefer fluid situations so as to use their managerial prerogative. Without proper checks and balances, liberty can become license. However, if there is sufficient transparency and a climate of learning exists then creativity and innovation will thrive.
- A good example of fluid systems, which permit the unit head to use his discretion, is the unwillingness to share a resource with other departments. This can be prevented through Strategic HR intervention, which creates a climate of openness and togetherness.
- Empowerment and accountability cannot be separated from each other so it is the Sales Manager who should call the meeting and invite the Superior Managers to attend.
- The problem must be posed openly at the meeting and the solution must come from the sales team. This will ensure commitment and ownership of the decision.
- All future contracts for delivery must have definite clauses for quality, non-compliance, penalty and all specifications. It should not be possible to change conditionalities in the midst of the contractual compliance very easily.
- Advertisement of a product may bend a fact or cover it slightly but should never contain false claims. It is illegal and unethical besides having long term negative impacts on the company image.
- Corporate Governance thus becomes an imperative for Strategic HR to succeed and cannot be left in the hands of Company Secretaries and Chartered Accounts alone.

❑❑❑

CASE 9

ALL INDIA METALLURGICAL LABORATORY

The All India Metallurgical Laboratory (AIML) was set up in Adityapur during the 1950s to service the needs of local industry in the Chota Nagpur Region of Bihar. In 1990 this Government of India body received a major boost with the CII intervening to promote industry. Teams of analysts were created by geographical location and by industry kind. So there were two teams that looked after Coal, one that looked after iron ore, one that looked after mica and manganese Ore, one that looked after imported ore like ferro chrome, two that look after Automobiles and four that looked after Steel Products. Each such dedicated team consisted of 8-10 top-level metallurgists taken from prime engineering colleges.

The Support Function consisted of three cost accountants, two chartered accountants, three security officers, two librarians, three stores and purchase officers and one personnel officer under whom the time keeping function came. Strict security was maintained and owing to the confidential nature of business neither summer vacation trainees nor outside consultants were permitted in the premises. HR intervention was unknown at AIML. The Director and his Senior Research Coordinator who sent the persons for specific need based training outside the organization decided upon technical training.

However, those who were recruited from any other industry with three to five years experience were offered a salary of something like Rs. 3.0 lakhs per annum. Those who had joined the laboratory straight from College through campus recruitment were given a salary of Rs. 1.8 lakhs on joining and after three years could expect no more than Rs. 2.5 lakhs per annum. The argument given was that good talent for research and analysis was hard to find and one had to pay a little extra to poach such talent from industry. Salaries very often depended on the bargaining ability of the candidate at the interview. Also, teams working with the Automobile Sector were usually given a higher rate of incentive so that they do not leave the laboratory and join industry. Teams working on mica and manganese ores were particularly hard done by.

During the period 1985 -1990 the annual turnover rate for manpower was fluctuating between 14% and 18% per annum. In 1991 it had risen to 20% and by 1995 it had touched the 35% mark. However, there was always manpower available from the vast reserve army of unemployed graduates in India. The real problem was that the new entrants had to be paid more than the salaries of those who left. This added to the cost of employment. Also, the new entrants took time to get set into the grove and there was a loss of output during this breaking-in period. Some of these new entrants had to be trained in specific skills and training costs mounted as well.

You saw that there was a problem, realized that it was not within your field of expertise and asked the Personnel Manager for an opinion. The manager hemmed and hawed but gave you no solution and offered no advice. You felt very frustrated. An expert from XLRI was called in by you to assess the situation and he recommended immediate wage parity be given to all groups. This was implemented after a four-month study. Everything seemed to have reverted to normalcy when in 2000 there was a sudden rise in attrition. The immigration policy to the USA has been one reason why people quit while the other reason was the expected turbulence caused by the formation of a new Jharkhand State within which the organization would fall. The Director has called a meeting. As the senior most managers it is your work that suffers most due to attrition and you are genuinely concerned. But you are a top research scientist at best and a mediocre technocrat at worst. You are willing to listen to an expert and you strongly believe that the Personnel Manager is not the right person to advise since he is 55 years old, has not been exposed to HRM and too set in his ways. You know that something should be done and some expert from outside should be called in. You had called in an expert from XLRI years ago and acted on his advice to good effect. Now the Personnel Manager is resisting your calling an outside expert and wants time to "solve" the problem himself.

How will you position yourself and put forward your views at the meeting? Will you do so at all? Should it not be the Director's job to think of such things anyway?

HINT:

All along you have taken decisions and were accountable for them. Why should it be any different now? What prevents you from taking a stand and not passing accountability upwards? The buck stops at our desk.

"Physician heal thyself" is an advice often reserved for tradition bound Personnel Managers who resist change and fear expert opinion in their field. Raise this issue clearly.

The emphasis should shift from employee recruitment to employee retention.

The changed political situation should have been discussed with managers openly so that doubts could be eradicated at the outset and attrition could have been curtailed.

Desired Discussion:

What is the position of the Personnel Manager in this issue? Was he ever consulted?

What is the real problem? Is it person related, process related or situation related?

Has anyone made a scientific study of why employees leave? Have exit interviews been conducted and the findings recorded? Were the findings communicated to the Director? Did the management act upon them?

In a situation where employees with the same age, qualification and experience profile in the same work unit get unequal compensation and recognition merely due to historical reasons, how would the Head of the work unit rectify the anomaly? There is a need for transparency and fairness not only to be practiced but also to be seen as being practiced. Wage salary and incentive differentials should be attended to at once so that de-motivation is nipped in the bud.

Desired Learning:

There must be some way available for wage bargaining at an interview but within certain limits only. People work for pay and recognition. The first fulfils an economic need whereas the second fulfils a socio-psychological need. HRD must address both with fairness and equity. A grid showing education, experience and salary must be developed and implemented.

Desired Solution:

This is a typical scenario when HR intervention is missing. Hence, an HR Consultant must be brought in at once so that a climate is created for forming a full HR section.

At the next annual increment exercise the managerial grid could be used to address anomalies.

Performance Appraisal Systems must be installed at once and operationalised. Evaluation of performance must be against stated and committed targets.

Complete transparency at the time of re-fitment is desired to offset feelings of favouritism.

Desired Caution:

(a) Experience shows that it takes 3 fitments (over 3 years) to set the house in order. Too quick or too drastic a re-fitment is not recommended.

(b) Disparity in wage levels gives rise to the feeling of inequality and negates teamwork.

(c) Unit Heads subconsciously may use these to show off their power to the detriment of organizational interests.

(d) The Personnel Manager must metamorphose into an HR Manager and intervention must be proactive and planned.

❑❑❑

CASE 10

BOMBAY INFOTECH LIMITED

Dr. Asutosh Dubey is a top-level specialist in just about anything that has to do with information technology. He is a much sought after consultant by the Government of India, has had a stint with the United Nations, is a Professor at the Indian Institute of Technology (Powai) and at the age of 60 was made Professor Emeritus at Bombay University. In 1992 by special permission of the Senate, the Academic Council of Bombay University permitted him to take over as the Executive Director of a software company named Bombay Infotech, owned wholly by the Government of India in Pune. Dr. Dubey reported directly to an ex-IAS officer who was named Mr. Chaugule and who was the Managing Director of the company since 1983. The company had been performing very poorly and in 1991 the Government of India was actually thinking of selling it off to private capitalists.

Mr. Chaugule is a polite, well-mannered and sophisticated person who also happens to be the cousin of a senior politician and has a lot of influence in Delhi. Policy making, reward allocation, target setting, recognition etc., fell within the purview of Mr. Chaugule. Leading the team, meeting the targets, delivering results and servicing customers was within the purview of Dr. Dubey. It sounded like a sensible arrangement and Dr. Dubey was glad not to be encumbered with administrative detail.

Dr. Dubey led by example, had excellent rapport with the team, worked day and night to turn around the company. In 1995, the company was awarded a major contract in Indonesia followed by a contract in the Middle East. Every newspaper published a lead story when the company bagged a major contract in the United States against competitive bids from Europe and the US itself. For a company, which had lost contract after contract in 1985, and had been declared sick in 1990 this been a remarkable feat! However, Mr. Chaugule being an astute person managed to project himself as the architect of the turnaround. Being a person wedded to his work Dr. Dubey did not seem to mind.

However, between 1994 and 1998 the number of software engineers who left the company had risen substantially and most used the newfound good name in the market to get lucrative jobs overseas. When he went deep into the matter, he discovered that the company paid its employees less than its competitors did and the training budget was very low. The young men and women who left the company sang the same refrain: Sir you are a great boss but this company has a lousy personnel policy. When he broached the subject with Mr. Chaugule he was told that he was a scientist and should not concern himself with company policy, since the Government of India had an ex-IAS man (in him) to do just that. In 1996 Dr. Dubey actively pleaded the case with the Central Government for a re-look at the entire personnel policy but to no avail. His major concerns were attrition and the declining morale of his team.

He told the Ministry of Science and Technology that he did not want to make personnel policy but unless the issue was addressed soon he was placed in an embarrassing position before his team. The Ministry replied that this was within Mr. Chaugule's portfolio and not his. Furthermore, he was a scientist who should not bother about pay scales etc., which were after all mundane issues. In frustration he resigned.

When the Minister of Science and Technology heard that he had resigned, Dr. Dubey was invited for a meeting at which the Minister of Human Resources was also present. They asked him, in the nation's interest to take back his resignation. At this, Dr. Dubey lambasted both men and said that if nothing were done in three months time, his resignation would stand tendered. He asked: "Why did you have to wait for me to resign before you woke up?" He added "What prevents you from going back to your old ways once I rescind my letter? Have you not read the book: Who Moved My Cheese? I recommend you do so."

You are the Minister of Science and Technology and you do not want him to leave. What will you do?

HINT:

Desired Discussion:

Should departmental Heads go to the extent that Dr. Dubey did? Was Mr. Chaugule guilty of any act of omission or commission? Are rules meant for the convenience of men or vice versa?

Desired Learning:

In a department where the No. 1 man controls the power and the No. 2 man is held accountable for delivery of work schedules but is not adequately empowered, what kind of top management intervention is called for to counsel the boss and prevent deterioration in the team's performance? A clear and equitable policy regarding rewards and expectations must be made clear to all, linked with declared targets and then implemented.

Desired Solution:

In any company where software projects are the main source of revenue, continued training is a very important factor in retaining talent. Hence, proactive intervention to give technical training to employees so that their knowledge and skill level is at an acceptable height is recommended.

Salaries are an important criteria no doubt, so this aspect needs to be addressed as well.

Bureaucrats usually make good routine bound administrators but very poor proactive HR managers. The time has come to address issues squarely with often-revolutionary solutions. Hence, Chaugule should either be given another portfolio or made to re-think his position.

Desired Caution:

In reality very seldom do people like Mr. Chaugule change their ways. Hence, the HR function tends to unfortunately become toothless, and as a result, the organization suffers. Change in the Executive Mind Set is important and must percolate from the top downwards. The greatest hurdle to progress is the human ego, and that affects all facets of work in one way or another. Guarding one's turf like Mr. Chaugule did can only impinge progress. How many of us subconsciously do so? Why? What breeds insecurity? Uncertainty and insecurity are ideal ingredients for organizational politicking, rumour mongering and facilitate the rise of the mediocrity. Eliminating this is the first hurdle in building a value based corporate culture.

❑❑❑

SECTION TWO

SHORT CASE STUDIES IN TRAINING AND DEVELOPMENT

CASE 11

THREE ASPECTS OF PERFORMANCE COUNSELLING

[This is a set of three shorter cases on the subject aimed at distinguishing performance counselling at three levels]

SENIOR EXECUTIVE PERFORMANCE COUNSELLING [Individual]

Modern Pharmaceuticals Limited is a medium scale company located in MIDC Marol and has taken full advantage of the fact that it is in Mumbai to expand its activities. It holds franchises from several Indian firms and has a very young and dedicated sales team as well as a workforce, which has contributed to its high market growth since 1993. Mr. Prakásh Desai (PD) is the Senior Manager (Sales) who heads this team. He is a B.Sc. (Pharma) graduate who has completed his MBA from the Institute of Global Management and Research at Bandra (Mumbai). With the spectre of 2005 A.D. looming large on the horizon, PD wants to increase sales revenue before the GATT strictures on patent rights begin to bite.

He addressed his sales team in January 1995 and laid down the cards face upwards. The team went in for a "hard sell" drive. Overall sales rose by 300% since then and revenues rose by 500%. Incentives rose by 200% and salaries by 100% between 1995 and 1997. However, during 1997 the attrition rate had increased from 10% per annum to 25% per annum (a condition which shocked everyone since the economy had entered a recessionary phase). The Manager (Sales), Mr. Bakul Parikh (BP) felt that incentives ought to rise but it is the salary component, which must be raised more if persons have to be retained. PD disagreed, felt that BP had got it all wrong and even accused him of becoming an unwitting spokesman for his team: something managers are not supposed to do. PD further added that it was the job of the salesman to sell and he was paid a wage for it. What he did extra was his incentive. The sales team all along felt that if wages were raised proportionately then they would not think of leaving the company, which had always treated them well.

In January 1998 the quarterly figures were analysed and it was found that sales during the fourth quarter of 1997 was 23% lower than that in the third quarter and this, in turn, was 40%

lower than sales in the second quarter of the year. Whereas, profits continued to be made, motivation levels had fallen and attrition rates had risen.

PD blamed BP for this situation and in the annual performance appraisal rated him poorly. PD felt that BP was not acting like a manager but as a team representative. Consequently, he was given a 5% increment in salary.

BP felt that PD was insensitive to the situation, misread the intention of feedback and wanted to shift the responsibility for failure to his subordinate so as to look good in the eyes of top management. Consequently, as a protest he has refused to accept the annual increment saying that the recognition was unjustifiably low.

PD has written a stiff letter to you as the General Manager recommending that he takes disciplinary action against BP, since refusing an increment amounts to misconduct under the Company Rules. You are the Head of HR and the matter has been referred to you.

Who will you counsel, what will you say and why?

HINT:

Apparent Issues:

- Proven insubordination which cannot be overlooked.
- Managers should not fan de-motivating feelings in the team.
- Converting a managerial conflict into a personal issue.

Real Issues:

- Managers need not be only task oriented.
- The problem perhaps lies with PD and not so much with BP.
- You will have to counsel both individually and differently.
- You will have to stress the fact that organizational goals take precedence over individual goals and all managerial behaviours should be value based keeping in mind the overall organizational interests.

❑❑❑

SENIOR EXECUTIVE PERFORMANCE COUSELLING [Group]

Greenfields Ltd. is a Company, which specializes in biotechnology. It has a well-equipped laboratory and research centre, a team of highly competent scientists drawn from various disciplines and involved in public awareness campaigns. It has a Projects Division, which looks after the development of "environment friendly systems" which would form a part of growing townships or rural development. It has a Biotech Division, which looks after the development and use of pesticides, fertilizers and chemicals for the agricultural sector. It has an industries Division, which is in charge of pollution control and industrial waste disposal. Finally, it has a Research Division, which is dedicated to the analysis of existing products and developing new products. Each division is an autonomous unit and a core group at the corporate office, which is involved in strategy formulation and corporate planning, supports the federal structure of Greenfields Ltd.

Mr. S. K. Gupta, a genuinely polite person who is considered to be a wizard in biotech development of new geographical locations, heads the Projects Division. He is the Vice President who is more concerned with his work than with anything else. His second in command is Mr. A. K. Sinha who is basically a town planner with a penchant for environmental concerns. Mr. Sinha is the General Manager under whom the entire division operates. There is a Senior Manager for each support service like Accounts, Personnel, Sales and Administration who reports to Mr. S. K. Gupta directly. It is generally felt that Mr. S. K. Gupta is a scholar who finds any administration cumbersome. It is also felt that Mr. A. K. Sinha is a hard taskmaster and an action-oriented manager whose bonafides, efficiency and effectiveness is unquestioned. But he is alienated from the rest of his division because of his status consciousness and reluctance to communicate his thoughts openly and freely. There is a feeling of "us" and "them" quite visible between the Management and the Techno-scientists, which perhaps adds to the feeling of alienation. Several attempts made to communicate this to Mr. Sinha by the HRM have failed. The team under Mr. A. K. Sinha consists of 30 very competent techno-scientists each with his own specialization. This team of 30 techno-scientists is divided into 3 groups of 10 persons each and each group has an office support team of 3 persons who look after clerical and routine tasks. Individually, the performance of the techo-scientific team members is very good but cumulatively it is not. The company is doing well as is the division. The moot point is that it is not doing as well as it should and therefore it is losing out on the opportunity cost front. The performance of the Projects Division found to be is well below par by the annual target evaluation exercise. You are the Vice President for Corporate Strategy and you find out (after interaction with the various persons in that Division) that there is a serious problem that must be addressed.

How will you counsel your colleague Mr. Gupta?

HINT:

Apparent Issues:

- Individual excellence but collective mediocrity.
- Energy and effort is not always channelled properly.
- Actually the Division functions as a Group and not as a Team.
- Trust relationships are low as there is poor communication from the top.
- Nobody has told the techno-scientists what is precisely expected of them.

Hidden Issues:

- The division is task centred and not person centred·
- The degree of inter-personal communication is low.
- There is little clarity of role, goal, and this leads to everyone doing their own thing at their own pace not knowing what is in store for them at the end of the day.

These are the group issues which you will have to address in the counselling session where the "us" and 'them" concept will have to be debunked. There is only a "we" concept if real progress is to be achieved.

❑❑❑

EXECUTIVE PERFORMANCE COUNSELLING (Organizational)

Bharat Steel Company manufactures stainless steel rods, flats and bars for export. It has a steel melting shop in Nasik, which produces billets. These are out sourced to several special steels plants for rolling into rods and bars. These are then sent to the Pune plant of Bharat Steel Company for annealing, pickling, straightening, grinding and despatching.

The General Manager (Pune) and General Manager (Nasik) report to you, who are the Vice President (Production) located in the corporate office in Mumbai. Both the Pune plant and the Nasik plant are individually doing quite well and the group quarterly incentive paid on the basis of output + dispatch has been consistently high.

Now, a major consignment sent to Germany has been rejected for poor quality and this has cost the company Rs. 1 crore plus a loss of goodwill. The customer is not even prepared to buy your product as an inferior quality steel and pay you less for it. Besides, you have to pay for its shipment back to India. This will also mean that the group incentive payable for that quarter will be low and this will cause a ripple effect in terms of frustration and de-motivation amongst the employees. You are very upset and have called both GMs separately for a close door meeting.

The GM (Nasik) blames the GM (Pune) for dispatching goods without proper inspection and the special steel plants, to which the work was sub-contracted, for rolling defects. The GM (Pune) blames the GM (Nasik) for defects at the steel melting stage and showing laboratory reports in support of his claim. Both GMs accuse each other (in absentia) of covering up for the incompetence of their respective units. The result is that the organizational interests are suffering and overall performance is being adversely affected.

You are not satisfied with what the GMs tell you, since you know that there is an element of truth in both versions. So you decide to discuss the matter with the Corporate HRM Manager who informs you that the calibre of staff in the Quality Control Cell is poor and since their organizational status is low, many a time line managers succeed in bulldozing their products past the inspection stage. You then call both the GMs in for a joint meeting for a counselling session to promote the overall organizational interest.

What will you say to them? Will you involve the HRM at this stage? Give reasons.

Should you not address the issue of organizational structure and design so that functional parity is maintained?

HINT:

Address the issue of organizational structure and design at once. Make accountability go hand in hand with empowerment.

Apparent Issues:

- Poor quality of output is costing the company both in terms of profit and goodwill.
- HR intervention is called for to create quality awareness.
- Senior Management should think in terms of organizational interest first and departmental or unit interest later.

Real Issues:

- Quality can neither be assumed away nor can it be inspected at the last stage of production. It has to be in-built in the entire process irrespective of the kind of industry. The QC team must comprise of senior and technically competent people who are empowered. Systems must be in place to take care that this disparity between functions and executives does not happen.
- You will have to emphasize the overall corporate goal in your counselling session and make the point that consistency and dependability in quality holds the key to competitive advantage.

❑❑❑

CASE 12

LAKSHYA CONSULTANCY SERVICES

Five students who successfully completed their PGDBM from Lakshya Institute of Management Studies and Research and since all of them hailed from Pune, they have got together and started a HR Consultancy Service. Since all the students had majored in Human Resources at the postgraduate level they knew each other well, understood each other's strengths and weaknesses and the comfort level for working in a cohesive team was high. They named their consultancy out of sheer love and respect for their alma mater whose name they even adopted i.e. Lakshya Consultancy Services (LCS) and began operations from Pune where they took up an office on Junglee Maharaj Road, which was the heart of the city. The motto of this LCS was to "deliver value based and value driven services to corporate houses and small-scale industries that approached them such that every single customer would be converted into a confirmed and reliable client." The background of the five members is given in brief below.

1. Richa: An amiable M.Com. postgraduate with a flair for numbers and data. She was comfortable with analysis of data using a computer but was by no means a computer programmer. She was an introvert of sorts and did not like to meet customers for the first time. But once the customer was prepared to discuss requirements then Richa would invariably sit in on the discussion, take notes, ask clarifications and then disappear in the back office to deliver the requirements. She has written short pieces for newspapers and even published some of her poems but had no work experience before joining Lakshya. She loved taking short training sessions and this was something she realised during her summer project with a Corporate Training Organisation. Her minor specialisation had been Finance.

2. Arjun: An extrovert to the core he was a B.A. in English Literature who boasted that he could sell a refrigerator to an Eskimo in the middle of the Alaskan winter. He handled media very well, did the publicity for functions at the institute when he was a student and now continued to do so as a partner for the consultancy. He could talk well and was an outdoor man but asking him to sit behind a desk was a tough job. He had worked selling space for a newspaper for two years after graduation and before joining Lakshya Institute of Management. His minor specialisation had been Marketing.

3. Charlie: An electrical engineer with a penchant for gadgets, he loved developing programs on the computer, assembling stereo music systems and repairing electrical goods for his friends. He was a hard worker who did not flinch at a challenge but when he relaxed on weekends he was the wild party animal. He liked abstract mathematics and people with the same zeal and so he was in many ways two persons built into one. He chose to talk less but when the time came to speak his mind he could be painfully forthright. In the Business Analysis Quiz held for leading B-Schools he had helped the Lakshya Team, which had bagged the first prize in India. Before joining Lakshya he had worked as a Data Entry Operator and then as a Team Member for two software companies in Mumbai for four years. His minor specialisation had been Systems.

4. Sangeeta: With a B.Sc. degree in Botany and Zoology she was a persuasive talker. She hated numbers with a passion but loved being with people. Her PR skills were excellent and preferred to liase and operate from an office desk instead of going into the field. She was the senior most in the group and had been a school teacher in science for seven years before going back to academics at Lakshya. Being on the Placement Committee she had good corporate contacts and invariably accompanied Arjun for the first customer call after she had set up the meeting. At present she was perusing a PG Diploma in Training and Development, which she hoped to complete in six months time. She had taken Marketing as a minor specialisation but was not really interested in the subject since she loved to teach more than to sell.

5. Gautam: A Mechanical Engineer who had worked for five years on the shop floor of an automobile company and developed a liking for People Management. He had been particularly successful with handling workers on the production line an his love for the underprivileged was known to all. This is what prompted him to go back to academics and join Lakshya. As a student he had excelled in Industrial Relations and his summer project was with an NGO that worked with educating workers in the small-scale industries sector. He was pursuing a Degree in Law and hoped to complete the same next year. He was always there to campaign the cause of weaker sections of society and was a great animal lover. In particular he had continued to be in touch with the NGO and trained taught workers in basic shop floor skills under its umbrella. He had opted for operations as a minor specialisation since this was closest to his work experience.

On graduating from Lakshya the five of them had taken up HR jobs in the corporate sector. But four years thereafter they met up in an alumnus meeting got on to sharing their frustrations and decided to set up LCS. All five of the partners are mature, in their thirties, and very serious about whatever they do. But LCS has been in business for two years now and there seems to be lack of clarity regarding their purpose, focus and division of duties. Very often they hire training facilitators to assist them in meeting customer needs but the experience with almost half of such facilitators has been far from satisfactory. There is moreover little linkage between one training session and another in the same programme. So the five have re-grouped for a re-think.

Break up the class into three groups. And each group will collectively address the following issues through discussion. Only when you have agreed upon a focus and a target area will you return to make a presentation. You have exactly one week to do so. Come back with a clear strategy and make a presentation in the next class.

Issue No. 1. What will be the HRD Consultancy Services that LCS will offer?

Issue No. 2. Who will be their target customers?

Issue No. 3. Will the services be niche'? Customer specific? Core competency based?

Issue No. 4. How will the organisation and functional structure of LCS be set up?

Issue No. 5. How will the services be provided and who will provide them?

Issue No. 6. If they hire outside facilitators how should the programmes be handled?

HINT:

There is no need to have core competency if the organisation is comfortable with having divergent competencies. However, for a new entrant into the market, it is necessary to create a market niche and a corporate identity.

❑❑❑

CASE 13

RADHA FERTILISERS AND CHEMICALS

RADHA Fertilisers and Chemicals was a small firm that had grown remarkably well in the face of competition from the other giants in the field. It also had sizeable exports especially to East Asia and West Africa. The name RADHA was an acronym for the five persons who had initially got together, pooled their capital and set up the company. Set up in 1960 it had registered modest growth up until 1980 after which things had picked up. Two reasons were generally ascribed for this. Their five sons, who ran the show and had a more international exposure, having studied abroad succeeded the first generation (founder) entrepreneurs. Corporate policy changed from admitting that while profits were needed for growth, people who worked for the organisation also needed looking after. What was badly needed was a long-term view of organisational growth that could match global competition. RADHA Fertilisers and Chemicals did not have any such well-articulated plan and virtually "managed in the moment." In pursuance of this ideal they have recruited you as General Manager from a multinational firm in 1982. There is no doubt that you being a Finance specialist from XIMB are forever looking at the bottom line without letting your long term development perspective being adversely effected. However, you understand very well that you are not an HR Expert but nevertheless people management is important for growth. Within three years of your joining the organisation you have recruited a young lad who has been trained at DYPIMR and is considered by his alma mater as a "small guru" in training and development.

The CEO wants the growth chart to register a visible increase and the financial standing to improve. You as the General Manager were hell bent on making as much money for the CEO before the year 2007 A.D. when the two founding fathers of the company would be superannuating. This was the message you gave to the Sales Manager who in turn conveyed it to his young sales force. After negotiation and consultation with the Sales Head you devised an incentive scheme, which linked rewards to sales revenue. The term value in context of the company when used by you in the early stages of the campaign to promote sales related only to value addition and this was measured in the form of returns on sales. You were looking at the financial dimension only.

The Sales Head believed that as long as financial returns were pouring in the manner in which sales were to be achieved was not important. At the end of the day it was profits that counted. Quality was controlled in terms of cost and the ability to force sales in the market. For instance, three products had registered very high sales levels since 1998 in spite of the fact that their efficacy was highly debatable. The first was a potency pill called Power Plus, which in fact was a strong multi-vitamin but sold at rate Rs. 200 for a sachet of four pills. The second was disposable syringes that cost Rs. 50 more than the best market competitor. The only reason municipal hospitals bought these were that they were not disposable could be re-used to last for a long time and bureaucrats' palms were greased with impunity to promote their procurement. The third was named Malarial Caps, whose process patent was blatantly pirated from Germany.

The sales force took up the challenge and in their enthusiasm to earn greater revenue fought zealously to guard their turf but thought nothing of cutting corners and encroaching on their colleague's market segment. To add to all this, delivery contracts with hospitals were signed with fluid specifications so the customer in the midst of the contract often altered conditions. Also, commitments were made only to gain immediate benefits with little concern for retaining the clientele in the long run. As a result, quality of product as well as service suffered. The market was sooner or later likely to realise that the three products were not quite what they claimed to be and that would adversely effect future sales. This was the fear of the sales team.

Claims of products were not supported by scientific evidence as well as market performance. So the credibility of the sales pitch itself was in doubt. Salesmen found newer ways to sell their products and outdo each other. Many a time separate teams approached the same client from the same company making a separate sales pitch. What had started as healthy competition in 1990 had degenerated into an undeclared cold war between factions and sales teams. Sales persons became more and more ruthless and trust relations at the customer level plummeted to an all time low. The market image too was fast losing its erstwhile glitter as customer complaints rose. In their zeal to better than the rest, sales persons did not share information and resources were not being used for the overall good of the organisation. There seemed to be no clear organisational bonding between teams.

In the summer of 1991-92 a student from XLRI was doing his summer placement program at RADHA Fertilisers and Chemicals and presented a very articulate, factual and candid report on the marketing function of the company. You had accidentally read it when you found it lying on the desk of the HRD Manager, asked for it and quite uncaringly it was passed on to you. You subsequently discovered that several such summer placement reports had been submitted over the years and routinely they were sent to the stores. Nobody including the HRD manager ever read them!

You as the General Manager, realise that what started out as a good intention turned sour because there was no clarity of strategy. Naturally, you are very concerned with the situation when you understood the gravity of what was happening and rightly realise that organisational aims and market goodwill were being overlooked for the sake of short run revenue. You took up the matter with the CEO and it was decided that the General Manager calls a "general meeting" and along with the HRD Manager starts laying down the do's and don'ts of sales practices.

You agree to the CEO's suggestion and tell the HRD Manager that the meeting is scheduled for the Friday and today is Monday. The HRD Manager insists that the Sales Manager be asked to call the meeting instead and that he invites you, the General Manager, and the HRD Manager to attend. Therein, he says that decisions should be taken democratically but enforced autocratically. This is not in consonance with what you and the CEO had agreed. It was a time-honoured practice that corporate decisions were taken at the top and no reasons were given to anyone as to why these decisions were taken. At the lower levels people met to democratically decide how to implement them.

- ***Did the Training and Development function fail to address the needs of organisational growth?***
- ***What is wrong with the company? Is it that values and ethics are not properly defined, accepted and communicated?***
- ***What should you, as the General Manager, have done in the first place?***
- ***What will your response be to the stand taken by the HRD Manager and why?***
- ***How can such a situation be avoided in the future?***

HINT:

Look at the entire situation from a strategic HRM point of view and subsume it within a general policy prescription for training and development.

Creating a program based on training needs analysis is needed along with complete clarity of vision, mission, role and goal at the level of the person, process and product.

After the training has been completed a detailed analysis of the impact of training is needed to dovetail future interventions.

❑❑❑

CASE 14

INTERNATIONAL INFORMATICS INCORPORATED

International Informatics Inc. (TRIPLE I) was an outstanding market performer whose base was in Chicago, USA, but which had subsidiaries in 21 countries across the world. It was well known for manufacturing computer hardware and gave stiff competition to the well-known names like IBM and HP. In 1985 it began to offer software solutions and within a decade made a mark for itself global market. Started by a migrant German Jew with a philanthropic bent of mind ever since its inception in 1970, TRIPLE I funded research projects in Universities on Management Informatics Systems (MIS) and Management Control Systems (MCS). This funding of projects was soon extended in the Third World and scholarships were offered to deserving candidates based purely on merit. The company treated its employees exceedingly well and as a result, the attrition (employee separation) levels at TRIPLE I was well below the industry average. When projects were not available the company paid the employees all the same and did not believe in retrenchment as an option. Instead, the lean periods were when training was given to the employees to keep them updated with technology and retain their morale.

However, the activities of the Personnel Department besides hiring and firing remained at the level of employee welfare and employee concern. Training and development did not feature in the scheme of things for Personnel Department that was very powerful but traditional. In 1981 the HR Department sent its entire workforce in batches for skill training in systems, marketing and finance. By 1993 the world economy had steadily become unipolar with the USA at the apex. It was a fact that TRIPLE I often sold the same or marginally different software solutions to different clients while charging them the full cost for developing the solution all the same. It similarly sold computer hardware with minor changes in the configurations for major clients claimed that the same were specifically developed and charged them for the entire cost. The research funded by TRIPLE I invariably came up with different patents and each of these was registered under the name of TRIPLE I with a token award to the research scholar/discoverer.

The US Press carried stories of how TRIPLE I found its way around the various tax laws and carefully cut corners to save millions of $. Nothing was ever proved. The Third World Press similarly carried articles highlighting the blatant exploitation of their resources by the company but the Governments did nothing about it. It was well known that the company had influential friends in high places. Competitors often accused TRIPLE I of indulging in industrial espionage and using high-level political leverage to gain an unfair trade advantage. Somehow the accusations never ended in a court case and a settlement out of court was reached.

Just then an eminent research scholar named Dr. Escobar of Portugal came up with revelation in his book *Exploitation Unlimited* that beneath that bright veneer of philanthropy hid a dark demon of exploitation. He questioned how contract after contract in the Third World was awarded to TRIPLE I when better-known players in the market existed and had a proven record of accomplishment, which was better. The scholar pointed an accusing finger at the nexus between the State and the Multinational Corporation, which was draining the country's economy. Value generation, he pointed out had been personalised and restricted to imply the generation of wealth by any means. The ghost of primitive accumulation of capital and wealth had returned to haunt the business, he further said. The Public Relations Officer went on the television and the radio to defend their company and stated that in a competitive world it was fair game to pull the rug from under your competitor's feet. Moreover, TRIPLE I was in business for profit and not in religion or for conversion. A two-page declaration to that effect in the leading newspapers followed next morning.

TRIPLE I took strong objection to the book and mounted a virulent personal attack on the author. It also pulled the right strings by doing which the Government of Portugal banned the book within weeks of its publication in 1998. But the text somehow appeared on the Internet site and journalists raised a public outcry. Other Third World countries, where TRIPLE I had business operations, like Pakistan and Chile followed suit and joined the outcry. The company mounted a public relations campaign to show that it had supplied quality products and generated employment in the Third World, benefiting the economy thereby. It also carried a cover story in Newsweek that showed pictures of its employees at various locations in an ebullient mood. It also seemed a classic case where the external customer was exploited to keep the internal customer satisfied. Which of the two groups of stakeholders was more important to the company was the issue at hand.

- ***Deliberate on the value system of TRIPLE I in the context of an organisation or an institution you are familiar with.***
- ***Are the values and ethics of TRIPLE I synonymous concepts?***
- ***Should Training and Development function be outsourced? If so should it not be guided by an internal HR policy?***
- ***Should Personnel Management be concerned with the welfare of the internal customer only or look after the interests of all stakeholders including society at large? Why?***
- ***Is it enough for an organisation to be Value Driven?***
- ***Should attitudinal and behavioural training not accompany skill training? If so, what ought to have been done and what can be done now?***
- ***What would you have done if you were to advise those at the helm of affairs at TRIPLE I?***

HINT:

Go into a discussion of beliefs, values and ethics before you embark upon any attempt to find a solution.What are the core beliefs of the leading actors? Are they acceptable to civil society?

❑❑❑

CASE 15

MAHAKAL ELECTRONICS LIMITED

With the opening up of markets and the globalisation of competition Indian business were in the throes of strategic alliances involving take-overs, mergers, and acquisitions. Mahakal Electronics Limited is an unusually successful firm. It was so named since it was located near a very famous Mahakal Temple and the owners believed that it was the great deity that had brought them all success and glory. However, it is relatively small and is being eyed for a take-over by several multinational companies. On its part Mahakal cherished its corporate independence and wanted to retain its identity. However, the current global recession of 2001-2002 has placed the company under considerable strain. The Chief Executive Officer was a financial wizard and his name was Deen Dayal Agarwal. He had good man management skills, was loved and respected by all, had a soft corner for his weekend golf and pursued an open door policy at work. Besides he championed the cause of fairness and equity at work with a passion. Mahakal Electronics Limited prides itself for having a vibrant and value based corporate culture. People fondly called him Chief. Deen Dayal was 58 years old and wanted to see someone who would succeed him in two years time. That someone, he felt, would have to share his zeal, subscribe to the values of the organisation, pursued a policy of egalitarianism and meritocracy, and also be able to successfully negotiate the company out of hostile hands and retain its identity.

The company had a Personnel Manager who looked after hiring, firing, welfare, legal compliance and personal records. However, the personal records of all persons including and above the rank of manager were maintained by the CEO's Secretariat and the Personnel Department was neither involved nor was it consulted in relation to matters concerning Managers. The company also had an HRD Manager but his department's activities were restricted to training workers and supervisors. As far as Managerial Staff was concerned the HRD Manager had no role to play and no say at all in respect of training and personal development. Generally, training was seen as something, which Senior Managers did not need and consequently they carried on working the way they wanted. The HRD Manager and the Personnel Manager were good friends but their functions seldom if ever overlapped or coincided. Both reported separately to the CEO of the Company who was benevolent, paternalistic and tradition bound.

A senior Vice President's position is about to open up at Mahakal Electronics, the internationally acclaimed maker of components for audio and visual equipment and computers. It is very possible that the incumbent would take over as the Chief in two years time. The head office of the organisation is in New Delhi whereas the factory is located in Jaipur. Whosoever fills the position will surely be one of the six most powerful people in the company and may one day become its Chief Executive Officer. So the whole company has been watching the political skirmishes among the three leading candidates: Anurag Singh, Jayanti Pillai, and Bharat Sinha. All three of them have proved their worth many a time. They are successful executives who are known to be personally very ethical but at the same time very ambitious. All of them command the respect of those who work under them and who have professionally dealt with them.

All three contenders for the position are known to lead from the front and lead by example. None of them canvassed for themselves yet did not prevent others from doing so, for them.

Anurag Sinha, currently Head of the Research and Development division, has worked this way up through the engineering ranks. Of the three candidates, he alone has a Ph.D. (in electrical engineering from BITS, Pilani), and he is the acknowledged genius behind the company's most innovative products. One of the current Vice Presidents, Hira Lal Yadav himself an engineer and a man with strong political connections both at the State and Centre levels canvassed on behalf of Anurag who is comfortable with figures, charts, and reports. He is, in true sense, a genius. He is often seen as a recluse and is visibly uncomfortable with man management. Instead of discussions and meetings he is more prone to issue memos and exchange e-mails with his peers. However, his stint as a new Vice President over the last year has been very successful. He has just turned 53 last week.

Jayanti Pillai has only a Bachelor's Degree who has spent years on the job and earned a reputation as an outstanding salesperson of Mahakal products. She has worked her way up the Marketing Division by sheer merit. She knows just enough about what she calls the "guts" of Mahakal`s technological network to get by. But she is very good at marketing the product and had has a big hand in promoting the brand image of Mahakal Electronics Limited. She is a very good leader and motivator. She was promoted as a Vice President about two years ago and has developed a reputation for being an honest go-getter. Ramanujam Nair, another Vice President, has always had a soft corner for Jayanti and has been filling the Chief's ear with praises about her. Jayanti however, did not quite understand Finance as well as he would have liked. She is a master negotiator and does not succumb to pressure. Though she is 48 years old Jayanti looks considerably younger. She is known to be efficient, loyal, truthful and trustworthy.

Of the three candidates, Bharat Sinha is the youngest being 45 years of age, and has the least experience at Mahakal. Like the Chief, he has a PGDBM from XLRI and a very sharp mind for Finance. He understands the stock market better than anyone else and the Chief has credited him with turning the company's financial situation around, although some others in the company believe that Anurag's product knowledge or proven selling ability really deserves the credit instead of his command over business finance. Bharat Sinha does not make enemies but has no particular champions among Mahakal's top executives, but he is the only other golf player the Chief has located in the company, and the two play a few rounds of golf every weekend. Invariably they would end up at the 19th hole for a few quick ones before going home. By nature he is flamboyant, charismatic and an extrovert. However, he looks tired and 10 years older than he is. Bharat Sinha seems to be indifferent to the race for promotion. He spent time on the phone and in front of the computer screen, reporting by e-mail to the Chief regularly on the company's financial successes. Although he kept his distance from the Chief at work, he never missed a golf game.

Hira Lal Yadav and Ramanujam Nair are already 58 years old and so the question of their succeeding the chief is ruled out. But they are efficient and reliable in delivering what is expected. They are both keen to have someone they like to grace that Sr. Vice President's chair. They have noticed that the company's financial decisions often get made during the cooling off period following a golf game. Both Yadav and Nair have a sharp mind but by nature are interested in minding other people's business and criticising others behind their back. They always take a self-righteous position and try to paint themselves as being "holier than thou."

In the month preceding the Chief's decision, the two Vice Presidents have been busy. Yadav was Head of National Engineering Association, (a professional body to which it was very prestigious to belong). He had been known to have worked very hard to help Anurag to win an achievement award from the association. He ensured a splendid press coverage of the event. And two weeks before the naming of the Senior Vice President, he threw the most lavish banquet in the company's history to announce the awards. When introducing Anurag as the guest of honour, Yadav made a long impassioned speech detailing his accomplishment and heralding him as "the future of Mahakal Electronics Limited". When this happened everyone including the Chief was embarrassed and their body language showed this.

Ramanujam Nair has moved slowly and subtly. Since the Public Relations function came under his ambit he used this to good effect. Over the years he would send news snippets and interesting articles to the Chief. Recently he gave the Chief one article from a psychology magazine about the "cloning effect" i.e. the tendency of powerful executives to choose successors who are most like themselves. He also passed on to the Chief a Fortune article arguing that many American corporations are floundering because financial people are running them rather than people who really know the company's business. To top it all, he submitted a Research Report from the IIM (A), which stated that women made better executives, and were less prone to corruption than their male counterparts. He also flooded bulletin boards and the chief desk with news clipping about the value of having women and minorities at the top levels of the company.

Deen Dayal Agarwal was a well-known name in IIM (Ahmedabad) as he had been invited several times as an expert guest lecturer to build industry-academic interaction. He lost no time in contacting two of his old acquaintances who were retired Senior Professors at IIM (A) and secretly invited them to come to New Delhi post haste. When they arrived Agarwal himself received them at the airport and whisked them away to a plush location on the road to Bhivani where he had made provision for their stay. For the next three days the three old friends debated and discussed who should succeed as the next Senior Vice President of the Company.

An idea of getting an outsider to fill the post was also mooted during these discussions but there was a genuine fear of his acceptance by those who were already in the company. This was because competition for the post had become quite intense and the atmosphere had been charged. So it was decided to give a special extension of six months to one year to the superannuating Senior Vice President so that the transition of the new person (whoever he/she may be) could be smooth. They agreed that corporate culture at the company needed to be reviewed urgently so that competition remains healthy and devoid of politics.

- ***Does HRD have a role to play in building corporate culture? What is that role?***
- ***Can the Personnel Function and the Training Function be allowed to operate as separate specialisations with no interaction and synchronised intervention?***
- ***As an HRD Expert which of the three contenders would you like to see as the new Senior Vice President and why?***
- ***What skills and aptitudes does the Senior Vice President of an Institution such as Mahakal Electronics Limited require? Can these skills and aptitudes be imparted?***
- ***Besides skills and aptitudes should values and ethics also not come under the HRD scanner?***

HINT:

Corporate culture building is part of the strategic HR responsibility. It is based on ethics and values on the one hand and on the goals and supporting systems on the other.

Review the dozen hats of the HR Officer and then look at the case afresh.

❑❑❑

CASE 16

BHARAT STEEL COMPANY

Bharat Steel Company was located in Bihar and began to be known for its good quality products as well as for its humane nature of man management. The company was set up fifty years ago by a group of entrepreneurs who had inherited ancestral wealth and wished to put the same to good use for the betterment of the national economy. They went out of their way to attract talent and created a Board of Directors from the professional experts to whom they entrusted the future of the company. The manpower strength of the company was 5000 workers and 500 executives.

Being one of the seven sons of a village mukhiya (headsman), A. D. Pandey was brought up in relative poverty. Though he had been given good upbringing the craving for money began to lure him quite early in life. He understood that to earn and retain money one needed power. So he set about single-mindedly to acquire power. He joined the IAS and as an officer, who had risen from rather modest beginnings, he served the Government of India well. He rose to the rank of Secretary and wielded a lot of power when he was posted in Bihar. He had also developed very good relations with the entrepreneurs who had started Bharat Steel Company. However, public sector and state sector salaries were no match for private sector compensations and so he began to think of switching jobs.

In the early 1960s there was a strong political movement to employ "sons of the soil" in the State of Bihar and accordingly A. D. Pandey grabbed the opportunity and resigned from Government Service to join Bharat Steel Company as its Director (Administration). It was well known that Pandey was hobnobbing with senior government officials and could make things easy or difficult for the opposition depending on what was at stake for him personally. The company placated the Government of Bihar by appointing Pandey, a son of the soil, as its non-executive Director. Three years later he was invited to join the Board of Directors and was appointed as Director-in-Charge of the Company. The company's ties with the state government improved, the offshoot of which was easy access to the License and Quota Raj that was prevalent in India at the time. Pandey played a proactive and leading role in facilitating the company's case before the government and all parties stood to gain as a result of this. Net profits for Bharat Steel Company doubled within five years of Pandey's joining the company. This was partly because the company could now get the license to import modern technology and thus the per capita productivity of labour rose substantially during the period.

In stages, Pandey had rendered the HR Department impotent. The Department was concerned with skill training, attitudinal training and behavioural training at all levels. It was also allowed to conduct these training programs but it was observed that these programs did not convert themselves into recognisable benefits once the employees returned to their workstations. The Personnel Manager was a stooge and could not assert himself. Hence, he became a pawn in the game plan of Pandey to whom he reported. When the profits increased, the Workers Union put up a demand for increased wages. They argued that the per capita productivity of the workers increased leading to higher profit and so they too must be given their due share. The workers went straight to Pandey.

Pandey argued that it was the imported technology in which the company had invested that was the reason for the profits. There was a major stand-off leading to a strike. Pandey played the waiting game, used the contacts in the government to brow beat the leaders, declared the strike illegal and terminated the services of 500 men who were taking an active role in the strike. Having sacked these men, he employed 500 sons of the soil in their place and thereby placated the government. The Board of the Company too was happy that relations with the Government had improved and the strike had fizzled out. Pandey became a blue-eyed boy of the entrepreneurs who gave him substantially increased powers. He then made a rule to the effect that 50% of all persons recruited in the company should be sons of the soil. He thus became a folk hero who had done well for the people of his state.

By nature he would help anyone who hailed from Bihar and was known (for them) to be a compassionate person by nature. But for non-Biharis he was quite the opposite. Pandey also began to sub-contract a lot of the work such as township maintenance, disposal of scrap and building of company quarters to his friends (who it was alleged) gave him a hefty cut from the proceeds. Pandey began to quietly build a small but palatial mansion in Patna from where he hailed and a bigger mansion in Muzaffarpur where his wife came from. He sent all his 10 children to study in elite schools and colleges in USA. In the state of Bihar, Pandey was hailed as a champion of the sons of the soil and songs of praise were written in his honour all over the state of Bihar. His village (just outside Patna) was truly proud of him as everyone said how much good he had done for his fellow men. It was done openly and so nobody suspected that the finance for these projects might have come from the coffers of Bharat Steel Company or from kickbacks.

Suddenly one day a dismissed union leader gave an interview to the local daily newspaper pointing out these lavish investments and raised questions about the way funds may have been raised for them. He even distributed copies of documents that supposedly substantiated this claim. The Workers Union began to take up the question and banners appeared in strange places on which was written *gali gali men shore hain, Pandeyjee chor hain*. Things were getting too hot for comfort. To save his own neck Pandey had to now break the unity of the workers so he played the caste card. His henchmen sowed a rift between the three castes among the Union leadership: the Rajputs, the Bhumiars and the Brahamins. Union leaders were so busy fighting against each other that nobody bothered with either Pandey or the Company any more. Profits continued to increase and the industrial relations scene remained quiet. This caste politics so divided the working class that they could not mount any strike action against the management. Business prospered and peace remained on the shop floor. Worker wages remained static even as market prices and company profits rose. Pandey took the credit for this.

Questions for Discussion:

- ***Should CEOs in the private sector also start hobnobbing with the government to get prime postings as is usually being resorted to in the public sector?***
- ***Can any organisation survive for long when the Personnel Function has been emasculated? Should the policy of divide and rule be encouraged?***
- ***What is your opinion as an HRD Expert about the way that Pandey used his power for the society at large in his state?***
- ***What sort of business scenario do you see unfolding for this organisation (unless things change) after the WTO regime comes in after 2005?***

HINT:

This is a case where values and beliefs come into play.

What are the work ethics of the organisation? Are they in consonance with those of civil society?

All power corrupts and absolute power corrupts absolutely.

❑❑❑

CASE 17

SUDARSHAN MILD STEELS

Mr. Pradeep Sudarshan was an old man who had come to India after the partition. It was clear that he was tired of life but the craze for making money had not left him even as he turned eighty years of age in 2000. He had inherited his family property after a bitter dispute with his brother whom he had deprived of his rightful share. A lot of skulduggery, arm-twisting and threats had been resorted to before the inheritance was gained. He then set up a small foundry in Central Mumbai, way back in 1965, wherein he manufactured steel strips. These were sold to industries that used it as raw material for their cold rolling plants and, in turn, manufactured finished steel for use in the housing industry as well as for the manufacture of household utensils. He had two sons who having completed their engineering in 1980 and had started to work in the family business. They believed in Training and Development but Sudarshan did not.

Despite the well-intentioned protests from his sons Pradeep Sudarshan continued to call the shots and his style of management was highly autocratic. He had no scruples about contravening the law of the land. He was well known for his polices of exploiting the workers and consistently paid them below the market rate of wage. His decision-making was never transparent and he believed in the managerial right to hire and fire at will without the need to give any reason. He had a lot of informers strategically placed in the company. These were the old timers that resisted all change. To them he was paternalistic. His policy was to check and cross check everything himself since he did not trust anyone. However, as far as his old timers were concerned he was convinced that they could neither err nor go against him.

When Navi Mumbai started to develop in the 1990s, he set up a steel foundry, which occupied an area six times, that of the Central Mumbai unit. Management of this unit was handed over to his elder son, Sanjay, who was a mechanical engineer. Although Pradeep liked to interfere and call the shots, technology had been quite advanced and the de facto control of the new unit was in the hands of Rahul, the second son. It was common knowledge that Pradeep and Sanjay did not see eye to eye on many matters relating to management policies and practices. Under pressure from the trade unions Sanjay had developed a Reactive Style of Management. Here there was a fair amount of delegation and mutual respect amongst managers but people took decisions only after the need arose to do so. Planning was always for the immediate to the short term.

The younger son Rahul was more liberal in his views and although he stayed back to assist Pradeep in the Central Mumbai unit he was surely but steadily moving into the proactive style of management. All marketing functions came under the control of Rahul. There was a lot of empowerment and accountability amongst managers. People were encouraged to plan ahead and take calculated risks in the interest of the organisation. However, whenever Pradeep Sudarshan came to know of individual initiatives he would interfere and get the managers to seek his approval before they proceeded further. Since Pradeep Sudarshan still controlled the purse strings the progress made by Rahul and Sanjay were limited. Moreover, there was no clear vision, mission, role or goal laid down for the two units of Sudarshan Mild Steels.

The only real change organisational structure came with the appointment of an H R Manager who would look after both plants: Navi Mumbai and Central Mumbai. The HR Manager was well meaning and competent in Personnel Management but when it came to Training and Development he would hire outside specialists for workers and send the supervisors/managers to some place like NITIE to undergo training. The HRD Manager had easy access to both Sanjay and Rahul who were willing to listen to him. The problem was that the HRD Manager was insecure, feared the wrath of the old man and despite provocation refused to proactively influence the pace of change.

The culture of Sudarshan Mild Steel was one wherein management operated in the feudal-mercantile – trader mode. But Rahul and Sanjay wanted desperately to move towards a culture where managers operated in the innovative-creative-entrepreneurial mode. Both Rahul and Sanjay would do consequently things behind the back of the old man and even managers began to ape this habit. As a result, whenever Pradeep Sudarshan found out about (what he thought was) an irregularity in management functioning he would throw a tantrum and become his old vindictive self again. Invariably it was the old timers who would spill the beans. He was prone to be very autocratic and singularly money minded, so each time there was a deviation from the norm, he perceived a threat to his dream.

When the recessionary spiral combined with the post 11th September 2001 scenario began to bite into the mild steel exports of India, Sudarshan Mild Steels began to reel under the shock. The old timer located in every pocket of the company went straight to the old man and told him that a liberal culture was the cause for the loss in profits. Pradeep then took away many of the powers from his sons, began to run the company in his own way. Many professionals who had joined the company during the last five years quit and profits plummeted further. It became clear that something had to be done and old man Sudarshan had to be convinced to tow the line since he still controlled the finances.

- ***Who would you have employed to do this task of convincing the old man of his folly if you were his son?***
- ***Had HRD not abrogated its corporate responsibility totally and thereby let down the organisation? Can organisational change be brought about without personal conviction?***
- ***What could have been done to avoid this situation had you been the HRD Manager in the company?***
- ***What would you have done to the HRD Manager if you were either Sanjay or Rahul?***
- ***What sort of a corporate culture would you try to evolve in such an organisation? Why? How?***

HINT:

HR is the conscience keeper of management and therefore ethics, governance and excellence falls within its purview of strategic concern.

Catching the bull by the horns is a good idea provided it is done tactfully. Do not give up your job for the sake of self-righteousness unless it is something you feel very strongly about.

❑❑❑

CASE 18

BRIGHT-WAY COMMUNICATIONS

Two former telephone executives, Deepak Mehta and Ashok Bhargav, founded Bright-Way Communications six years ago, in 1995. Their goal was to create a long-distance telephone company that would compete with the larger long distance Sea and road carriers without imposing the bureaucratic culture associated with the larger government companies. The company with 400 employees now provides long-distance service to the entire Thane Belapur zone and is still owned and headed by its enterprising founders. Both employees bring a lot of energy and spirit to the company and seek employees with similar levels of drive and determination. Bright-Way Communications recruits many entry-level managers from several top business schools. "Newly minted graduates have no pre-established ideas about how communications companies should operate", says Deepak. "They are like a blank slate on to which we transfer a new work culture". Employees at Bright-Way are energetic and youthful, the average age of the workforce being 31 years. Their work life is best described as "one great jamboree".

In an effort to turn Bright-Way into a viable nation-wide long-distance carrier, employees are encouraged to seek innovative solutions, try risky alternatives, and work long hours. Most salaried employees work between 50 and 60 hours a week. From the start Deepak and Ashok have maintained open lines of communication with all employees. The official policy states that any employee can discuss problems, issues, or ideas with any other employee at any time. According to Ashok, "We're in the business to foster communications. We have an obligation to our customers to facilitate open communication both within and outside our corporate boundaries. Many inside Bright-Way credited the open communication policy for allowing innovative ideas to circulate throughout the company. Employees bounce ideas off one another and proposals often develop into tangible services offered to the customers. To maintain an invigorating climate the employees are eligible for a general annual bonus based on individual and team performance and on company profit measures. Both Deepak and Ashok are avid cricketers and the company cricket team frequently participates in local matches. Employees who score a 'century' in any match receive a personalised decorative wall plaque denoting entrance into "The Century Club". Similar plaques are awarded to the maximum wicket takers and they find their entry into "The Best Bowler Club". Through these and other acts, all employees at Bright-Way are made aware of the importance of achieving difficult goals. The work life revolves around meeting short run targets and everyone lives in the present moment only.

- ***Describe the quality of work life at Bright-Way Communications. What are its main features?***
- ***List examples of Bright-Way Communications' observable work culture, shared values and common assumptions.***
- ***Given what you know about the quality of its work life, is Bright-Way Communications the type of organisation that you would like to work for? Why or why not?***

If you as an HRD Expert were to be given a free hand in changing the quality of work life of the company in order to make it value based as well as value driven, what would you do and how would you go about introducing the desired change? Facilitating change, we know, is the greatest gift that a transitional leadership can possess and for this the leader must be personally ethical and strictly adhere to good governance principles so that excellence can be approximated. In importance, he must place the means before the ends and make it a point not to cut corners.

What should be the vision, mission, goal and role of HRD in this kind of a situation? Is being given a free hand enough? Should some guarantees of support from top management not be solicited before implementing the intervention? Can HRD deliver unless it is empowered and held accountable? Elaborate.

HINT:

Let the mind wander and think in an upside down fashion.

❑❑❑

CASE 19

MODERN SOFTWARE LIMITED

Modern Software Limited was started in the High Tech Zone newly created in Navi Mumbai. It was a spin off from a small computer software firm established in Pune by two friends and which came to be known as the Page-Patil Group. The original company in Pune was a proprietorship firm that assembled personal computers for sale through retail outlets to private consumers. From its very modest beginnings in 1985 it had grown in size and expanded its operations. Its products were relatively dependable and its after sales service was above average. In 1990, the company started writing customised computer programs for small firms operating in Pimpri and Chinchwad industrial zones. It had two distinct units: a hardware unit headed by Prakash Page located in Chinchwad and a software unit headed by Chandrakant Patil located in Pimpri. In 1991, there were 175 employees in the hardware unit and 80 employees in the software unit. With encouragement from the Ministry of Industrial Development and the computer-aided technology aptly leveraged by the calculated risk-taking attitude of the two entrepreneurs, there was literally no looking back. The company was relocated at Navi Mumbai in 1990 and there it made steady progress in the next seven years. Both Page and Patil were both basically honest businessmen who have a keen eye for detail and wanted to make a quick buck but stopped short of indulging in downright unethical practices.

The company's sales turnover had been Rupees 60 crores in 1991 and it rose to Rupees 450 crores in 1998. Its manpower strength in the hardware unit was 350 employees at the time and in the software unit it was 220 employees, most of whom were computer professionals of one sort or another. Patil was a B.Sc. Degree holder with specialisation in Mathematics who had a keen sense of business. Page had a B.Sc. Degree who had specialised in Physics and also completed a Diploma in Management Studies from a Management Institute in Pune. Both of them had a fascination and a penchant for computers from the very beginning of their careers. In 1989-90 they had gone public with their shares on the equity market and made huge profits playing the bull market.

In 1997, they met the proprietor of a small construction company with a dubious reputation, called SEAFACE (because he operated from Bandra Seaface where he had havala links with partners in Arab countries) and through him they were introduced to a wheeler-dealer located in Mauritius. He was commonly known as Rafique. He had more recently came to be known as the "king of havala". He visited India once or twice a year and was usually accompanied by gorgeous ladies of questionable integrity. One of them was the wife of a noted journalist who helped cover his tracks through her husband. He had convinced the Page-Patil Group that it would pay them well to deal in foreign made computer spares as an offshoot of Modern Software Limited. He had even arranged for the two friends Page and Patil to meet some underworld dons based overseas, but sanity prevailed and the two friends backed out of the meeting. However, they could not evade the guile and deceit of either Rafique or his smooth-talking friends.

Modern Software Limited entered a series of contracts to import computer parts, microprocessors, and other telecommunication equipment from East Asian countries. Through a carefully planned program of under-invoicing imports and over-invoicing exports, they had amassed huge profits between 1989 and 1992.

They had also made a large profit when the stock market had plunged after the scam in 1992-93. The Page-Patil group had traded (speculated) on futures and now played the bear market successfully as well. In 1998, Chandrakant Patil went to New York to assess the market since he was thinking of starting a body shopping operation in Mumbai. While in New York he had attended a seminar on "developing core competencies" to which he had been invited by a business contact. He came back duly impressed and employed a senior level HRD Consultant named Milind Desai to help develop the company. He strongly believed that if the company had to thrive in the next century it would have to first identify and then enhance its core competence. He set about this task with missionary zeal.

In 1999, Prakash Page especially went to attend a six-week program at a Summer School in England on "building corporate culture." He returned home full of new ideas and a few contacts too. He wanted the Modern Software limited to have a corporate culture founded on trust, transparency, and teamwork. Page came back duly enthused and asked the HR Consultant to come on board as a Vice President HR. He detailed the two main thrust areas for Milind Desai: to create a vibrant corporate culture and enhance its core competency such that the company could develop into a major global player. He gave Milind Desai a free hand, empowered him, but also asked him to set his targets and benchmark his progress with other players in the market.

Both Page and Patil always wanted to lead from the front and were known to walk their talk. So they began by setting their own targets and made these targets known to all employees. Their decision-making processes became more transparent each month and very soon, the three Ts (trust, transparency, and teamwork) became the watchwords of company policy. Simultaneously, Milind Desai introduced a system of group target setting and objective performance appraisals. He also asked Page and Patil to adopt an open door policy like him. Employees could walk in and speak to any of these three gentlemen in confidence and rest assured that even if they disagreed with the company, they could be sure that there would be no victimisation. The work climate dramatically improved and with it also improved the per capita output and net profit figures. The software development team, the maintenance team, and the quality team began to work in harmony and the usual frictions, during project work, between them began to ebb away. The mood of employees was buoyant and the external customers, judging from market feedback, were more satisfied than before.

Soon, it became apparent that a group of managers was opposing these moves to liberalise the internal environment. As weeks went by, their opposition became more vocal. Sensing trouble, Milind Desai immediately handpicked a group of eight young lads whose potential appraisals had showed that they had future promise. He formed a core team of these eight men and brought in a reputed firm to introduce Corporate Governance in the Company. The Corporate Governance team started to examine each function and department in detail. Organisational structure, chain of command, authority flows, and accountability norms were examined and modified whenever it was required. All such modifications were made in association with the people involved so that change was never imposed but agreed upon.

The groups of managers, opposing liberalisation then made the Corporate Governance team, its target and started a smear campaign. Milind Desai stepped into the breach with urgent dispatch. He looked into the personal files of each of these managers and found that in someway or another they were linked to Rafique. They either had regularly dealt with him on behalf of the company or had been appointed on his recommendation. On further scrutiny, it became apparent that there was a great reduction in the twin tasks of under-invoicing and over-invoicing. In two cases it was found that funds were even siphoned to militant outfits operating from Pakistan. Yet profits had not stopped rising. This convinced Milind Desai that there was more to it than met the eye. He confided in Page and Patil who agreed with his observation. They then made some discrete inquiries and found that when the under-invoicing and over-invoicing tasks were at a peak, Rafique had made more profits, as the principle middleman, than had the company. It did not take them long to understand that the managers who were objecting to liberalising the environment were doing so at the behest of Rafique.

Page and Patil called a joint meeting of all senior level managers and declared that Corporate Transparency and Public Accountability were there to stay and anyone who did not agree with the company policy could flourish elsewhere. Of the disgruntled managers, 50% resigned and 25% visibly changed their ways of work. The rest were known to be on the look out for jobs elsewhere. This meant that attrition of high-level managers became a reality and would likely increase. Milind Desai was unruffled and prevailed on Page and Patil to remain cool.

- ***What kind of a change leader was Milind Desai? Was he too laid back for his own good? Explain.***
- ***Did Page and Patil do the right thing when they were confronted with the facts? Should they not have acted earlier?***
- ***How could a middle man-fixer like Rafique make such inroads into the company and why did the leadership allow it to happen all along?***

HINT:

Never allow the mediocrat-bureaucrat to call the shots.

Always keep a tab on what is going on and this does not mean spying but keeping a daily check.

Page and Patil did the right thing by confronting the people responsible but they ought to have acted earlier.

The importance of a good HRIS cannot be under estimated.

❑❑❑

CASE 20

RAJASTHAN TEXTILE MILLS

The year was 1970 when Girilal Arya, the benevolent patriarch from Jodhpur in Rajasthan had chosen to move to Bhivandi in Maharashta to set up his small-scale textile mills. Arya himself was a textile engineer who had passed out with distinction from that elitist institute, TITS Bhivani, and had gone to North Western University Chicago to do his MBA. Having returned in 1960 he joined the Birla Group of Companies and within a few years decided to use his ancestral wealth to set up a medium scale factory of his own named Rajasthan Textile Mills. Having decided he planned well and within no time at all was ready to set up shop. Those days Western India was a safe haven for investing in textiles so he opted to set up his plant there and in Bhivandi on the outskirts of Mumbai. Business grew and his manpower strength rose from 300 employees in 1970 to 5000 employees in 1990. There were now four separate units set up and which were linked up a scientifically designed process chain within a single compound. There were security guards that manned the two entry-exit points (one to the north and the other to the south of the Mills). The first unit was the Spinning Plant being looked after by Dinesh Kapoor, a finance specialist who also looked after security, administration and the colony related functions. The second was the Weaving Plant being looked after by Pradeep Ray, a specialist in production management. The third was the Dyeing Plant that was looked after by Jacob Abraham, a specialist in law and chemistry. The fourth was the Packaging and Export Unit that was looked after by Arvind Naik who was a specialist in strategic marketing. All the four CEOs had sufficient autonomy, powers were delegated, and accountability was clearly assigned. All four were located in a single sprawling compound. Though independent in functioning and style these four CEOs worked in harmony with one another. They also shared Arya's views on social responsibility of business. There was a monthly meeting presided by Arya and a weekly meeting where the four met and compared notes so as to reset targets. Since the license and quota raj was still going strong in India Arya became involved in corporate finance and high-level liaison with the government, leaving the production, administration and sales to the four CEOs. By 1985 Rajasthan Textile Mills was already the jewel in the crown of Bhivandi and its export orders were flattering, as was its high quality. No worker was exploited, no child labour was used and the women were given more than an equal opportunity all along. This was very unlike what went on in other textile companies in Western India.

The top management style in the company was originally paternalistic but soon evolved into being reactive and by 1985 it was clearly proactive. The corporate culture was based on trust, teamwork, and transparency. The management-labour relations were congenial and in its entire history there had never been even a single day's production lost in the company due to trade union problems. Even when the Datta Samant led wave of labour unrest swept up Western India (1983-88) this company had remained unaffected. For Rajasthan Textile Mills it was business as usual. All the four CEOs were highly respected persons who knew how to handle their men, materials, machines and money very well. More importantly they worked, as a homogeneous team whose decisions were always value driven and. whose style of management was value based.

As per company policy, every employee was comprehensively insured and a school bus was provided to take their children to Thane City every morning and bring them back in the afternoons. Children in the bus came from all types of families and mixed freely irrespective of caste, religion, or class considerations. Students, who were wards of employees, and who did exceptionally well in either studies or sports got scholarships to see them through their graduation.

There was a medium scale workers colony near the company premises where the workforce was housed. There were three categories of flats, which provided for workers, supervisors, and managers respectively. The colony was on the northern side of the Mills while the senior management resided on the southern side of the Mills. This had more to do with land availability than intentional social segregation.

The sanitation and health aspects were also not forgotten. Besides, the colony had one co-operative store, a medical store, two restaurants, a cyber cafe, and a textile showroom cum sales centre. There was also an arrangement with the Thane Hospital for free medical treatment to the workers and their immediate family. In addition there was a small clinic with two company doctors and two nurses who were available on call throughout the day and night. There was a Transport Officer under who were one jeep, an air-conditioned ambulance, two school buses, and a mini-bus to be used in emergencies.

In addition there were five beautiful row houses in which Arya, Kapoor, Ray, Abraham, and Naik lived a little away from the factory on the southern side. There was also a corporate guesthouse, which could accommodate 4 VIPs and their spouses at a time, and to which was attached an excellent dinning room and bar. This is also where the five would retire for a tipple after their monthly meetings and spend weekends playing Bridge. The housing colony on the northern side had a workers clubhouse, an officers club, a gymnasium, a park and a playground. Both management and workers were a happy lot and attrition levels never exceeded 8% per annum. In addition, Arya was well known for his sense of charity and worked ceaselessly with the International Centre for the Advancement of Philanthropy (ICAP). His was clearly a socially responsible management and he was an ideal corporate-social citizen.

The 1991-92 watershed followed and the first generation economic reforms ushered in a climate of liberalisation. The license and quota raj was withering away and so Arya increasingly concentrated on philanthropy and social projects. The four CEOs became more production and quality conscious than before as competitive pressures mounted. It was quite common for one CEO to visit the other CEO's office to sort out issues then and there. One day Arya convened a three-day brainstorming meeting to share his views and agree on the strategy for the future of the company in the light of economic changes. The five retired to a hotel in Khandala to sort things out away from their daily business.

There was general agreement that owing to their predisposition all four CEOs were good people managers and did not need an HRD Expert to tell them how to treat their employees. The employees too, they agreed, were efficient enough and worked well.

They agreed that Rajasthan Textile Mills had a vibrant as well as a robust corporate culture that had stood everyone in good stead. Change in the way they did business, however, was the need of the hour. Now the company must go for an ISO 9000 certification since global buyers increasingly insisted on it. They also agreed to appoint a high level Quality Assurance Expert to facilitate this transition. However, on the question of further expenditure on workers facilities and social causes there was a difference of opinion. This was because the company had to increasingly convert its core competence into competitive advantage in the global markets. In spite of all this their export performance needed to be enhanced since Indian textiles were losing out to the products from Indonesia, Malaysia, Thailand and China. In addition foreign players would soon be entering India giving them tough competition on the home front. Salient features of what the five actually said (on this point) are given below in such a way that no part of the argument is lost.

ARYA: I have all along believed that we are the trustees of society above all else. God has granted us money and we cannot be niggardly with it. Charity is our sacred duty to society and we must not forget that we are mere stewards of social wealth for the time being. We were born with nothing and shall take nothing back when we pass on to the other world. All that will remain is evidence of our deeds and history will judge us thereupon. And charity is also a great corporate brand builder. But what of our employees? Today every big company has an HRD Manager and we do not have one. Let us not forget that.

KAPOOR: Please, Girilalji let us not get carried away. We wanted a level playing field all along and now that we have got one, let us use it well. There is only one social responsibility of business and that is to generate wealth without cutting corners or slitting throats. All else is a luxury that we cannot afford in a competitive world. There is nothing like a free meal any more. People Management through HRD is a window dressing and an additional cost. Why add to our cost when we are doing so well anyway?

ABRAHAM: Hold it friends! Do not forget Dinesh that we are loyal to nothing but to our own values and are responsible to nobody but the larger society. Today we have power, wealth, and all else. If we fail to use it in a manner that society things is appropriate then we will, in due time, lose it. Remember what happened to the Russian Tsar? So let us temper our new found free market ideology will restraint. Let our self-interest be an enlightened one. Let us get a consultant in to study the situation and tell us whether we actually need an HRD Manager and do our employees really need training?

RAY: Maybe I would prefer to take each social issue on its merits and not take an all-encompassing view like Jacob suggests. Let us first recognise the issues at hand in its correct perspective, analyse it threadbare and only then try to resolve them. This will take time and we must give the process due time. Do you not think we are rushing things? Also let us review the way we think. For one, we should start talking of social responsiveness rather than social responsibility? Let us wait and observe the environment and then respond to changes in it in an appropriate manner. HRD and all other things can wait till we have made more money and are comfortable enough to splash it around.

NAIK: Being a marketing man I would desist from clubbing everything together as my friend Pradeep has already suggested. Let us isolate issues and then deal with them one at a time.

If a goal or core belief is threatened we shall react appropriately and ward off the threat. If our competition comes across strongly we shall take steps to ward of their challenge through advertisement. We shall ask around for the public opinion in the changed scenario and fall in line. But above all else, let us put our heads together and see how events will unfold in the post reform era and pre-empt it through Strategic Intervention.

ARYA: All through my life, you know that I have stood by and acted on my ideals and held my basic value system as being something sacred. They have not let me down. We have all along acted on the principle that the basis of social responsibility lies in our inherent values and beliefs. Having heard each other, we shall recognise the changed situation and act without compromising either the future of this lovely company that we have built or my cherished beliefs we have all so far shared. Let us go back, think things through and when the new Head of Quality Assurance joins, let us meet again in three months time. In the meanwhile I will see if we can locate a trustworthy consultant who will do what we ask him to. By then our Dr. Manmohan Singh would have also completed his first year in office as the Finance Minister and things would be clearer. Reality cannot be seen in terms of black and white. There is a lot of grey area in between. Things are not as clear as the distinction between chalk and cheese. We may have to make selective civic interventions based on what we can do best. But are our employees really happy and do they have unsatisfied needs? How do we know that they too are growing like our corporate bank account?

On this note the five agreed to re-assemble for another three day brainstorming session in July 1993.

- ***Assume that you were the invisible bystander who witnessed this three-day meeting and heard the varying positions taken by the five Functional Heads. What would your precise stand as an HRD Expert be on the new company policy with regard to its responsibility towards its employees and the society at large?***
- ***In a competitive world where organisations must thrive on the cutting edge of market competition and be more technology savvy than their competitors, what will be the importance of HRD as a specialised management function?***
- ***Is it acceptable to have organisations without HRD Managers? Should the entire HR function be out sourced? Can a good line manager not be a good people manager too? Why employ HR experts with hefty pay packages if you can do without them?***
- ***Take a logical position as an expert and then explain your stand.***

HINT:

Go by your gut feeling and take an ideological stand.

❑❑❑

SECTION THREE

SHORT CASE STUDIES IN HUMAN RESOURCE PLANNING

CASE 21

JHARKHAND MOTORS LIMITED

Jharkhand Motors Limited is a very prestigious company with a track record especially since 1980 in Planned People Development. It was originally set up in 1950 and it manufactures chassis that can be used for either a truck or a bus depending on the kind of body that is built on it. What rolls out of the assembly lines is a chassis with a cabin for the driver and no other embellishments attached to it. The plant in the year 2002-2003 produced 60,000 chassis a year, with a manufacturing cost of Rs. 10 lakhs per chassis and the rejection rate is 0.5%. The total number of manpower employed by the company numbers 30,000 and is distributed between the Forge, the Foundry, the Machine Shop, the Auto Division and the Assembly Line. The company has a full-fledged Materials Management Department that looks after stores, purchase and raw materials. It also has full-fledged Accounts and Finance Department, which looks after wages and salaries, costing of production and fund flows. In addition it has a well-equipped HR Department, which has a sub-section for HRP, one for IR, one for HRA and one for HRIS besides a very well equipped HRD section.

However, the comprehensive climate survey conducted recently threw up the following issues and which top management would like the HRD section to address expeditiously and effectively.

Attrition rate had risen from a benign 8% per annum to a whopping 20% among graduate engineers below the age of 30 years. They lacked a sense of belonging to the corporate ethos and saw themselves as being above the traditional manager who had slogged up the hierarchy in a hard way.

The Managers in turn looked upon every graduate engineer as a renegade who was getting too big for his boots while being still green behind his ears and needed to be cut to size at the earliest opportunity.

The supervisory staff was highly skilled in very specialised tasks and very unaware of other functions even within the same department. Hence, job rotation was becoming difficult. Attrition at this level of staff was little less than 2% per annum and those who left were either superannuated or had died on duty. Nobody at this level had resigned in the last five years.

The Managerial staff looked upon workers with an attitude of "us" and "them" with the result that communication between these two categories usually was routed through informants or supervisors.

The workers distanced themselves from both the Managers and the Trade Union leaders and made their own norms of behaviour, which were not always conducive to either discipline or efficiency.

The Trade Union leaders were a pampered lot and did not actually work on their jobs. They spent their time politicking. They had chauffeur driven cars and behaved like managers. There was a sense of alienation amongst the workforce that had been responsible for trade union leaders becoming managers of discontent, which was a role they often created to justify their position.

Target setting exercises had not been very successful nor had been small group activity. These initiatives had been started with good intentions but had remained there just for the namesake with nobody taking them seriously.

The company was now on the eve of a major expansion to meet the needs of the newly liberalised economy and globalised markets. Top Management felt that an overall HR initiative was called for to enhance skills, make supervisors multi-functional, improved attitudes to work and condition behaviour to suit the challenges of the new market competition.

You are the Chief HR Manager and you have a team of Senior Experts as well as bright eyed and efficient MBAs working under you who have been exposed to training and development both at their postgraduate level and at subsequent industry sponsored programmes to XLRI and IIM (A). Formulate a comprehensive Planning Intervention so as to address the problems highlighted above and prepare the company for the new business environment. Explain how you propose to implement the Training Intervention and evaluate its impact.

HINT:

Three steps are imperative after employing the Sadri-Jayashree methodology, in HR Planning.

1. Training needs analysis
2. Training process monitoring.
3. Training evaluation.

Benchmarking and using the balanced score card in such conditions is an added advantage.

❑❑❑

CASE 22

HINDUSTAN COMPUTER CORPORATION

Hindustan Computer Corporation better known as HCC was a software company set up by a group of Non-Resident Indians who wanted to invest in their own country since the political economy of East Africa had been in such a turmoil during the late nineteen seventies that they wanted a secure source of income in case things really went wrong for them. Consequently, an Indian business house from Nairobi and another from Kampala joined hands and floated a company in Pune.

Since they were essentially traders who knew nothing about computers but knew just enough to invest in that industry as a safe bet, representatives of the promoters went to the USA and hired five Indians who would come back and use their funds to set up a company for them. These five Indians were all specialists in various aspects of software technology who were given a clear mandate: To give the investors a good company within three years using the state of the art knowhow.

With such a broad but clear mandate, and virtually no interference from the promoters, the five technocrats set up HCC in Pune in 1980. Restrictions imposed by an almost closed Indian economy, on the transfer of technology made their task very difficult and they restricted themselves to taking on projects that used low-end technology to begin with. So they started to take on contracts from Indian book and journal publishers to key in their texts so as to publish. Desktop publishing was a new concept in India and so they did not make much profit. This was especially because the low budget journals preferred the conventional printing to desktop publishing and partly due to the conservative mindset of the publishers and editors. HCC also went into software development and customized their programs for meeting the needs of local industry. HCC undertook jobs such as devising computer controlled assembly line production systems, computerized on line material flows for inventory control and computer controlled panels for furnace monitoring.

By 1983 their manpower strength increased from a meagre 15 technicians and 25 data entry operators in 1981 to 50 computer software engineers and 50 computer hardware engineers plus a support staff of 100 data entry operators. By 1986 the strength had almost doubled on all three levels. HCC had now started to take on small export orders in respect of porting jobs for bigger clients. HCC had also tried to make an entry into data warehousing but had fallen short of it and started taking on electronic processing jobs for scientific journals in USA. By 1986 the five initial technocrats from USA who had started the company decided to divide the company into three separate and smaller companies. These would have separate Chairmen but these five gentlemen would be on the Board of Directors of each of these companies. Each of these was formally set up within the same year 1987.

HINDUSTAN COMPUTER CORPORATION

Hindustan Computer Co. Hindustan Software Co. Hindustan Publishing Co.

There was one Director from each of the promoters on the Board of each of the three Companies. The Chairman of each company was an expert in the field of business chosen by HCC and the other Directors had a free hand in running the company. However, the Directors on the Board who represented the two promoters also had executive powers in respect of finance and portfolio management. However, they seldom interferred with technical decisions.

HCC did not give up its identity. It housed the registered offices of the three newer companies and took care of common functions as Human Resources Management, Corporate Communications, Finance, Corporate Planning and Company Secretariship. Moreover, all persons of the rank of General Manager and above in the small concerns were termed as "covenanted staff" and were employees of the parent company HCC. They enjoyed many benefits and were given a share in the profits of the particular (new) company they helped to manage. Hence, they had a financial stake in the future of the company.

The new companies were Hindustan Computers Company (HCC), Hindustan Software company (HSC) and Hindustan Publishing Company (HPC). Everyone below the rank of a covenanted staff belonged to the payroll of the particular company to which they were attached. Each of these companies had their own Personnel and Administrative Function, their own payroll cell with their own salary scales and fitment norms. This was because they were treated as separate companies with a separate identity and separate clientele. Job rotation within the same company was not always encouraged and inter-company transfers were unheard of. Management would prefer that disgruntled employees leave the organization rather than be transferred to a sister company. This was because, they believed that giving one transfer would open flood gates for people trying to switch over and gain newer skills.

Each company had its own marketing function and its own training cell. It was the task of top management in each of the newer companies to earn profits and expand its business. Since the infotech industry was market driven and there was always a demand for the products, marketing as a function did not have to be very proactive. Similarly, since the technology was so rapidly changing, training had to be skill based and need/client based. Since the two functions of developing markets and clients as well as training of employees both incurred a cost, which ate into the profit margins, it was felt that this could be kept to a manageable minimum. Each company managed its own manpower and recruited its own personnel.

HINDUSTAN COMPUTERS COMPANY

Hindustan Computers Company (HCC) was accordingly floated with a clear vision that it would be involved in the assembly of personal computers for sale in India. They would also be involved in setting up and executing Annual Maintenance Contracts (AMCs) for both their corporate and their private/individual clients. This company required both hard ware and software engineers and assemblers. However, the bulk of the specialist manpower was from an Engineering background with a specialization in electrical or electronics engineering. They were, in short, computer hardware engineers with an aptitude for software development and/or marketing.

The company began by manufacturing and selling its own assembled personal desk top computer with the brand name of Hind P C. It later went into manufacturing lap top computers with the brand name of Hind Lapo. For this, the manpower requirement was of a rather loosely defined kind: It grew into setting up customized systems with electronic circuit boards using CAD/CAM, in-house security systems and modems according to customer specifications. For this the kind of activity, the manpower required was specialized and came from a formal engineering background.

Manpower in HCC was of five kinds. (a) The front enders were those who serviced clients and interacted in the market place. (b) The back enders who were involved in tasks such as contract creation and account maintenance. (c) The support persons who would provide software demonstration to the clients and write programs and reports of a non-development nature.(d) The persons who actually assembled the computer with the help of drawings and circuit diagrams provided to them. (e) The administrative, accounts and security support persons.

The administrative, security and accounts personnel had skills and training of a general nature and so finding persons with the correct profile was not a problem. The assemblers were college and school drop outs with hands on experience of a year or two, as well as persons who were on their first job after graduation. This category was replaceable and persons tended to stay on in the company between six months to four years. Attrition in this company for the other three categories of staff also showed a healthy trend and since the skills were not so unique that they were not irreplaceable, and staffing did not present a major problem. Moreover, the front enders, tended to be those who loved to work in the market place, interface with clients and were generally outspoken, so management would know if someone was disgruntled and no surprises would be sprung by way of resignations. It is only later when HCC went into Report Writing by introducing the Graphic User Interface (GUI) that attrition levels became slightly high. However, the reserve army of unemployed persons in the country and the low-end specialization skills needed by HCC ensured a steady flow of jobs seekers.

The company had its own distribution network and operated both directly and through accepted and accredited vendors who were carefully selected and consciously developed. Since the vendor network existed, attrition at the sales and marketing staff levels did not create immediate problems of staffing.

Similarly, the mushrooming of industries in the wake of the Central Government's Policies of Liberalization, Privatisation and Globalisation ensured a steady clientele that needed the specialized skills and products of HCC. Hence, too much attention was not given to developing newer client accounts or expanding the market share. Demand seemed to be pulling the supply. However, there was an attrition level lower than the industry average because HCC salaries were comparatively higher and the style of management was such that it believed in delegating responsibility and holding persons accountable for their performance.

In spite of the fact that salaries were not below the industry average and the level of technology was low, attrition levels created problems. First of all, in terms of knowledge, there was a low value addition and this was not attractive for potential entrants, Although the hardware and the software engineers were performing complimentary functions, the former were treated better than the latter and this created friction and this led to lower productivity and the rise of one-up-man-ship.

HINDUSHTAN SOFTWARE COMPANY

The next company floated was called Hindustan Software Company (HSC), which would be involved in customizing requirements for industrial and non industrial business clients as per the client's specifications. They were involved in setting up a vast array of facilities ranging from low end security systems such as time keeping machines to highly automated and sophisticated computer aided production systems for the textile mills, automobile manufacturers and the steel plants. In many cases, the projects undertaken involved knowledge of CAD/CAM which invariably every young engineer possessed.

Each activity in HSC was project related and had a long time frame for completion. There would be a new learning curve on each occasion since each customized requirement would be unique. The top man in each project undertaken was either an accounts person or a general operations manager. Since he had no real unique functional specialization he was easily replaceable. Only if the top man was a functional specialist that his leaving could have led to a structural collapse, as he would take key personnel with him. One such experience had convinced top management at HCC not to repeat the error of appointing a functional specialist for such a position. By the very nature of the company's functions software developers were crucial to its success and were treated as blue-eyed boys.

In so far as customizing software for industrial use in the manufacturing sector (steel, textiles, automobiles, general engineering and chemicals) was concerned, the company had a very good name. The clients were quite pleased with the product quality. as well as after sales service. When it came to the question of customizing software in the banking industry or in the transportation industry was concerned it came within the range of the second or third best players. However, when it came to the question of porting, re-engineering or migration, it was no match for bigger players like Satyam, Tata Consultancy Services and Infosys. Hence, it wisely stayed away from this market.

However, this company had its own problems. Once a project had started the contingent of manpower employed to nurture and service, the project was not stable. Young persons in the infotech industry were known to be job hoppers and there was a problem containing them. Clients would get un-nerved when they found that upwards of 30% of the project team had left the company between the beginning and the end of the project. Projects similarly went through a cycle of phases and when the level of activity was at low ebb, attrition levels rose.

The dependability and quality of deliverables was not below par but despite the fact that systems were in place, monitoring of projects did not seem to be adequate. The very idea of functionally dividing a project group into a development group, a maintenance group and a quality assurance group was questioned. The inability of persons to move from one dedicated and functional sub-group to another caused a little bitterness as did the fact that everyone wanted to work on development projects irrespective of the level of their talent or their conditioned ability to do so.

Knowledge sharing between sub-groups within the project group was low and this added to the feeling of alienation. Communication channels were unclear and there was an air of uncertainty about the fellow employees' attitudes towards one another. On the plus side, management was ethical and benevolent and took individual care of the employee's welfare in a paternalistic manner.

The problem faced by this company was chiefly that the younger engineers looked for overseas placements, did not have patience to stick on and grow with a company and looked for short run benefits. Salaries were above the industry average so recruitment was relatively easy but salaries were not sufficiently high to retain persons. Moreover the bigger players in the industry would attract the better talent and this company was left with the second rates.

When deadlines had to be met, the manpower force worked literally round the clock and made sure that the company was not let down. Those who were at the high end of the knowledge worker scale, were very ambitious and ego-centric. Hence, they had to be constantly placated. As a result, the compensation policy was not as streamlined as might have been desired and over a period of time a lot of subjectivity had unavoidably crept in. Since the management was paternalistic, decision making was not transparent and this aggravated the feeling of alienation.

HINDUSTAN PUBLISHING COMPANY

The last company set up was Hindustan Publishing Company (HPC), which was the first large desktop publishing company of its kind. It brought out a quarterly semi-academic journal named International Computers and a monthly business journal called Infotech World. For this it had hired two editors, three full time consultants and a dozen editorial staff. This company also took on electronic publishing jobs on behalf of outside clients.

The company had a huge sunk cost in terms of a large number of desk top computers, customized programs and a minimal training to the operators so that functional accuracy can be attained. Manpower required for this company was of two kinds. At one level were the developers, researchers and programmers who made the Data Warehousing job possible. At the other end was the employee operating at a low end technology. These varieties, composed of college drop outs, housewives, and semi-retired persons with computer operations knowledge and reliability in data entry work. It also needed some persons with an artistic bent of mind to create Web Sites and source clients.

Since the nature of the job was repetitive and there was little value addition by way of knowledge, people tended to take on this job when they could get no other. To that extent the manpower employed was relatively stable. However, at the higher levels (tool developers and program writers) attrition levels had reached an all time high of 45%.

COMMON ISSUES

The company was a very reputed employer known for its ethics and fairness. It did not believe in the American system of hire and fire and nurtured its workforce paternalistically. Its salaries were not low nor were they very high. Therefore, attrition levels remained from 30% to 50% amongst the three companies. Job rotation was desired but not possible so that created a little bit of frustration.

It is felt strongly in certain circles that if the company does not grow, it will be overtaken by competition. With this end in view the companies have taken a conscious decision to grow the size as a well as the scope of their business both in India and overseas. With a consistent record of operating at increasing returns to scale the mood is buoyant on the part of the Board.

The Board of Directors deliberated at length for several days on the issue and has come to the conclusion that growth is the only option open to them. But to grow systematically they need a corporate image and a common corporate culture, which appears to be lacking now. This group culture in the short run is aimed at consolidating the policies and practices of the three companies with two clear objectives: To plan for the effective allocation and utilization of manpower. To develop into a major market player by planned expansion program.

In the end the group wants to play in the major league and emerge as market leader in the niche area of addressing the software (development, maintenance and quality control) needs of other local corporate clients. It does not want to enter into the export sector for another five years.

In the immediate future, the Board has had trained its sights on bidding for an upcoming Y2K contract of the Government of India. As a senior consultant with years of experience behind you, what will you recommend and why? Should the company that is doing reasonably well risk an expansion program?

It is well known that the Y2K or Year 2000 problem for the computer industry would cost India a conservatively estimated sum of Rs. 700 million. If Indian expertise is to be used gainfully in the export market to service this problem globally there is a potential market, which is considerably higher in value and waiting to be tapped. This is what the company wants to do. It has started building the infrastructure required for it and developing its marketing function for the last one year. The major issue before the company is sourcing the manpower required for this expansion of business.

HINT:

If the three companies have to operate as a unified whole then they need a corporate image, a common purpose, and a clear direction. A Quality Policy, a Governance Policy and Competency Mapping exercises must be mooted. Strategic HR must initiate this.

Although it is tempting to do so, do not go in for a corporate culture building exercise at once. When you do so, dove tail it with a corporate image building exercise. The former addresses the external customer (the client) while the latter addresses the internal customer (the employee).

Step 1. Undertake to calculate the production function of each company.

Step 2. Simultaneously undertake a Management Styles or HR Audit.

Step 3. Undertake a climate survey and start taking action on the findings within the quarter.

Step 4. Moot a target setting exercise and make every executive as well as department set their own targets and be judged according to the deliverables.

Address the knowledge worker squarely. He works for money and for skill enhancement. Hence, re-work the compensation package and undertake a fitment exercise. As long as there is a degree of transparency, the disequilibria in salaries can be managed.

Based on the findings of the climate survey which cannot be independent but must be born out of the production function and styles audit, undertake a well planned HRM intervention through (a) training (b) counselling and (c) clear communication.

HINT:

For effective manpower planning the following ratios must be known:

$$\text{Wastage Rate} = \frac{\text{Number of Leavers} < n \text{ years of service}}{\text{Average No. of Men on Rolls} < n \text{ years of service}}$$

For the infotech industry n should be taken as 2 years to be on the safer side.

$$\text{Labour Turnover} = \frac{\text{No. of Levers in a Year} \times 100}{\text{Average No. of Men on Rolls in that year}}$$

This is expressed as ratio in terms of percentage. This will give us the rate at which recruitment must take place.

Attrition beyond 20 % is not acceptable under any conditions since there is a cost attached to recruitment and leaving. If investment in training is made properly the attrition levels can come down considerably.

❑❑❑

CASE 23

MARKS AND SPARKS (INDIA) LIMITED

As a result of the IMF conditionalities in 1991 the Indian Economy was forced to liberate its market mechanism, privatise its means of production and globalise its competition. This caused a substantial devaluation of the Indian Rupee *vis a vis* the US Dollar and made India an attractive venue for direct private foreign investment. However, rather than an influx of infrastructure building industries with the exception of power generation, most investments were in the areas of FMCGs and the service sector (both financial and non-financial). Among the notable contenders for establishing outlets in India was the famous Marks and Sparks Chain Stores of Europe.

As soon as it was known that M and S was interested, a well known firm, based in Goa, D'Souza Consultants, entered the fray. Based on the subtle hint received from a Business House, D'Souza Consultants organized a team of experts, which flew to England to study the way the Chain operated. This was done in a hurry and in a rather clandestine manner. Their analyses were genuine guestimates of what would be entailed. The team flew back and reported the findings to its Firm, which in turn got in touch with a large Business House in India. This Business House got in touch with its subsidiary Information Technologies Limited (ITL) and passed on the findings of Messrs. D'Souza Consultants to them. Accordingly, the Chief Commercial Manager Mr. T. Srinivasan was deputed by ITL to go to Europe and begin consultations with Marks and Sparks. Along with Srinivasan went the Marketing Manager Ghanshyam Boriwal. Srinivasan was always perceived as a man from the Business House rather than from the Subsidiary Company. Boriwal functionally reported to Srinivasan and they got on well.

Based on that report, ITL made a bid against other contenders for setting up the MIS for the Indian operations of M and S. ITL had an indigenously developed ERP package, which was operated on Windows 95 platform and which, was being used by several leading warehouse chains in India. Being the lowest bid it bagged the order. The Business House sent its marketing team to England to negotiate the deal and very soon a contract was signed. The figures given by Messrs. D'Souza Consultants were taken as benchmarks for the tender bidding and for the estimate of costs and expected profits.

In their hurry to enter India Marks and Sparks gave a rather loose Systems Requirement Specification and assumed that the bidding firm would do all the necessary homework. Their policy was not to hide any detail from the bidding firms while at the same time not to give out more than absolutely necessary information on its own. They required an Indian Company to set up their MIS and invited open tenders. It was visibly delighted when the lowest bid belonged to Information Technologies Limited (ITL), which was a very respectable company in its own right. The contract was awarded a team of software experts was dedicated to the project.

Ghanshyam Boriwal was a seasoned Marketing Manager with several years of experience and successful projects to his credit. He was an ambitious go-getter and wrapped up a neat contract before long. There was a kick off meeting followed by a press conference and a cocktail party in Delhi.

Marks and Sparks is well known for high quality products and a higher quality of service to its customers. Over the years, it has built up enviable brand equity. In England except for the British Home Stores, Harrods, and a few more chains that could be counted on one's fingertips, M and S is a jewel in the crown of Europe. It's strict standards of deliverable deadlines, its commitment to customer service and its penchant for excellence in whatever it undertook made its products sold under the brand name of St Andrews a household name universally. After detailed deliberations and prolonged negotiations with the Indian governmental bureaucracy, M and S set up eight major departmental stores in India and they were simultaneously opened to the public on 01.01.1998.

As per the terms of reference 51% of the equity capital was raised by Indians and M and S put up the remaining 48%. There was a public share issue in Delhi, Mumbai, Kolkata and Chennai for the 51% equity capital and the National Stock Index showed a prolonged Bull Run for its share prices all through 1998 and 1999. The Headquarters of M and S in India remained Delhi where the Registered Office was located but its stores in Mumbai, Kolkata, Hyderabad, Chennai, Bangalore, Chandigarh, and Cochin operated under the independent charge of Heads of these Strategic Business Units. Policies on all matters were uniform as was the systems they adopted. A thin silver line ran through the chain and the control finally rested in Delhi Office and through them in London.

However, as far it was concerned, before it opened its doors to the customers, M and S had done its homework well. It had chosen the most prestigious Business House in India to set up its MIS (Management Information Systems) but unknown to the Business House it had transplanted its MCS (Management Control Systems) from England. This Business House had a Subsidiary Company named Information Technology Limited or ITL, which was assigned the task of setting up the MIS for the chain of outlets in India.

ITL appointed C. M. Fernandes to head the project. Fernandes was a hard worker who did not have a good technical background but years of experience had helped him to scale the corporate ladder. With a lot of publicity in the press the project was kicked off on 01.03.1997. ITL had perfected an oracle based software which would operate as an ERP mechanism for all functional specializations ranging from personnel to sales and from stocks and inventories to receivables and from quality assurance to sales and marketing. This was implemented without much ado and the Chain of Stores opened to the public. It was an ERP package, which was a hybrid of sorts. The best features of Peoplesoft, BAAN, SAP and others were taken to develop this new package, which was implemented for the first time on a large scale on the M and S project.

It was an open secret that Boriwal and Fernandes did not see eye to eye on several matters. Fernandes was miffed about the fact that he had been invited to the kickoff meeting in Delhi but nobody had consulted him about the project all through.

Fernandes was a stickler for detail and was often termed a slow coach. However, he would seldom stick his head out and his over cautious nature would easily be mistaken for him having a negative attitude. Consequently, Boriwal did not take him along for any future negotiations with Marks and Sparks

Srinivasan who had a major hand in the decision to appoint Fernandes argued that with Fernandes's penchant for detail the cavalier attitude of Boriwal would be compensated for. With Boriwal's savvy for Marketing and Client Relations, the abrasive nature of Fernandes would be off set. Mr. Fernandes would look after the technical side while Mr. Boriwal would look after the commercial and client relations side.

Fernandes set to work and began to find fault with the contractual arrangements. As could be expected by Boriwal the client-contractor relations began to suffer. Marks and Sparks would call up Boriwal who was based in Delhi and he would somehow pacify the client. Marks and Sparks were very happy to deal with Boriwal who was an amiable person with the gift of the gab. They preferred not to deal with Fernandes the Project Manager since there were too many ifs and buts in everything that Fernandes did or said. As on 01.01.1998, the chain of M and S began operations without a fully reliable MIS but a time-tested MCS.

There arose five specific problems at the very outset.

- The new ERP package had not been suitably pilot tested and there were a lot of bugs that needed to be removed before it could be fully implementable. It had worked well on Windows 95 but M and S had introduced Windows 98, which caused problems for software implementation.
- The price of the ERP package was bid low as Boriwal argued, ITL did not have to spend time and money to develop the MIS and could adopt its ERP package with minor alterations. So the ERP package was introduced to take care of the major managerial functions. It was however not equipped to handle specific functions like linking incentives to sales and multiple products which were differentiated by their brand and thus by their price. Similarly, it could not handle Euro-Conversion, which M and S had assumed since its base was in Europe.
- The ERP package had been developed on oracle keeping in mind Compaq Personal Computers. M and S on the other hand had their own brand of British Computers, which were not 100% compatible with Compaq. Fernandes had pointed this out but since he was dubbed as a person with a negative attitude, his objections were taken lightly.
- The cost of implementation worked out (according to Fernandes) to be three times more than what was originally quoted, since a lot more alterations to the ERP package were called for before it would be fully implementable.
- Finally, the MIS program was incompatible with the MCS program and this caused major hiccups for M and S since there was a 18 month project overshoot.

Fernandes took up the matter with Srinivasan who was unable to resolve the issue since he had all along assumed that Fernandes would raise objections. He had counted on Boriwal to make up for this lacuna through his personal charm with the client. Boriwal maintained that Fernades was making much ado about nothing while Fernandes argued that Boriwal had no business to by-pass the Project Manager and deal with the client directly.

Fernandes adopted the position that since he was not taken into confidence when the deal was negotiated he should not be held liable for any delays. Boriwal took the position that Fernandes was a born bureaucrat who would never flourish in a competitive world. Further, Boriwal argued that Fernandes never bothered to speak to him and resorted to going straight to Srinivasan each time a problem occurred. And every time Srinivasan would manage to cool the tempers.

Boriwal indirectly encouraged Marks and Sparks to deal directly with him. To this the foreign company readily agreed and relations between Fernandes and Boriwal on the one hand and between Fernandes and Marks and Sparks on the other hand suffered further.

The situation deteriorated steadily until a point was reached in February 1999 when communication between Fernandes the Project Manager and Marks and Sparks ground to a halt. All communications from the foreign firm would go through Boriwal and when they were routed to Fernandes he would raise objections and work would not be done. Things came to a head when team of senior executives flew in from London and threatened to sever connections with ITL and sue them for the cost incurred in finding another firm that would fit the bill on the terms laid down by M and S.

The local executives of ITL called this dirty imperialist politics and a war of attrition ensued. The Business House intervened at this juncture and a hastily summoned meeting revealed the following.

(a) The team sent by ITL consisted of marketing experts with only a working knowledge of MIS and MCS. Hence, their assumptions of compatibility of systems were flawed.

(b) The Project Manager had a serious attitude problem, which was not brought to the notice of HRD and kept under wraps.

(c) There was low client involvement in decisions taken by ITL and therefore a lot of paper work was generated. This could have been avoided if they had just bothered to amicably talk to one another.

(d) ITL was at sea regarding many of the expectations of Marks and Sparks since the standards of quality expected by them were far higher than what the Indian clients had earlier expected from ITL.

The Business House made it a prestige issue, intervened directly and took over the control of the project de facto from April 1999. Srinivasan who had excellent relations with the Business House was asked to personally deal with M and S and see that the project was completed. Boriwal resigned and Fernandes went on long leave on medical grounds. Replacements were found and the project was back on the rails before long. M and S was happy and things were running smoothly. In the meanwhile, ITL had incurred sufficient losses and would be lucky even it broke even at the end of the day. However, the project would be completed by the target date of 31.12. 99, and about this there was no doubt.

Analyse the entire situation from a critical and Strategic HR viewpoint.

What would you say about the insider information used by D'Souza Consultants?

ISSUES:

- ***Who was ultimately responsible for the mess-up?***
- ***Could the project delay have been avoided?***
- ***Did the Business House do the right thing by appointing Srinivasan to complete the project?***

HINT:

- Total Quality Management is the crying need of the hour especially in competitive markets.
- Accountability without authority breeds slaves, while authority without accountability breeds tyrants.
- Never enter into a technical contract without a technical expert in the initial negotiating team. Never have a project team without a commercial/ marketing person in it. Multi-functional managers are not easy to find. Therefore, a project team must have divergent functional expertise but a convergent goal.
- Complete clarity of vision, mission, goal and role is necessary for all companies that have to flourish on the cutting edge of competition. It is fatal to look at short run actual costs alone. Long run opportunity costs are vital for software companies.
- Continuos communication with and between all stakeholders is vital to every project success.
- Trust transparency and targets are the three Ts that must never be compromised if project outcomes are to be positive. This is possible if HR is involved from the very beginning to the end.

❑❑❑

CASE 24

CUBIC ZIRCONA SYSTEMS

Om Prakash Gupta was an entrepreneur with a social conscience. He was from a small village in the Punjab, had joined the navy and become adept in fields of wireless and transmission. On retirement after the Indo-Pak war of 1971 he set up a small workshop in Gazhiabad where he repaired television sets, transistor radios and tape recorders. His business grew and he acquired a dealership in a leading brand of television sets. From then on there was no looking back for him or for his business. He retained his workshop but purchased a show room in Delhi.

A man of sound principles and morals, Gupta always liked to play according to the rules and never tried to circumvent the law. However, Om Prakash Gupta (or OPG as he was fondly called) was highly trusting and yet superstitious by nature. Consequently, attributed his success to a very large cubic zircona that graced the gold ring on his left hand. During his travels when in the Indian Navy he had gone to Madagascar where he had met a gypsy woman who divined into the future by gazing into her crystal bowl. This woman had advised him to wear a ring with a cubic zircona on it for luck. This was in 1965 and ever since then his personal and professional life had improved considerably. He had bought a row house in Delhi and named it Cubic Zircona Villa, he had named his workshop similarly (Cubic Zircona Radios). Now the same name stuck on to his showroom too (Cubic Zircona Televisions).

During his attempts to increase his business ventures Gupta had met a retired civil servant with some experience in agriculture management who managed to gain OPG's confidence with his smooth talk and persuasive manner of conduct. This man was Vivek Mohan Thakurda who originally hailed from Bangladesh but who had settled in Mumbai and had been all around the country, knew a number of politicians on a personal level. On premature retirement from the civil service he had become an effective middleman between businessmen and the state bureaucrats, which made him quite important for those who traded on the fringes of the market. The day Mr. Thakurda joined the company OPG bagged a large contract from the Army General Stores to supply television sets. Being superstitious he thought Thakurda brought him good luck, even though the purchase order agreement had been signed a fortnight before Thakurda joined the company. That the period was marked by the great stock market boom of early 1990s did not convince OPG that the growth was market driven.

Over the years Thakurda had developed a friendship with OPG and gained his trust. In return, Thakurda ran odd errands for OPG at the Mantralaya and the Customs Office, for a retainer. Thakurda was a very smooth talker and could charm anyone with his words. However, he was unscrupulous and would stoop to any level to gain his desired ends. He had, it was reported, left the civil service under a cloud. That notwithstanding, he could work his way into many a corridor of power and get government clearances with ease. That had proved to be an asset for the company.

Thakurda's sons and daughters were well settled abroad. So he and his wife took a small flat next to the company guesthouse and lived just outside the premises of the company. This enabled Thakurda to drop in at odd hours to see if work was going on well. This spot-checking helped the company keep its supervisors on their toes all the time. However, it also created a feeling that management did not quite trust the supervisors completely and "big brother was watching you".

However, Thakurda had other merits. He had succeeded in extricating the company from a serious legal tangle in which it had inadvertently walked in and would have had to be shit down had matters not been controlled. Thakurda had spent endless hours in the Delhi Offices of the government bureaucracy sorting things out. On another occasion he had flown to the Gulf countries on a whirlwind mission covering six countries in a month and procured orders for the company, which helped it out of a financial fix. If not, the company would have had to go in for a bank loan to finance its expansion plans.

Nature had blessed OPG with three sons who had been educated well and all of who had secured their Masters Degrees from BITS (Pilani) successfully. In addition all of them were straight forward, upright social citizens who would scoff at the very thought of politicking. They respected their father immensely and consciously did not wish to cross his views for fear of hurting the old man's sentiments. The eldest was Alok Gupta who took over the workshop and expanded it. The second son was Ashok Gupta who managed the showroom and began to rake in profits at every turn. The third and youngest son was Arvind Gupta. He was a computer buff and wanted to start a software engineering firm in Noida. He prevailed upon his family to support his idea and grudgingly they agreed to do so. Accordingly, Cubic Zircona Systems was set up.

It was decided to merge the three ventures under one corporate umbrella and a Board of Directors was appointed to look after the entire investments. A bank loan of Rs. 30 crores was obtained to update the technology and a further loan of Rs. 20 crores was taken to open marketing outlets all over India and some offices abroad. OPG was the Chairman of the Board, his sons were the Directors and Thakurda became the Group Head (Administration). The three sons did not like him and had warned OPG against trusting Thakurda but to no avail.

The chartered accounting firm appointed by Thakurda was a well known medium scale business owned by some young men who had put together their personal funds to start the business ten years ago. The firm had all along given the Zircona Group of Companies a clean chit. So the sons did not doubt the stories of success.

For a while all went well but then Thakurda started playing favourites. He had his henchmen who would report against their bosses and through threat and sheer blackmail Thakurda began to control the senior officers. Those managers who wanted to curry favours used to sit for long hours with Mr. Thakurda after office hours, chit chatting and bad mouthing managers who were not present there. Thakurda who has little else to look forward to welcomed these gossip sessions because it gave him vital information about what was going on, and thus tighten his grip.

All administration would no longer be the task of human resources department but rest directly in Thakurda's hands. Human Resources was reduced to recruitment, training and legal compliance under Indian Labour Laws. Thakurda was apprehensive of self-confident and efficient managers in whom he visualized some threat to his position. So he would adopt the *divide and rule* policy whereby all managers began to distrust each other and could put up a united front against Thakurda.

Telephones were regularly tapped, e-mail messages were intercepted and security guards kept a record, (for Thakurda), of which senior officer came to work, when and with whom. An atmosphere of mistrust developed and fear psychosis reared its ugly head. Creativity went out of the window and everyone was too busy guarding their back to have time to look in front. It seemed that Thakurda derived an insidious delight from this.

Things came to a head when it was discovered that Thakurda had conveniently placed a clerk in the office of each of the sons and had a very efficient though unofficial reporting chain built up. Nothing that the sons did in the office escaped Thakurda's knowledge. This included when they went out for lunch (and with whom) when they left for home and who were the visitors everyday that called on them. When OPG was confronted with these facts, OPG tried to shield Thakurda and asked the sons to give the old man another chance. In his heart OPG was scared that if Thakurda left the company, his good luck streak would follow out and/or Thakurda knew enough to shop the company. The sons tried in vain to debunk that myth. In June the three sons privately and jointly conducted a management audit. The sons found that things were not as rosy as they had been made out. Three major questions arose.

Alok asked a simple question: *how did the company continue to invest for the last three years when the cost of borrowing was less than the rate of return?*

Ashok stated that *the payment made for procurement of technology was higher than what it would generally fetch in the market.*

Arvind wanted to know why *the level of motivation and trust relationships were at such a low ebb when the three brothers had all along been transparent in their dealings and the wage rates were market competitive.*

One question that plagued all three of them and remained unanswered was: *why is Thakurda, who is so comfortably well off and whose family is well settled still working as if his very life depended on it? He certainly did not need the funds and the remuneration he got was not really worth the bother. Unless, of course, he had sources of income they knew nothing of and/or he had an ulterior political interest in knowing how the company functioned.*

However, none of the brothers was actually sure of what Thakurda was doing or besides liaison what his core competency was. Quite perturbed, the three brothers jointly approached OPG to call a meeting of Senior Managers and find out the real state of the business. But owing to pressures from Thakurda on OPG, who feared loss of market goodwill if the news leaked, they did not raise the issue publicly.

In the meanwhile (November 1998) business fortunes began to visibly and rapidly falter just as the stock market fell. The fall in average stock prices was less than the fall in the prices of the company shares even when their financial fundamentals were supposedly strong. Alok smelt a rat and called his two brothers over for an *official* dinner one evening leaving Thakurda and

OPG out (for the first time in years). They agreed that they were not themselves competent and had to get professional help to have the entire business audited properly. They also agreed to keep OPG and Thakurda out of it. However, they wanted to get their own facts right so they wanted to involve the three chiefs (human resources, accounts and production). This move was to ensure certain cross-referencing of information could be made possible,

A week later they met again for a confidential official lunch meeting in a hotel away from the city and this time the chief of human resources, the chief of accounts and the chief of technology joined them. The meeting continued well into the evening and by then the whole Group's operations had been fairly well analyzed. They all decided to call for expert opinion before confronting OPG with the facts.

Next day Ashok contacted his close friend in Hyderabad and got a very notable Professor of Finance from ASCI to agree to come down and see the factory. Arvind knew a Professor of Industrial Engineering who was an authority in Production Management as well. So he telephoned him in NITIE and had him come over too. Their cousin was a Professor of Human Resources at ISMS in Pune and they roped him in as well. All along Thakurda and OPG were kept in the dark.

In January 1999 at the monthly meeting, Alok announced that three Professors were going to be in Delhi and they had been asked to visit the business premises and give a considered opinion. OPG welcomed the move but Thakurda wanted to know more about each of the men visiting and stated that he wanted to know whether they were working for the competitors. For the first time, the three brothers united publicly, overruled Thakurda and OPG was candidly but politely told that it was time for him to retire. Being a very amiable person OPG agreed but Thakurda opposed the move tooth and nail. The meeting ended when the three brothers stormed out after Thakurda started talking in a very arrogant and highhanded fashion and OPG did not object.

The trauma of the fall out was too much for old OPG to take and he suffered a cardiac attack that very night. The doctors told him to take things easy for a while and so he accepted that he would leave the matter of running the business in the hands of his three sons and Thakurda. Not wanting to displease the father, the sons agreed. Everything went well until during Divali of 2000, OPG suffered a massive cardiac attack and could not survive it.

Thakurda became the self appointed boss of the company and started running things the way he wanted. The sons were still recovering from the shock of losing OPG and did not realize this until the much delayed and much awaited management audit by the three Professors was due in December. To their shock, the sons found out that three weeks before the demise of OPG, acting unilaterally Thakurda had cancelled this audit. The professors were surprised but had waited for clarification to follow.

Immediately they shot of letters of apology, explained the mix-up without casting aspersions on anyone including Thakurda. They also revived the exercise and asked the professors to indicate when their schedules would permit another long visit to the organizational premises.

Thereafter the sons reacted swiftly and called a meeting of the Board. At that fateful meeting, they stripped Thakurda of his financial powers, identified every one of his known reporters and terminated their services (without further inquiry but with a golden handshake). Thakurda reacted by getting the state and central government bureaucrats to make things difficult for Cubic Zircona in every possible way. The Board agreed to induct an expert in Corporate Governance at once and start setting things in order within the Group. They pledged that trust and transparency would be practiced to the letter as well as spirit of the avowed intention. They were preparing for a bureaucratic crack down from the civil service. This never happened but the organizational climate improved as a result of the new transparency. The much delayed management audit was conducted and a lot of skeletons began to tumble out of the cupboards.

Six months later, in late 2000, the Board asked Thakurda to put in his papers and steeled themselves to face the bureaucratic aftermath, which could follow such a decision. {Just for records, nothing untoward happened.}

Was the top-level managerial mindset in dire need of change? Why? How?

What went wrong? Why was the management audit delayed? Why was an HR audit not conducted?

To what extent was OPG to blame and to what extent were the three sons to be held answerable for the delayed reaction?

Should Thakurda have been empowered without being given adequate accountability?

Why was Thakurda still working when he clearly did not need to?

Is this not a case where the corporate culture needs to be re-examined and the position of strategic HR needs to be re-asserted?

HINT:

Whenever corporate growth is market pulled rather than market driven, managers overlook the need to conduct a thorough diagnosis. The diagnostic process is an ongoing one and cannot be conducted only when the business is to be started or expanded or when things are going wrong.

Senior Managers should speak their mind at the slightest sign of trouble and not let subjectivity cloud their logic. That does not imply that they should dis-regard the fact that there is a human being behind every mind-body genome whose respect is inviolate. The culture must also be able to absorb these criticisms and take the feedback positively and for improving processes and functions.

OPG's superstition and trust in Thakurda made him forget that accountability and empowerment cannot be divorced. The reluctance of his sons to come out into the open earlier cost the company quite a lot. Had they acted earlier, perhaps Thakurda would have been out and damage to the organization would have been controlled.

Continuous management audit is not the answer but a *periodic* audit is. The former inhibits creativity and hampers growth. The latter acts as a mid-course corrector. The auditing body's bonafides must be beyond reproof. It must be aimed at improving conditions and not finding faults. So that exercise too must be objective, have a defined goal and should be approached with an open mind as well as a positive attitude.

Four aspects of Strategic HR are brought out by this case: the need for having a value based corporate culture, setting up a system of corporate governance, installing a proper HRIS, and the practice of continuous monitoring of systems, practices and performance. Other issues exist no doubt and the facilitator could bring these out.

Danger signals were raised when Thakuda started taking over the HR function but nobody paid heed to this. Had adequate diagnosis been conducted perhaps this situation would not have arisen.

As for Thakurda, he as either mentally sick or so insecure that he needed to work to convince himself that he still had not lost any of his marbles. Alternatively, he had an ulterior financial or political interest. Otherwise, there is no justifiable reason for him to be in continued employment.

❑❑❑

CASE 25

KOLKATA MANAGEMENT CONSULTANTS

Kolkata Management Consultants (KMC) is a private firm with a small group of professionals located in Turbhe (Navi Mumbai) and they service the Finance and Accounts needs of industries, which fall within the purview of the Howrah Industries Association. Basically Mr. Pradeep Mahajan ran a series of highly successful training programs in company costing and accounts under the auspices of the Howrah Industries Association in 1995. It then dawned on Mr. Mahajan that if he were to have a small group of highly specialised professionals he would effectively be able to service the needs of industries in that belt. He conducted a pilot survey and employed Mr. Thomas Mathew a well-known placement agent and management consultant to recruit a team of young professionals with the express idea of floating KMC.

Given the expected and promised revenues from industry the pay scales offered were lavish by local standards. Those recruited were First Class graduates in Cost Accountancy with an (AICWA) qualification. With this group were thrown in three Chartered Accountants, one Lawyer and one person with a qualification in Company Secretariship.

KMC started with a bang and got seven retainers in one year. However, from the group of 21 persons recruited initially only three remained with the company in December 1997. The reason for this high rate of attrition was puzzling and Mr. Mahajan called in an expert from TISS to analyse the situation. Records were examined and ex-employers were spoken to at length.

What came across was that very few had left the company due to salary reasons. The main thing was that Mr. Mathew had taken the task seriously and employed the cream of the accountants from institutes of higher learning. But the job content offered by the industries was what a bookkeeping clerk or an accounts assistant could handle. There was no challenge and no job satisfaction as a result of which the incumbents thought that they were spoiling their time and missing out on better opportunities elsewhere. Clearly the goal of KMC was unclear, as was the role of the incumbents. In between project assignments there were lull periods during which the accountants had no workload and no value addition took place as a result thereof, this added to their frustration.

Armed with this finding Mr. Mahajan re-approached Mr. Mathew who now went to Under-Graduate Colleges in the area and recruited replacements with a simple First Class B.Com Degree and a flair for oral communication. They were selected after a group discussion followed by a brief interview. Some PGDBM students from lower level management institutes also came for the interview and were recruited. These recruits were very satisfied with the salaries they received, did not have high expectations from their job and in January 1998 all of them were still working with KMC.

The wage bill of the company fell as the demands of these new recruits was modest. The clients were happy with the turnout of reports, the employees were happy and there was some amount of stability in KMC. Now the company was looking at the possibility of lending software support to the industries in the area by developing and servicing their EDP Departments. However, when the Howrah Industries Association sent them the new contract to service ten industries in the area, they asked for Electronics Engineers with Postgraduate Qualifications in Computer Software Technology and Hardware Maintenance. This idea did not please Mr. Mahajan but he wanted this contract very badly since he would thereby be able to rake in a lot of funds even during a period of recession in the economy. He was on the horns of a dilemma.

If you were Mr. Mahajan how would you react and why? You do not wish to make the same mistake twice and yet you need the new contract. You also know that getting qualified manpower is not a big problem but retaining them is.

HINT:

- What is the vision, mission and goal of KMC? Has it been crystallized and communicated to all?
- What is KMC's core competency area and who are the target customers? Is the new contract within the ambit of the desired target customers?
- Do not forget that IT is not an end in itself or a stand-alone project, as some tend to think. It is only an enabler. If the manufacturing, processing and service business itself does not exist what will IT enable?

Desired Discussion:

When a fast track company in the arena of Business Consultancy has a major problem with attrition, quality of work and adherence to target schedules the chances are that there is little goal and role clarity. And when that happens, the external customer is less likely to be satisfied. Conversely, if you employ mediocre personnel for low level knowledge jobs then it is unfair to expect high level performance from them on the knowledge-technology front.

Desired Learning:

Manpower recruitment is a specialized activity, which takes place in a planned manner. It ensures having the right person for the right job at the right time.

Effective allocation and effective utilization of manpower are twin concerns of HRP in so far as manning is concerned.

There is no reason to employ high calibre personnel when the job demands a medium calibre manning. This will prevent frustration.

To use these low level recruits to develop high level deliverables is a challenge.

Desired Strategy:

Contracts are signed so those end use products are reliable and delivered on time.

Quality of manpower when specified in a contract implies low trust relations on the part of the client.

When negotiating contracts, care should be taken not to jeopardize long run goals for short run benefits.

Always employ some study to gauge the organizational – job- employee fit. It could be a rudimentary O & M (organization and methods) study or it could be employing the Hay Methodology.

Desired Solution:

Negotiate from a position of strength. This strength usually comes from your past record, your expertise, realizing your core competence and knowing what kind of manpower the project demands.

Negotiate at the level of deliverables; emphasize quality and reliability of product delivered and stay away from the conditions, which specify the kind of personnel to be employed. This is because you and not your client will have to put up with attrition, frustration and associated human issues.

Arrange to add value whether by Training or by Job Rotation or both during periods of lull so that frustration is not allowed to creep in.

Candidly ask the client to justify why a particular employee profile is needed to do the stated job and convince the client that it is your task to deliver an end product which is reliable and dependable. So you should decide the kind of manpower needed.

❑❑❑

CASE 26

THE UNESCO PROJECT

Professor Ikenna Nzimero was given the task of formulating socio-economic indicators for Africa. He was a very well known social scientist and an astute theoretician. But his problem was that he spoke very little and assumed that every one understood him completely. He had succeeded in getting a UNESCO funding for the project and promptly appointed 26 well known scholars to man the project. He also appointed Mr. Makhdoom Khan to head the project team since is extremely good at writing software programs and making computer based analyses for large research projects. Mr. Khan had stated that the research would take at least 18 months with 30 persons working, but Professor Nzimero wanted the funding so he quoted the time required as 12 months with a team of 26 persons working on it. Against competing bids from other Universities, the University of Nigeria represented by Professor Nzimero, Mr. Khan and their team got the project. Their bid was the cheapest and needed the least time for completion.

Mr. Makhdoom Khan is a hard working project leader who has a dedicated and hand picked team working for him on a project involving the development of socio-economic indicators for Africa. The project is very well funded by UNESCO and consists of persons drawn from diverse disciplines like economics, sociology, anthropology, statistics, political science and history. All the team members were computer proficient though only two were involved in writing the program. The amount of data generated by the investigation was large by any standards of social science research. However, the modalities of the investigation are such that not all persons are gainfully employed all the time and whereas some were involved in the project formulation stage, others contributed to the data collection while some were involved in data analysis.

All the variables were placed on the computer and a complicated simulation program had been developed to compute a Single Index Number (SIN). The higher the SIN recorded for a country, the higher was its stage of economic development.

When the final result came out it was found that countries like Chad and Niger were placed higher on the developmental scale than countries like South Africa and Zimbabwe. Clearly something was wrong. Professor Nzimero dismissed the finding out of hand. Time was running out and the deadline for submitting the report to UNESCO was fast approaching. Mr. Khan stated that the deadline was unrealistic and wanted an extension to be sought. But Professor Nzimero would have nothing of it. He said "why did you not put your foot down earlier if you felt so strongly?"

A crisis meeting was called and to his horror Professor Nzimero discovered that each scholar knew his onions but had little idea of what the colleague was doing. Both he and Mr. Khan had assumed to the contrary all along. And nobody had bothered to tell them that they were wrong.

This was clearly a case of individual excellence and a collective mediocrity. There was no way in which the UNESCO deadline could be breached, since it would mean that no future research projects would come their way again. And the University of Nigeria badly needed funds, which such projects could generate.

Mr. Makhdoom Khan rose to the occasion. He took the data generated by each of the 26 research scholars and keyed in the data again, reformulated the simulation and came up with the more realistic answers. UNESCO officials were very pleased and secretly told Professor Nzimero that they had not expected the deadline to be met since the estimate had been too ambitious. The deadline was met but Mr. Khan fell violently ill due to overwork and mental fatigue. Mr. Khan swore that he would never be a part of Professor Nzimero's project again.

As a dispassionate and objective observer with years of managerial experience, what do you think went wrong? What lessons can be learnt from this?

HINT:

A team has some definite characteristics. The group has magnitude and mass, as does a team. However, a team also has direction, which a group need not have. Secondly, a team has members of divergent skills but convergent objectives. Also, the whole is greater the sum of its parts.

A team leader makes a correct assessment of team capabilities and resources. Then alone does he make a commitment to a client for time, quantity, quality and cost of deliverables. Such decisions are taken democratically ensuring the involvement of every team member.

Desired Discussion:

How should a team consisting of specialists in different fields but working on a specific project interact?

Does a Project Leader have the moral right to fix unrealistic targets?

If a target is unrealistic either in cost, quantity, quality or time dimensions, should the expert who finds it unrealistic make an issue of it before the project begins? How?

Desired Learning:

Quotations for contracts should be realistically made. Also, communication is fundamental to the success of a team especially if it has to meet target deadlines, also maintain expected quality standards. If communication is not smooth, transparency cannot exist. Then people become unsure of themselves and their position in the team. Consequently, the goals are not achieved.

Desired Message:

(I) In such a business scenario product is the people and so the Human Resource must be nurtured.

(II) Wherever knowledge workers are involved as against manual workers, their loyalty lies not with the organization or the team or even themselves but it lies with their values. Development of technological competence could be one of the values cherished and pursued. Hence, their intellectual interest must be kept up through job enrichment and total team involvement.

Desired Strategy:

Strategic HR intervention was sadly missing. As a result some essential elements were forgotten.

It is the task of Prof. Nzimero to detail the proposed project step by step with a time frame.

Goal clarity must accompany individual role clarity.

Each specialist must be clear about what he is expected to do and how it fits into the overall scheme.

There must be a project plan against which progress is mapped and everyone is privy to this information.

Regular monitoring of progress against well-established benchmarks helps to team in line and avoids last minute shocks.

Desired Caution:

In all such cases the manager is advised to use the 5 D Methodology to ensure project deliverables.

What would have happened if Makhdoom Khan had been unable to rise to the occasion and deliver the results?

If UNESCO officials also knew that the deadline set was over ambitious, can Prof. Nzimero be excused for his risk-taking bid?

Was the cost of failure ever taken into cognisance and if not, why not?

❑❑❑

CASE 27

T & L INCORPORATED

Sree Bhagwan Tibrewal (SBT) and Bajrang Lal Agarwal (BLA) were childhood friends who were partners in T and A Inc. They hailed from the same school in Udaipur and went to the same university for their Bachelors Degree. However, at the postgraduate level BLA went to Cambridge U.K., and specialized in finance and economics. He earned a Doctorate and returned home to serve the House of Tatas. SBT in the meanwhile had gone to Cambridge Mass., and specialized in materials management and systems. He too earned a Doctorate and returned home to serve the House of Birlas. Both friends were located in Mumbai at the respective head offices in Bombay House and Industry House ever since their return to India in 1970.

In 1975 BLA left the service of Tatas and went to Noida near Delhi to set up his own small scale unit in the manufacture of ball bearings. His younger brother had expertise in this field of manufacture. The following year S. B. Tebriwal and B. L. Agarwal's decided with the consent of their children that SBT's daughter Tara be married to BLA's son Lalit. The ball bearing factory was re-named T & L Incorporated, after the newly weds, and SBT agreed to move to Noida and become an equal partner in the new firm.

T and L Inc. began with a modest sales turnover of Rs. 5 crore in 1978 and by 1988 it had reached the Rs. 50 crore mark. In 1996, the sales turnover rose to Rs. 75 crore and the partners were more than pleased with their progress. Growth though gradual was well planned. The men on roll position (m o r) rose from 100 in 1970 to 500 in 1980 and 1500 in 1990.

Most employees has at least 3 years of work experience, after graduation, before being hired by T & L Inc. The average age of the employees was 30 years and the average age of the executives was 40 years. Annual employee turnover varied from 7% to 10 % although the salary scales were 15% above the industry average in the case of employees and staff while they were 20% above the industry average in the case of executives. The employers paid well and looked after their staff well but they expected a lot of dedication for the facilitation of which a climate was painstakingly created. Both BLA and SBT were scrupulously honest and their managerial practices were well above board.

However, they recognized that they did not have the required managerial talent in the field of marketing. They then scouted for talent globally and in 1992, found Vijay Poojari from Gwalior to head the effort as Senior V P (Marketing), when the sales turnover had stood at Rs. 52 crore per annum. On joining T & L Inc. Poojari scanned the markets and gave the partners a detailed report. Arising out of this report T & L Inc. appointed Young & Ernst Consultancy to find them a person who would facilitate the expansion effort internally so that Poojari could develop the leads externally. In three months time the hunt ended and Tinu Prasad Shah of Ahmedabad came on board as Senior V P (Human Resources).

Soon thereafter, a top-level management meeting was called in December 1992. Three decisions were taken:

1. T & L Inc. would have a sales turnover of Rs. 700 crore by 2000 AD.
2. To make that happen the company would have to go public to raise equity capital.
3. The company would be divided into Strategic Business Units (SBUs) and Strategic Service Units (SSUs). The former were profit centres while the latter were cost centres purely for purposes of account keeping.

T and L Inc. had a very good infrastructure, a dedicated workforce and an excellent credit rating so the expansion plans were not wildly ambitious. BLA undertook to source the market for funds since he had excellent relations with the financial institutions. SBT undertook to liaison with the stock exchange and the Governmental bodies since his strength lay in that area.

What should be the intervention from a Strategic Human Resources viewpoint, which must now be undertaken to make T and L Inc. a Rs. 700 crore Company?

HINT:

Desired Discussion:

Just as a cantilever bridge stands up by sheer tension distributed scientifically through its segments, so too does an organization. However, that cantilever bridge needs to be firmly grounded at the ends through pillars. One pillar is the market support, which brings in the revenue and the other pillar is the human resource support that helps to bring in the revenue. The company must decide first whether it wants to just grow or also develop. If growth is the only desire then the company operates with a trader-mercantilist mentality and the management will forever be stuck with bottom line figures and short run actual costs. If development is the desired objective then infrastructure needs to be built up. This takes the shape of a well-manned and well-equipped marketing network so that the hit rate is improved and accounts are not lost to competition. What will concern management is not just how much revenue was earned but how much could have been earned and was not. For this to happen internal customer satisfaction must be at a high pitch and for that to happen a well-manned and well-equipped human resources intervention is needed. Having just part time trainers who come for the money, chitchat with staff and maintain good public relations for continued association is the nemesis of most companies. The constant question needs to be asked: what value is added through HR interventions? And the task of the HR facilitator here will be to advise management strongly to develop the marketing function first and empower it.

The common theme of dividing Company Functions into SBUs (Strategic Business Unit) and SSUs (Strategic Support Unit) is a fallacy in the modern day. Since all functions are important and the acid test is: do they add value to the organization? Whether a function is a profit centre or a cost centre is inconsequential to the issue. When this acid test is applied we will see that the distinction between SBUs and SSUs does more harm than good. Research indicates that since immature managers keep their eye on the bottom line, expect the CEO to do all the thinking for them and start building little empires for themselves at the cost of the overall company objective.

Desired Strategy:

Get top management to re-examine the SBU-SSU distinction and if called for, re-engineer the systems and processes. HR intervention should beckon and initiate this process of change:*

- Crystallize its vision and mission.
- Clarify its goal and role at crucial posts.
- Detail its priorities in the long run and in the short run.
- Democratically arrive at a solution so that these are met.
- Once agreed, these must be relentlessly pursued to the end.
- Make executives in all functions accountable after they have been empowered.
- Every function including HR must be benchmarked with the best practices in the market.

❑❑❑

CASE 28

NAINAN AND SON

Major Gopal Nainan was a straightforward gentleman who had sacrificed his career many a time at the alter of his principles. He had retired as a Major in the Indian Army when his colleagues had retired as Colonels. Nevertheless, he had no regrets and had even been decorated for bravery in combat. He had his own brand of ethics but was very paternalistic. He certainly did not have a mind set fit for business. So he went back to his farm in Trivandrum and began to cultivate bees. This was his secret hobby and passion. He had no children save a son named Rakesh who grew up to be a lawyer and had joined a software engineering company. He knew how to bend rules without breaking them. Unlike his father, who was a straight talker, Rakesh was very diplomatic and was particularly good at the play of words. He was good-natured, kind and got along with people at all levels.

Rakesh had made a lot of money and by the time he was 30 years old, he had made his first million. He had made some astute business deals and cut corners in the process. In 1992 Rakesh entered the arena of real estate on behalf of his employers and by making some questionable private speculative deals he had made his second million by 1994. The following year, he quit and joined his retired father in Trivandrum. He used the old Major's land to use as mortgage and pledged his own shares as well. Together they planned to set up a software factory in Trivandrum since Rakesh had married a lady named Dr. Asha Nair who had a Doctorate from Chicago and presently was a Professor of Computer Applications at IIM Calicut.

Major Nainan wanted to do something that would *add value* and use high-end technology. He did not wish to see Indians being used as sophisticated wage labour by foreigners. Rakesh wanted to do something that would *rake in revenue* and he was not concerned with the level of technology needed. After a lot of argument, it was decided that they would not, after all, set up a software factory which is another name for a dedicated manufacturing unit for a principal company abroad.

Nainan and Son as a partnership firm had been formed. They employed Arthur Anderson to provide them with a project report so that they could set up a firm that would service Y2K orders from USA and Japan in the first instance. They planned to then go into software architecture and develop specific systems for client needs. Dr. Nainan (Rakesh's wife) liked the idea and agreed to quit her job to take over the Technical Director's post in the new family owned company.

However, the three Nainans have three different decision making styles. Major takes long to decide but once he makes up his mind he does not waver or change easily. Rakesh is easy to convince and very impulsive. He has a razor sharp brain but he ends up contradicting himself quite often. Dr. Asha Nainan cannot take a decision since she is engrossed in too many imponderables

At no point in time could any action taken by any of the Nainans be called even remotely immoral, although it was clear that their decisions were not always identical. The heart of the matter was that their core values were more or less the same. E.g. do not exploit the poor and needy, do not commit theft, do not commit what you cannot deliver, or do not break the law of the land.].

You are a Management Consultant with a strong HR background and who specializes in Business Process Re-engineering and Organizational Change. You enjoy the confidence of all the three Nainans. Hence, they have approached you for advice. You were given a copy of the report submitted by Ander Arthurson, a highly respected consultancy firm, and asked to study it carefully. You have been retained as a permanent consultant of the firm.

After a series of meetings it was agreed that:

- Nainan and Son would set up its company headquarters in Cochin.
- It would remain a proprietary firm.
- It would employ 50 software engineers in the first instance and add 50 more each year.
- It would employ a marketing man to source the markets for Y2K abroad.
- A well known head hunting firm called Change Proactive from Chennai was retained to recruit manpower.
- The State Bank of Tranvancore and Cochin has agreed to finance the project.
- A ready-made and air-conditioned building with three floors has been rented to start operations.
- Computers have been ordered and the operations will be on line within three months of initiation.

There are three aspects that you wish that the Nainans did not lose sight of.

(a) The product of the company will be people driven:

(b) The loyalty of knowledge workers lies in their ability to enhance their technology skills.

(c) The bottom line must be well managed but long-term development cannot be overlooked.

In response, to the above, the Nainans have asked you to draw up a clear vision, mission, goal and role for top management. In addition:

- Major Nainan insisted that everything should be ethical and above board.
- Doctor Nainan wanted the company to operate professionally at all levels.
- Rakesh Nainan wanted to ensure that both the client and the employee are kept happy.

How will you go about the assignment?

HINT:

Do not go in for setting up the vision mission goal and role clarity without the clients. In fact make them arrive at their objectives. You merely facilitate the process.

Desired Discussion:

This seems like a case where everything has been done right. The proprietors have taken conscious decisions, taken strategic actions and defined their position while laying down their core beliefs. In such a situation the task of the HR facilitator is simplified since he does not have to spend time trying to change the mindset of those at the top before implementing his solution. Therefore, the discussion must move on to strategy formulation at once.

Desired Strategy:

There is no doubt that the proprietors have clarity of vision. Now the task is to convert their vision into a concrete mission statement. The HR Consultant should help them to first concretize their mission. The pass on to stating their goals and finally their objectives in terms of quantity, quality, cost and time. Ethics is like a pregnant woman. You can be pregnant or not pregnant: you cannot be somewhat pregnant. So the company must have a set of core beliefs, which must be committed to paper and not just place all over as decoration but something that must be followed. These are what the company stands by come what may.

Once this is done, the company must delineate three areas of concern. In the software area these are:

(a) To create a sense of belongingness.

(b) To constantly upgrade the technology base of the employee.

(c) To pay the employee sufficiently well to retain him.

(d) To set up a reward scheme that recognizes merit and promotes innovation.

Companies that pride themselves on not being the best paymasters delude themselves since the cost of attrition and the cost of training is lost when a person leaves. It is always beneficial to know what each employee is worth to the company, to himself and then equilibrate the two kinds of worth to arrive at a win-win situation. This is easier said than done especially because the HR professional hardly ever addresses himself to this issue, most unfortunately.

The thing to avoid in such a situation is for top management to believe that they know all that there is to know about HR and dictate policies to the specialist. In proprietary firms that are still in the mercantilist grove, the HR man is supposed to say *yes sir, yes sir, three bags full sir*. If the HR Consultant has any professional self-respect he must put his foot down firmly but politely and help the proprietors along. Since they may be unaware of the actual damage, they may be inflicting on the organization and the employee morale he should educate them on what their policies could result in.

This can happen only when the HR Consultant:

- Knows his job well and is confident of his skills.
- Is able to walk his talk and stand up for his beliefs.
- Constantly adds value to his job and this value addition is visible.
- There is no conflict of interests between the consultant's various businesses.
- Stops being a consultant and acts as a facilitator instead.
- The task is not extended knowingly so that more fees can be collected.

Perhaps what the proprietors need to do is to empower the HR Consultant and insist on accountability for pre-arranged deliverables. Unless they show and carry forth their trust in the HR Consultant he will be at sea and unable to deliver results. Unfortunately, this happens many times, and since the HR professional does not put his foot down and the proprietors walk all over the consultant, real development remains a pipe dream even with the best of intentions. Ideally, the HR Consultant acts in tandem with the line manager and the internal HR expert for value based intervention. Hence, it is very necessary that his relationship with the company should be strictly professional, his contract is time bound or task bound and if possible there is a clause inserted so that non-performance is penalized.

❑❑❑

CASE 29

BROACHA STEELS LIMITED

Sarosh Broacha was an MS in Metallurgy from the famous Carnegie Mellon Institute of Technology USA and had inherited the steel company, which his illustrious father and his two uncles had started way back in 1940. Due to the untimely death of his father and his uncles in a plane crash, in spite of a good technical degree, Sarosh had to learn how to be a Director of a well known but privately owned Steel Company, in the school of hard knocks. Ever since he took up the post of Director in 1960 he was uncomfortable with the returns to scale generated by the plant which was located in Chaibasa, a mofusil township 30 miles from Jamshedpur and which was also the District Head Quarters. Things came to ahead in 1991 when the Indian markets were liberated by reforms. This was in spite of the fact that the company had up to date technology, which was both efficient and competitive.

Sarosh had long since realized that the Chota Nagpur Region of Eastern India is the lifeblood of raw material needed for Indian industry. And yet, it is the one of the poorest geo-physical areas that one can come across. Entrepreneurs with a mercantilist-trader mentality from Rajasthan and Punjab have a set up industries in the small-scale sector as have the erstwhile landed bourgeoisie from North Bihar who exploit the people of Jharkhand with impunity. The Christian missionaries who proliferate in the area are often more keen to convert people to their line of thought than their socio-cultural up-liftment. In this regards, the Jesuits were the only exception. The much-needed political platform has been debauched by the scams that have rocked the party representing these tribal peoples. To add to this was the fact that the State owned companies within the mining industry in that region were not doing too well since their captive buyers were now free to buy from the best seller. Moreover, the super structure of the state owned mining industry is too heavy for the infrastructure to withstand. The situation in the manufacturing sector is quite similar. And imbalance (in and between both sectors) is creating a greater disquilibrium as the battle for competition raged on.

The question was begged: how much value addition does a factor of production make? The answer to that question exposed the behaviour of the capitalist in respect of investment. Conventional Human Resources specialists invited as consultants by Sarosh did not have the answer since they were forever trapped in the vicious cycle of conducting climate surveys, compensation surveys and performance appraisals. Since they did not take up projects, which have to be designed, developed and then implemented, their exercises remained at the level of the intellectual fornication. Despite his Four General Managers (finance, manufacturing, marketing and human resources) maintaining that all was well Sarosh had his doubts.

So he employed the services of three young MBAs who had joined the company from prestigious institutions like IIM(A), IIM(C) and XLRI to do some fact finding research for him.

From the table given below, it was clear that although there had been a decline in productivity for all the steel plants during the period 1976-77 to 1980-81, there had been a steady increase in nominal earnings. On the face of it this appeared to be a clear violation of the marginal productivity theory. It did not take a genius to realize that along with the rise in nominal wages if one considered the rise in price level, one would find that there had virtually been no increase in real wages.

On the contrary the rise in the money wages had not been sufficient to offset the rise in prices. During the period of late 1970s and early 1980s prices rose at the rate of 12-14 % per annum. The increase in nominal earning had rarely succeeded in maintaining the level of real wages. Thus, Sarosh found that a declining trend in productivity had been accompanied by a virtually unchanged or at times slightly falling real wages.

TABLE 1

AVERAGE EARNING PER EMPLOYEE PER YEAR WITH CORRESPONDING LABOUR PRODUCTIVITY INGOT TONES PER MAN-YEAR

PLANT	*1976-77*		*1977-78*		*1978-79*		*1979-80*		*1980-81*	
BHILLAI	13311	82	5657	87	16294	80	19519	76	20383	69
DURGAPUR	11635	49	12890	49	14837	43	18956	40	20393	33
ROURKELA	11955	62	12046	56	15084	52	15563	49	17873	43
BOKARO	8752	70	9863	59	10477	67	12582	69	13953	48
TISCO	N.A.	NIL	12504	72	13065	65	16151	62	16380	63
BROACHA	N.A.	NIL	7550	50	9980	55	12020	58	14050	60

Next, the three MBAs considered the productivity and average earnings of his employees over the five-year period ranging from 1989-90 to 1993-94. In this case study, "employees" include all employees working inside the works and does not restrict itself to the definition of "worker" as given in the Factories Act, 1948. Moreover, they had considered the production of both hot metal as well as work saleable steady during this period so that the analysis is made more relevant.

TABLE 2

YEAR	*No. of Workers Inside Works (making steel)*	*Total Hot Metal Prod. (Tons)*	*Per Worker Prod. (Tons)*	*Total Workers Saleable*	*Per Worker Prod. Steel (Tons)*
	1	2	2/1	3	3/1
1989-90	25571	2268959	88.75	1966046	76.88
1990-91	26516	2320628	87.52	1944338	73.32
1991-92	27703	2400932	86.67	2037958	73.56
1992-93	28395	2427659	86.15	2123675	75.05
1993-94	29140	2597755	89.15	2153725	73.91

As any economist will tell, the theoretical instrument to be used for the measurement of the relative worth of the capital and the labour inputs respectively is the Constant Elasticity of Supply (CES) Production Function. The Cobb-Douglas Production Function is a more malleable function to be used in the case of the primary industries like agriculture. Whereas it could be used in the case of raw materials also, it needs to be explained precisely why it was chosen, as many have. A short description of the two can be gleaned from any textbook and need not be entered into here.

It was found that the elasticity coefficient of capital for Hot Metal Production is 0.25. In other words, a unit increase in capital increased the output by 0.25 units. The issue of Factor Intensity was then taken up. In case of Cobb-Douglas production function, factor intensity is given by the ratio of *a* to *(1-a)*. Hence, in the case under study, factor intensity is a/(1-a) = 0.75/0.25 = 3. Therefore, the Hot Metal production in the company was found to be highly labour intensive.

TABLE 3

Year	*Average Salary per month (Rs.)*	*%age increase over previous year*	*Rate of inflation*
1989-90	5966	—	6%
1990-91	6460	8.28	11%
1991-92	7003	8.40	12.62%
1992-93	7601	8.54	9.15%
1993-94	8259	8.65	6.45%

Thus, the MBAs found in case of the company, over the five-year period from 1989-90, there was virtually no increase in productivity either in hot metal production or in MS steel production. On the other hand, there was steady increase of more than 8% per annum in salaries. This would seem to contradict the marginal productivity theory. However, if we were to take into consideration, the MBAs argued, the rate inflation during the same period, they would find that in real terms the wages were in fact falling or at best they had remained constant.

They further realized that the same reasoning held true for the entire iron & steel industry in India. While they found that the productivity had remained constant or showed very little increase, wages had always shown a steady increase. However, one must take into account the fact that inflation rate has been high throughout the planned era (with the notable exception of the First Five Year Plan). Hence, what appeared as a very little increase in productivity was actually a constant or even slightly declining level of real wages. Therefore, it could be concluded that marginal productivity theory held true for the Indian iron & steel industry in this limited sense only. In other words, a more or less constant level of real wages had accompanied an unchanged productivity of workers.

It was apparent to Sarosh that with the markets opening up, an increase in productivity will lead to an enhancement of the competitive edge and therefore growth which will invariably lead to more effective employment in the aggregate. With this in mind he called for a high-powered meeting to be attended by the four general managers, their technical assistants and the three MBAs who had prepared the report. With everyone armed with a copy of the report submitted to them well in advance, Sarosh laid down the future manpower planning strategy.

- Have a lean and mean organisation structure.
- To gauge whether or not any activity actually adds value to the organisation and dispense with those persons, processes and products lines that did not add value.
- To emphasise on the growth of the efficient vital few and dispense with the inefficient trivial many.
- To create a healthy work culture where people come first but where empowerment and accountability go hand in hand.
- To have quality built into the process rather than be inspected at the end of the value chain.

This meant clearly that a Voluntary Retirement Scheme was on the cards and many of the old guards had to leave.

The four general managers found this to be a complete turn around from what was practiced in the past. They vehemently objected and stated in a uniform voice that things should be allowed to remain very much as they were, and not rock the boat. Sarosh argued that since there was enough disequilibrium in the market caused by foreign players entering the field at lower prices and better quality, Broacha Steels had to change or perish. There was an obvious deadlock so the meeting was adjourned and they agreed to meet again in a week's time.

Assuming that you are the three MBAs, put up a stiff defence by way of a policy report, on behalf of Sarosh such that the four general managers have to accept this change of manpower strategy.

HINT:

- It is well known that when a company is operating at increasing returns to scale, recruitment is advisable. When it is operating at constant returns to scale, training interventions to increase efficiency must be mooted. When it is operating at decreasing returns to scale, retrenchment was advisable.
- Prepare a technical note on the microeconomic production function.
- Calculate whether the company is operating at increasing returns to scale, constant returns to scale or decreasing returns to scale.
- Calculate also whether the company's production process was capital intensive or labour intensive.
- Then take a rational stand advising Sarosh Broacha so that he can defend his policy with the help of data.

Remember well that a working knowledge of economic theory and basic mathematics is vital for undertaking meaningful manpower planning exercises. All students of HR must take special note of this fact if they wish to succeed in their careers.

❑❑❑

CASE 30

INDO ARAB OIL INC.

Indo-Arab Oil Inc., the petroleum giant, with an annual turnover of over Rs.10, 000 crore and being over 20 years old, was going through a massive modernisation phase in the late 1990s and early 2000s. The Indian partners were the landed gentry who had become rich by using the license and quota raj effectively for massing personal wealth of the Directors, who shamefacedly used political connections to get lucrative contracts and the concomitant kickbacks. The reason given was that global markets had opened up, that Europe was re-uniting as a customs union and the company wanted to exploit the situation to its fullest advantage. Oil prices were rising and technology needed to produce oil at competitive prices was just not adequate to absorb the fall in demand and resultant fall in profits. It had all along dominated the pricing policy of the Government of India and many of its welfare measures even preceded state legislation on working class rights and privileges. With foreign oil extracting technology having been rated more efficient than its Indian counterpart, the interests of Arab countries shifting towards a global jihad, it was time, the Indian Directors of the company felt, to sever the Arab-link and depend on the crude found by the Ambanis and others in Western India. In addition, the level of quality requirement having taken quantum leaps, Indo-Arab Inc. was fast losing that pride of place it had enjoyed for decades. Due to vertical and horizontal integration of the production process, and by virtue of government patronage the company had a controlling interest in a number of smaller oil concerns all over India. The company was based in Rajkot and the management policy was to deal with the working class directly. Dialogues were a regular feature and there was a progressive union in the company, which was alive to employee welfare, market conditions, as well as managerial constraints.

The company has grown from strength to strength and was ranked No. 3 on the turnover rankings, up until it lost that position five years ago. The company had always been associated with far-sightedness and had started thinking in terms of export in a big way with the goal of becoming one of the major global players at least a decade before India liberated its markets. Exports had always been a part of the company's turnover, but it never was able to rise above the 15% mark.

Top Management made a historic decision in 1995, according to which the Arab connection was severed. Simultaneously, complete modernisation of its plant, in 5 phases, was scheduled to get over by 2003. What Manojbhai Patel, its feudal-mercantilist minded Chairman, did not anticipate was the global recession of 2001 would hit the industrial sector so devastatingly, and it was only through the financial wizardry of Sailesh Hude, their Director of Finance, that they managed to avoid defaulting payments to suppliers of raw materials. Even in 1999, the financial liquidity position was not very impressive. The Company no longer remained the "byword" as far as petroleum went in India. The erstwhile public sector giants were doing better than expected and even the business deviousness and underhanded dealings of Kasande Bhai Kumar its Director of Production and Marketing, could not rescue the company's fortunes. They very reluctantly called up a professional agency to look into the matter. This was especially a sad thing to happen since all along Patel, Hude and Kumar had boasted that they could handle almost any situation.

The findings of this agency were:

(i) The company was overstaffed by 30% and about 50% of the manpower performed below acceptable efficiency levels.

(ii) Modernisation was the need of the hour and the Arab connection had to be severed.

(iii) Lines of responsibility were not specific so goal and role clarity was needed.

(iv) There was too much centralisation of management control and not adequate willingness to play by the rules.

(v) Costs of production had to be reduced at any cost if the company was to survive global competition.

(vi) Per capita productivity of labour needed to be raised by at least 100%.

(vii) The company needed to generate revenue for financing the proposed modernisation programme.

(viii) The Director of Personnel, the Vice President of Finance and the Vice President of Corporate Affairs should be located in a central office, if diversification of control was not an acceptable proposition.

(ix) Both authority and accountability should be delegated down the line and horizontally in a clear manner.

(x) Directors should stop taking frequent trips abroad ostensibly for business purposes but in reality to maintain their bohemian lifestyles. Audit reports had thrown up quite a few questions that were difficult to answer with a straight face.

Since the plant modernisation programme was already in progress, top management focused their attention, primarily, to just one major problem at a time. They zeroed in on another issue, that of over-staffing, hoping that in so doing, they would also be addressing the question of per capita productivity of labour. They further argued, that even if 30% manpower could be reduced, it would lead to cost reduction and the profit cycle could start moving upwards again.

Options: Top management, which was known for making delayed decisions, studied the problem for full two years and only then decided that the various options could be narrowed down to three areas viz.

(i) Retrenchment: On paper, this was the most effective method of reducing over-staffing and its chief advantage was that the dead wood could be weeded out but not quite comfortably. The corporate culture was such that the word "retrenchment" was anathema since many caste and village affiliations dictated who got which position in the company. Top management struggled with the idea of retrenchment knowing that cost reduction could take place easily. Using this option would have to be at the cost of goodwill and since it did not have a good name in the market for ethical practices anyway, they did not want to make matters worse. It was decided, therefore, to forego this option.

(ii) Re-deployment: This was the second option open to the top management. It was reasoned that the surplus manpower could be shifted to those companies where the Directors had a controlling interest or sent to the village where they had sizeable agricultural land and even a brewery. The plan was that there would be a mixture of the "good" and the "bad" who would be shifted to the villages so as not to upset the vote bank, since one of the patriarchs of the family was in active politics and make the allied companies have the worst of it. However, when a study of the allied companies was conducted, it was found that apart from the new ball-bearing plant in Cochin, none of the companies had any openings.

(iii) Voluntary Retirement Scheme (VRS): This third alternative was agreeable to top management and not opposed by the union, since it was offering a benevolent golden handshake and there would be no socio-cultural fallouts in the villages that could upset the vote bank. Furthermore, it was made optional and not compulsory to soften the blow.

The report of the agency were kept strictly confidential and all that the senior managers were given was a covering letter signed by the Chairman, giving a short summary of what the Chairman thought the problems were. The primary reason for this was that the Director of Finance had gone on record to state that the company did not have enough liquid cash to embark on the VRS. His objections were steam-rolled by the Chairman, who felt that he could use the VRS dole-outs to be re-cycled into the company exchequer to finance the modernisation scheme.

The Chairman constituted a task force to formulate the terms and conditions of the golden handshake. Yet another task force was formed to liase with the governmental bureaucracy. It sought the approval of the Central Board of Direct Taxes to enable the company to have operationalised the VRS. A third task force, headed by the Director of Personnel, the grandson of the political patriarch of the family took charge of the implementation of the VRS. The task force, which was to deal with the state bureaucracy, reported directly to the Vice President (Corporate Affairs), located in Mumbai. The task force, which was to work out the financial package, reported to the Vice President (Finance), who was also the Managing Director of the ball bearing plant at Nasik. The Director of Personnel reported to the Managing Director at the headquarters located at Rajkot.

Implementation: The Director of Personnel, first of all, decided to formally confer with the Union. Interestingly, the Union decided to remain "neutral" on this issue supposedly since the level of trust on top management's commitments was low. A circular was then sent out to all the departments through pre-chosen heads so that the scheme could get due publicity. Every employee received details about the financial offer, terms and conditions. Suggestions were also given on how to utilise the "cash carrot" being offered. This circular was designed chiefly to eliminate all communication gaps and quell the possibility of rumour mongering, while opening the door for re-investment of employee funds into the company's exchequer.

Terms and Conditions: The worked out terms and conditions had the following salient features:

- Employees should be 40 years of age or should have at least 15 years of completed service to their credit.
- While every eligible employee was free for VRS, the acceptance of the application was discretionary. This was in accordance with the provisions of the Finance Act 1999. The aim was to stop the 'critical workers' from leaving the organisation.
- The financial offer was substantial and generally quite acceptable.
- The company paid an annual interest equal to what the banks paid but far below what the workers would get if they invested in the share market.

Effect: In a dialogue with workers, the Chairman stated that preference would be given to those who were willing to re-invest funds in the company. A fortnight later, the scheme was launched with a lot of pomp and pageantry.

Three things happened on the morning when the VRS was announced:

(i) An editorial in the Gujarat Samaschar appeared stating that it was improper for any company to offer VRS on the condition that funds would be ploughed back.

(ii) The statements issued by the Vice President (Finance) to the Indian Express, by the Director (Personnel) to the Sakal and by the Vice President (Corporate Affairs) to Lok Satta were incongruent. The first stated that VRS was introduced mainly to cut production costs. The second stated that the VRS was introduced mainly to help the workers who could invest funds and live off the interest. The third stated that the VRS was introduced to streamline the organisation, making it lean, mean and effective. The local Gujarati paper, "Lal Vavta", as well as its Hindi and Marathi editions highlighted this point.

(iii) The President of the Union, when interviewed by the local All India Radio Station, Vadodra, stated that he had not agreed to the VRS and there was no signed document to prove his acceptance.

The VRS scheme was launched on 31st. December 1999. Employees declared extra to the standard force by the Industrial Engineering Department were targeted for the VRS. As of 18th February 1995, only 500 out of the targeted population of 5,000 workers, took Voluntary Retirement. 1000 non targeted manpower, however, left the company using the VRS. This was an unexpected blow. 60% of the managers in the Computer Services Department opted for the scheme and left the country. The Voluntary Retirement Scheme was more favourably accepted by executives rather than the supervisors and workers. According to the terms and conditions of eligibility for VRS, the employee had to be either '40 years of age or have 15 years of experience'. Young executives in their mid-thirties, who had joined straight after college, fitted the requirements of the VRS and started leaving the organisation in search of greener pastures with solid work experience under their belts and a solid bank account, thanks to the VRS. There was no favourable response to the VRS from people who originally hailed from Rajkot or had already built their own houses in the city.

This was the situation in which the oil giant found itself in early 2003. The VRS was ignominiously scrapped.

ISSUES RAISED:

- ***Where lies the accountability for the failure of the Voluntary Retirement Scheme? Where did the Manpower Planning exercise go wrong?***
- ***Was it good managerial practice for the top management not to divulge the consulting agency's report to the managers? How can there be trust without transparency?***
- ***What were the main reasons for the exodus of good men from the company?***
- ***Was the union's attitude to the VRS politically proper?***

HINT:

Is it not good management practice to have lines of communication open all the time, keep employees informed and maintain relations of trust through transparency with the workers' collectivity. Any downsizing exercise needs proper planning, clear communication and objectively set targets that lend themselves to transparency. Manpower planning involves the future of human beings who have been working with the company for years and therefore has to be handled with a clear conscience. If this is not done, even the best of policies has a high chance of failure. Remember that many an industrial relations dispute has arisen due to improper manpower planning and poor communications. The link between a value centred corporate culture and a manpower planning exercise may not be apparent but it is nevertheless crucial to the success of any HR intervention as well as to the financial future of the organisation. Corporate communications play a major role in all such exercises where messages must be correctly conveyed, in the proper time and the appropriate manner so that interventions are accepted. This especially true during exercises involving downsizing, mergers, takeovers and acquisitions.

❑❑❑

SECTION FOUR

SHORT CASE STUDIES IN CORPORATE CULTURE

CASE 31

BABY CARE LIMITED

In 1980 a group of eight ex-students from XLRI joined hands to start a venture in Mumbai. Through their old connections they managed to get a franchise from a Swiss Multinational Company for manufacturing baby care products. Each was a specialist in one core aspect of management and so his expertise complemented that of his partners. Each had served industry for a period ranging from 8 to 12 years before tying up with this venture. Each as prepared to invest Rs. 10 lakhs at once and a further Rs. 5 lakhs by 1982 the factory was set up in MIDC Marol in Mumbai.

Each founding alumnus took charge of one core function viz.: finance, marketing, strategic planning, systems and control, administration and liaison, production and quality control. All major decisions were taken jointly and collectively, which invariably took time. But once the decision was taken it was implemented with complete devotion and precision.

By 1990 the sales turnover had reached the Rs. 300 crore mark, and their childcare products were fast becoming household names due to their unrelenting emphasis on quality. It was the only partnership firm, to get both an ISO 9000 and an ISO 14000 certification within ten years of going into business.

It was agreed that at least 80% of the net profits would be ploughed back into the company for developmental work and expansion. The firm believed in converting every customer into a client and their advertisement read: *Our Product is so damned good that it sells itself. Our service is better!*

Market reports were very favourable and in every possible way they were an ideal employer. However, unknown to most people the eight partners had set up a research facility in MIDC Mahape (Navi Mumbai) some 50 kilometres away from their factory. There they had set up a smaller company called Strategic Research Facility but known only as SRF. Some of the best brains in pharmacy, pharmacology, chemistry, biology and nutrition had been employed there at very good salaries. 70% of the annual budget of the company was diverted to SRF. The partners (rightly) saw SRF as their insurance against the year 2005 A.D. when GATT strictures on patents and trademarks would ring the death knell of many third world pharmaceutical companies.

The two companies Baby Care and SRF were separated not just by distance but also by work culture. SRF had one General Manager, one Administrative Manager, thirty Senior Scientists, fifty Scientists, seventy Laboratory Technicians and thirty Support Staff.

The work climate in MIDC Marol was thoroughly professional while that in MIDC Mahape was absolutely bohemian. Both units, although located within Greater Mumbai, had their own separate agenda, budgets and targets, which were more than adequately met. The annual climate survey using the Udai Pareek — T. V. Rao methodology consistently gave Baby Pharmaceuticals a very good rating. The annual HRD work ethic survey using the XLRI methodology consistently gave a very good report to SRF. The spirit of stakeholdership pervaded both the companies by design since this was the culture they had brought with them when these ex-students of XLRI had got together.

In April 1997 one Senior Scientist committed suicide and the autopsy revealed that it was a case of *suicide under influence of hallucinogenic substances*. Nothing like this had ever happened before. In fact nobody had ever misbehaved under the influence of drugs or alcohol. The partners wanted the matter investigated thoroughly by experts. An industrial psychologist from Sri Ram Centre of HR and IR (Delhi), a sociologist from Bombay University and a Social Work expert from TISS were invited to study the problem. Dr. Theo Mathias was invited over from XLRI to lead the team of experts. After a complete study, it revealed the following:

Negative:

- Alcoholism and the use of drugs was rampant in SRF.
- Almost every employee was sexually liberated and had multiple partners.
- Fifteen of the staff admitted being homosexuals while six admitted being lesbians.

Positive:

- Productivity and creativity per capita was at an all time high.
- There was no instance of disorderly conduct within the premises.
- Each employee added value at about 10-15 times their salary on an average.

Neutral:

- Everyone lived in their own world and worked for the sheer joy of it. However, there was no team leader and people often worked divergently rather than convergently.
- Although there was a high level of professional ethics, there was a low level of acceptable social morality.
- A spirit of detached interest in everything that went around them pervaded the psyche of most employees.
- Everyone had either no domestic life or a disturbed one.
- Nobody worked with a specific competitive spirit. If they competed then it was against science, their own knowledge and against time.

The committee of experts submitted the report and purely out of his missionary zeal, Dr. Mathias stayed behind in Mumbai to help the lads through this rough patch. Faced with a copy of this report the eight partners sat down in silent cogitation to deliberate at length on the findings. The four questions uppermost in their minds were:

1. Can competition not be converted into cooperation?
2. Is discipline a necessary condition for companies to perform well?
3. Can there not be a highly productive but leaderless group?
4. Is there any case for HR intervention?

As an HR specialist how would you deal with such a situation and how would you answer the three questions, which have been posed above?

HINT:

Desired Discussion:

In the strict Hegelian sense the very antithesis of freedom is slavery. Discipline then becomes a specific condition of slavery. In the strict Kantian sense however, there must be order in everything and the antithesis of order is disorder. Discipline then becomes a specific condition for maintaining order. However, discipline too must be questioned at every stage with the same questions: Is it necessary? Does it add value to business? Is it in consonance with our core value? Only is the answer to **all** three of these questions is in the affirmative discipline must be pursued zealously. If not, rules will become the reason for the existence and behaviour of man rather than instruments meant for his convenience.

The moot question then arises when does liberty become license? Where does the HR facilitator draw the line? Visualize the picture of a knowledge-based worker sitting up late in his office and going home at midnight. His is to meet a deadline and entirely in the overall interest of the organization. Now to expect that employee to clock in with the rest of the office staff at 9:00 am the following morning is asking too much and then to penalize him for coming late, say at 11:00 am is ridiculous. But such things do happen. However, artists and specialized workers often work in spasms and short bursts of activity are followed by a lull. Hence, it is quite acceptable to have such persons like those in the case take liberty with time and manner as long as the rights of others and the interests of the organization is not in jeopardy. Freedom then should mean allowing others to exercise their rights and not imposing one's will on the others. [Liberty is not license]. No abuse of power or authority of conflict was reported. So no action can be taken. But what the HR facilitator must do at once is to issue a code of conduct and a code of ethics, which while respecting individual eccentricities, makes allowance for such behaviour. The HR facilitator is not a schoolteacher or a class monitor or a *havaldar* in a police *chowkie*. He has to recognize and respect the fact that these persons are *adding value* to the organization and not causing any damage to each other or to the organization. For instance, it is quite common to see Professors living on the campus going to their offices at 4.00 am and not going in to work for days. As long as the students do not suffer nor does the institute earn a bad name, these professors are adding value all the time and their eccentricities must be respected. So is the case with research scientists and other knowledge based superior workers.

❑❑❑

CASE 32

I.I.M.E.E. (CHENNAI)

Chanda Murmu was an extremely good looking, polite and well-mannered young lady who hailed from a modest tribal background in the Chota Nagpur Region of South Bihar, now Jharkhand. She was dark skinned but the simplicity of her nature only enhanced her beauty as an individual. She carried herself with dignity, was always well composed and spoke little by choice. In addition, she could write very well and had excellent analytical skills.

Having graduated with industrial psychology from Ranchi University, she had earned a scholarship to come to Mumbai for her second Masters Degree, in industrial sociology. On completing her second MA she was recruited on a reservation quota as an HR Executive in the Indian Institute of Managerial Excellence and Entrepreneurship (IIMEE) in Chennai.

IIMEE was set up by the Central Government and came under the joint purview of the Ministry of HRD and the Ministry of Economic Development. It began in 1970 by training supervisors in the art of management and then took on consultancy assignments in the small-scale industries sector by 1979. In 1982 it started a specialized wing to promote entrepreneurial talent and had set up its own gobar gas plant as a part of this scheme.

The institute was located in the heart of the city not far from the University itself. It had a staff strength of 700 personnel of whom there were 60 trainers, and unfortunately not even three had any national level standing. Chanda was the de facto administrative head reporting to the Registrar, Mr. Jose Abraham. She was also the Chief Examination Officer of IIMEE.

The Director of the Institute of Dr. Kumar Guruswamy who, by training was an engineer, but over the years had become an administrator. From a small institute in 1960, today IIMEE had a name known nationally as an institute for training. The credit for this went entirely to the Director and the Registrar. They had worked hard and built the institute together. Unfortunately, Dr. Guruswaamy was very casteist and known to have been openly partial towards persons and especially Brahmins from South India. He was sometimes disparaging in his remarks about the persons from the lower strata of Hindu society. He did not apologize for it: indeed he thought it was a sign of his superiority.

Mr. N. Abraham was lay preacher and loved his alcohol. It was common knowledge that in the evenings he would be usually inebriated. He also liked the company of young women and although he had a family he was a known womaniser. There were several nefarious rumours about his behaviour and secretaries would shiver at the thought of going to his room to take dictation. Although he had been known to molest several of them, no woman dared to complain for fear of losing her job and gaining a bad reputation by default. He would employ people and not issue appointment letters but leave the matter at an offer and an acceptance letter. Therefore, the full terms of employment were never spelled out. This gave him room to be choosy about what he did with whom and how.

One afternoon when Chanda was working in her office, a girl named Rohini Kamath rushed in and started hysterically sobbing. It transpired that Mr. Abraham had called Rohini under the pretext of giving a dictation and started acting quite intimately with her. Rohini resented this and he tried to molest her. When her requests for leaving her alone, fell on deaf ears she had panicked. To avoid her dignity being violated, she had hit him on the head and ran out of the office in the nick of time.

Chanda Murmu offered her a glass of water, ordered tea and then took a signed statement from Rohini in front of a witness. She then sent Rohini to the local doctor (not the institute doctor) and obtained a medical report, which confirmed her fears. The girl bore evidence of fresh and deep scratches on her bosom and gash on her belly. Her sari too had been torn in three places and her blouse was ripped open at the seams. Chanda advised the girl to go to a lawyer and get an affidavit signed.

Next morning Chanda went to Dr. Guruswamy with the Doctor's Report, the Affidavit and the Signed Testimony of Rohini. At first Dr. Guruswamy dismissed it as a malicious rumor, but when Chanda was unrelenting, he said:

> *Chanda, this is the real world and such things happen. You too are a very good-looking woman and you live on the campus. Did Abraham not approach you yet? I am surprised. That must be because you are a tribal. May be that is why you cannot understand Chennai just as yet. I can always get another clerk but where will I get another Registrar? IIMEE needs Abraham and does not need Rohini. See if you can her pay her off and ask her to resign. If she does not agree, then call for an inquiry, find her guilty of hitting the Registrar, and sack her. That is an order.*

Chanda was visibly shocked and stated that she did not expect this from the Director.

> *Do not forget that Abraham is your boss and you are inciting employees against him. By the way, have you got your confirmation letter yet?*

Next day Chanda took a flight to Delhi and went straight to the Ministry of HRD armed with the evidence. You are also an alumnus of Madras University but now you are the Under Secretary to the Ministry of HRD and Chanda is now sitting in front of your desk. She has told you that she intends to go to the Ministry of Tribal Welfare in the afternoon. You know Dr. Guruswamy well and also know that Abraham has a cousin who holds a high rank in the Central Civil Service.

What will you do, as a senior bureaucrat and an HR man yourself?

What should companies do to prevent such an occurrence in their premises?

HINT:

Some Theoretical Input: Harassment of any sort may be defined as behaviour, which an individual finds offensive and unwanted. Physical sexual harassment is a charge that can be brought arising out of unnecessary physical contact such as touching, patting, pinching or brushing up against another person. It can arise out of seeking sexual favours for promises of employment, confirmation, promotion, transfer, sanctioning of loans or any other reward or benefit. An outright sexual assault or an attempt at it could cause it. Verbal behaviour tantamounting to sexual harassment could be caused through sexual propositions; continued suggestion for social activity outside of work after it has been made explicitly clear that such suggestions are unwelcome. Offensive flirtations, embarrassing remarks, innuendoes and lewd comments could amount to sexual harassment. Also harassment non-verbal behaviour amounting to sexual harassment could be in the form of that display of pornographic or sexually suggestive pictures or leering or staring suggestively at another person's body and making sexually suggestive gestures.

Ethnic or racial harassment is a hostile and offensive act or expression by an individual or group of one ethnic or racial origin against an individual or group of another racial or ethnic origin. It could take the form of physical abuse, intimidation, use of derogatory language, mockery, racist jokes, patronizing remarks, racial name calling, unfair allocation of work or responsibilities, threatening behaviour to incite violence, offensive comments about appearance or attire.

In law, it is always easy to prove an attempt to rape than to prove rape. So too, an insult is a cognisable offence if it is proved that it was premeditated and caused by malafide intent. This must be borne in mind when HRD facilitators are addressing employee grievances on the subject. In a society dominated by male chauvinism like that of India, sexual harassment often goes un-objected and un-noticed. That does not make it excusable and the offender cannot be condoned. The case, given above, involves both kinds of harassment and has been taken from a real life situation.

Desired Discussion:

It is quite common to find instances of victimization as well as examples of harassment in the work place. However, what cannot and should not be tolerated is discriminatory practices of any sort. Now, we know that man is a social animal and is subjective in his likes and dislikes but that does not permit him to blatantly discriminate against a person because of his looks, sex, ethnic origin, religious beliefs or political ideology. However, a prima facie case must be established. In this instance, there appears to be enough circumstantial evidence to initiate an inquiry. This must be started at once and the findings must be arrived at expeditiously. Not only should justice be done but it must also seen to be done. Moreover, justice delayed is justice denied.

The inquiry officer must be a reputed person who has no links with the institute and all evidence must be examined according to the rules of natural justice. Once this is done and supposing the person(s) are found guilty, then immediate action must be taken. However, a humane approach is always recommended. If the charges are proved, both the Registrar and the Director should be held responsible for (alleged) misuse of power and be asked to resign at once. This will send out a clear signal that such victimization will not go unpunished. In smaller and proprietary firms this is not always easy since personal equations between senior individuals usually come in the way of justice. Nevertheless, for such a thing to happen in an institution of national repute is not only morally despicable but also inexcusable.

On the other side of the coin is the fact that many a time under the guise of exploitation, personal vendetta is taken and scores are settled. In cases of sexual molestation, many times the victim keeps quiet for fear of adverse publicity, which in a male dominated society, is always biased against the woman. This seems to have happened in the past.

Above all, do not be shocked since this kind of incidents are common. The mediocrat-bureaucrat is either hand in glove with the perpetuator or willing to sweep matters under the carpet "in the overall interest" of the organization. This tendency has to be negated at once.

Desired Strategy:

This is a case where corporate governance has a role to play as has the HR specialist who is supposed to be the conscience keeper of the organization's values. The following actions need to be taken from the point of view of a value based management and these can be summarized thus:·

- A code of conduct must be laid down and displayed wherein sexual or any kind of victimization should be designated as an offence.
- A proper inquiry should be initiated and all evidence should be fully documented as well as cross-examined.
- There is always a possibility that a wily woman can be used to set up an innocent man so as to settle personal/professional scores. Hence, this too must be borne in mind while investigating the case.
- A system be set up for reporting such cases and a proper system be set up for redress after proper and unbiased inquiry: it is better to let off three guilty persons for want of adequate evidence than to convict an innocent man.
- In such cases, a person cannot be pardoned in the organizational interest since the long run ramifications of such a pardon are cathartic.
- It was professionally correct for Chanda Murmu to report and equally correct for you to take stern action against the Director and the Registrar. Discipline always begins at the top.
- If all fails then advise Chanda Murmu to take the matter to a civil court and make the issue public. Blowing the whistle in such cases is justified. Unfortunately whistle blowers are first hailed and then ostracised in most civil societies.

❑ ❑ ❑

CASE 33

MEGA SYSTEMS LIMITED

You are the Chief Project Manager employed by a software management company in Nashik named **MEGA SYSTEMS LIMITED**. It is a family owned business, which is tightly controlled, and as a matter of policy, its figures are not divulged to Business magazines. Hence, the managers have to accept what top level says about its performance. Of late there have been whisperings about the company losing a lot of foreign contracts to competitors and rumour has it that the cash flow statements do not appear encouraging. To add to all this the company has major problems with manpower attrition. By educational qualification you are a Commerce Graduate but who learnt about computers as a part of your Masters Degree program. The company is small and the HR Manager is a young man, full of ideas but still green behind the ears in experience. You have obtained a Masters Degree in Business Economics from MIT (Cambridge) and ten years work experience (but not in software) to your credit. You got the job because you are a good man manager and a brilliant trouble-shooter. Your job besides looking after the line functions is (a) to help HR in recruiting the correct talent required by the company and (b) retain the talent that is on rolls. The issue addressed is how can we retain staffs that are attracted by greener pastures overseas? Most of the migrants or potential leavers are knowledge workers who have a high self-esteem and know that there is market demand for their skills. Your first task is to try and understand the system. So you go to the root of the technology used in this company and the following are your findings in brief.

There are different kinds of software. The first type relates to Network Software and Systems Software. The second kind relates to Applications Software of various kinds. The third kind relates to Data Management of various sorts including Data Warehousing, Data Storage and Retrieval and Data Entry. The fourth type consists of tools, utilities and aids such as case tools, de-buggers, sorters etc. Hierarchically one could see the first type as the Architecture, the second as the Builder, the third as Production Worker and the fourth as a Maintenance Worker.

The computer itself could be either a Main Frame, a Mid Range Machine, a Personal Computer or a Notebook. The expertise for the lower end technology is not easy to get hold of, since it is something, which the developed countries are not interested in. In the Third World, labour is cheap and available for these low-end technology jobs. There are some well known packages developed by companies such as Word Lord developed by the Software Research Group, Hospital Management Systems developed by Thermax, Tally developed by Peutronics, Signbank, Microbanker and Easydeal developed by Citil and Banks 2000 developed by Infosys. Indian labour is used for these conversion jobs and both head-hunting as well as job hopping become lucrative trades.

Also, there is the Legacy Systems or the old systems, which have long since not been used in the developed world but which are still being used in the third world. Skills that are required to man the legacy systems are no longer plentiful in the devolved world. But nevertheless there are programs which were developed on and which work on legacy systems. These need to be made more client friendly and so they have to be "migrated" on to another platform for which a case tool may have to be created or the system itself be "ported" from one platform to another. For this kind of work, contracts are given to Indian companies and Indian workers are body shopped to foreign customers. For both sides of the wage-negotiating table this is a good proposition since the Indian Rupee is weak and the Indian Labour comes cheap to hire.

On subsequent reading of available literature in the company you learn that way back in the 1960s a number of systems across the United States were linked by a computer network called DARPA-NET (Defence Advanced Research Project Agency). The Department of Defence, (D of D) which had the three Cs firmly in its grasp, controlled this: *command, communication* and *control*. In the name of strategic defence of the country, various networks spread across the USA and various universities could be linked but only the D of D could uncode and decode the various outputs and make complete sense of it. In 1967 Norman Abramson was responsible for putting up a link between Hawaii and an Indonesian satellite named PALAPA. This linked Hawaii to the computer network in the rest of the United States and was known as ALOHA-NET. The modern Internet is an offshoot of the old DARPA-NET so it stands to reason to say that the controls still lie in the hands of the US Department of Defence. Hence, the claim that Internet is an independent international network is questionable. This, of course, is just one and covert aspect of US attempts to dominate the capitalist world economy.

You also discover the softer and overt side of US imperialism: the concept of setting up dedicated units in India also known as Software Factories. This idea appeals to you and you discuss it with your CEO who listens patiently. You float the idea gingerly amongst your top management team and find that there is no opposition to the idea in principle.

But you original problems persist: How do you retain talent? How can attrition be prevented?

HINT:

Software Engineers are basically knowledge workers who can be retained by attractive remuneration/ rewards and by recognition. There must be a constant up-gradation of technology so that the engineer is motivated to stay on. This can be done through proactive skill up-gradation and executive development programs. It is really no use saying that *why can we not pay below the industry minimum* and then cribbing about high attrition. There is a cost of recruitment, a cost of attrition and this all adds up because the useful time lost while the new entrant is getting into the grove is an additional and avoidable cost. Moreover, the software industry is improving the lot of mediocrity along with the market pulls. As with every trade cycle, this cycle too will dip. That is when the employees who have a *sense of belongingness* will stay on. Companies who can retain manpower when the going is rough will make it to the top such as TCS. Another example of Tata Unysis in the year 1995 is also worthy of note. It was precisely because of the Tata Culture and the belongingness need that was addressed, that people stayed on and with a new leader it revived as Tata Infotech and was doing well in 1998-99. (Subsequently, of course, its performance fell and strategic HR intervention could well have prevented this.) However, if this is mistaken for complacency then, like several other software companies, stability will transform into inertia and any company may well head for trouble. This seems somehow unlikely to happen.

From the political-economic viewpoint what India is supplying the world in Y2K projects is *sophisticated wage labour*. Whereas, we are having our engineers engaged in software development work, we neither own the technology nor do we have a control over the desired end use. Production in a manner of speaking is sub-contracted to us due to low labour costs. We are far away from the real cutting edge of technology where we are in the whole ball game of software architecture and other high tech modes of operation. This means that the brighter youth will migrate to places that can provide them with this latest technology and India will lose out. HR intervention has a social responsibility as well and it must make sure that national interests are not side lined for short run profits, as is unfortunately happening today.

From the long run viewpoint the HR intervention has a historical agenda. And, that is to prevent *development less growth*, which is sure to occur if industrialists behave like traders and the mercantilist attitudes prevail over the entrepreneurial attitudes. The only way is to build on our core competence, which is sometimes mistaken for profit making. The emphasis on technological growth and research and development activity needs to be enhanced. Today R and D within the software industry is just a *cliché'* since hardly any company is investing in long term research. Why C-DAC in Pune is doing so well even when salaries are not among the top players? The answer lies in the fact that management gives the employee sense of belonging, a climate of a learning organization has been created and technology rather than profits drive work climate. An investment in research has been consciously made there. Sure, profits are a necessary condition of being in business but it just cannot become the corporate objective of business. India being on the periphery of the capitalist word economy cannot avoid being prey to US surveillance. [The pressures being placed on India to sign the CTBT after the successful nuclear tests in the summer of 1998 prove the point being made, many times over].

However, all that notwithstanding, India can continue to blaze a trail by capitalizing on its strengths. One should ask why do Indians do well overseas and just stagnate at home? Part of the reason may be that only the cream migrates. A larger part of the reason is that Indian industry does not provide a culture where innovation and creativity can blossom. Every new idea is seen as a threat by those who are already there and is quickly squashed, in the name of safety, custom, convention, tradition ... the list goes on. The trick then is for HR intervention to work towards creating such a climate and this is easier said than done. Nevertheless, for that the project manager is equally responsible since the HR merely facilitates. As the Chief Project Manager you will have *no choice* but to work in tandem with the HR Manager and jointly take charge of man management. Both of you must make the people realize that you are adding value to their worth by equipping them with modern technology and giving them invaluable experience on prestigious projects.

It is a fallacy that project managers are the line executives and HR managers are the staff executives. In other words, it is wrong to speak of project managers as being involved in profit making functions while the HR managers as being a part of the support functions. The key lies in value addition functions which both the project manager and the HR manager are performing. This must be done in unison and there must be complete synergy between the two.

The climate in the software industry changes rapidly, and therefore, quick and decisive action is called for. But this must be well thought out and only then should it be well executed. If not, management might end up shooting itself in the foot. To prevent that from happening a corporate culture has to be evolved around three key words: *value addition, belongingness and ethical conduct*. It is the task of the leader to blaze a trail and rise up adequately to the challenge that the situation poses. You have to think *globally* and act *locally* making sure that you mean what you say and say what you mean all the time.

The solution needed to build a vibrant culture is not ready made nor can the same solution be applied uniformly in all cases. But there are certain common elements, which form a part of any strategy for a Line Management aided HR intervention. Ideally that *joint strategy* unfolds in eight stages:

- Involve the technical personnel in decision-making and only then hold them accountable for decision executing.
- Remunerate enough to retain their level of motivation without affecting the cost structures. Create a climate of trust and faith by promoting teamwork.
- Make sure that there is enough transparency and clear communication to offset doubts regarding possible *mala fide* intent.
- Continue to upgrade their knowledge level by adding value to them as professionals and thereby adding value to the organizational capabilities.
- Create a climate of stakeholdership whereby the need to belong is enhanced and people at all levels are motivated to give their best to the organization, which *must* adequately reciprocate that gesture.
- Rotate persons regularly so that boredom does not set in.
- Undertake a technological as well as behavioural skills survey and have open meetings wherein employee career development issues are taken up and then followed through.

But do we live in an ideal world?

❑❑❑

CASE 34

WHAT PRICE SUCCESS?

Raipur Engineering Systems (RES) was a company set up by seven friends who pooled in their life's savings to set up a software company in 1990. Each came from a different discipline and so each took over as the Director-in Charge of one function viz: Production and Maintenance, Technology and Research, Marketing, Finance, Corporate Governance and HR, Legal and Secretarial Matters, and PR and Liaison with the State Bureaucracy. There was complete synergy between the Directors but their subordinates began to isolate themselves and there was little interaction between them.

Initially the company concentrated on body shopping and even took on small projects for the leading giants in India like Tata Consultancy Services, Wipro and HCL-HP but soon began to make a name for themselves. In 1992, they got their first big chance when a Saudi Arabian banking company asked RES to develop a computerized software package. The package would link the 15 branches of the bank throughout the country and enable clients to get up-to-date balances of their accounting transactions. The project was completed in 1994 and RES had entered the global software market. A year later the same company approached RES to develop a migration tool to port an existing program from an RDBMS platform on to a Windows 95 program. Despite many glitches the project was completed and RES seriously started moving into the European and American markets. By 1996, RES had marketing teams in Tokyo, Osaka, London, Chicago, New York, Zurich, Milan and Paris.

The growth of the company was sporadic and there seemed to be no time for rules to be structured and codes to be formulated. Role and goal clarity often emerged by default and was never clearly laid down. But the software market was buoyant and the global demand pulled up the company in the market. It had a very able workforce, which helped matters a great deal.

Dynamic young men and women with degrees in software technology as well as a flair for marketing, who were given the title of Overseas Software Consultant (OSC) headed the external offices at various locations. He/she were remunerated well and earned extra bonuses for every lead, which they could successfully into an account. These bonuses did not always come in terms of monetary sums but were converted into additional annual increments. Hence, the OSC was keen to get more accounts for RES. The OSCs reported to one of the seven Directors who was exclusively in charge of Marketing. The OSCs were involved in outsourcing manpower (body shopping), getting new customers and converting old customers into clients. A corporate level decision was taken to update the knowledge and skills of all senior managers including the OSCs.

At first the OSCs did not wish to attend the program on the excuse that there was too much pressure of work. But HR prevailed on Top Management and convinced the company that training was an investment in the future not a cost to be met in the present. Consequently, it was made mandatory that all OSCs should attend seminars organized by RES.

So when in 1996 two senior professors from IIM (A) addressed a three-day seminar at the Taj Mahal Hotel every OSC was nominated for it. Everybody so nominated had to attend it. Three messages were communicated to the participants by the learned professors. (i) Whereas actual costs are important, do not lose sight of the opportunity costs. (ii) Always keep communication lines open and share information unflinchingly with everyone in your company. (iii) A sale is not completed until the revenue from it has been received. However, as events unfolded, the OSCs were so keen to make their own mark that they forgot that competition is not necessarily contradictory to co-operation. A dog eat dog mentality crept in unsuspectingly upon the OSCs and they began to vie with one another for more leads.

Traditionally the OSCs looked down on the Project Teams and vice versa each waiting for the other to goof up and appeal for help. Each watched the other minutely and waited for mistakes to be made so that they could pounce upon them. Information was concealed and invasion of another person's turf in the name of capitalist competition was rampant. Consequently, an atmosphere of trust was lacking and as a result of which there was little transparency in the activities of each of these sets of knowledge workers.

After the Frankfurt Trade Fair in February 1997, Dinesh (a dashing young OSC) reported to Mumbai that he was about to tie up a deal on a contract which he had been negotiating for the last six months, for the ESIS1-800 Rapid Reporting System. This came as a surprise to the RES team in Mumbai who wished they had been consulted or at least informed that such a deal was in the offing. The OSC conducted a full systems study and the SRS as well as the partial database design on site for the project and came to India to give RES the good news of his having bagged a project.

Earlier RES had struck a deal with another client regarding the SVR Project (which was still in process and running simultaneously with the 1-800 Project). Here again it was Dinesh who had brought home the new account. Dinesh told the new client that since RES already had experience on the SVR project and since the two projects were so alike, there would no problem in executing the same. Dinesh had assumed that a large portion of the database could easily be copied from the SVR system. The GUI as well as the source code for the Master Screens could similarly be picked up from the SVR System. The same was the case with the 57 State Reports required for the new project and Dinesh brought back a prototype screen from the site. The client wanted the delivery date hastened since Dinesh gave the impression that project delivery was going to be easy since two identical projects were being executed at once by RES. Dinesh made a presentation in Mumbai and was commended by all. All that the team in Mumbai had to do was develop one master screen, the main transaction screen, one query screen and a few extra reports.

Sudhir, the technical genius of the company, and who had been there from the start had been employed as a high level trouble-shooter. Sudhir had his doubts. He was uneasy by the way in which Dinesh had charged into the project and was unhappy with the claims that he had made at the presentation. He wrote a confidential memo to Dinesh pointing out the following:

1. He would have been more comfortable if Dinesh had conducted a feasibility study as well so that they could be sure the database could be copied from the SVR System.
2. Whereas there was common functionality between the two master screens, SVR was an Internet based project while 1-800 was a Client Server project. He did not see any option but to re-write the entire codes.
3. RES had earlier developed Controllers and Code Generators for the GESCO Project, which were in-house libraries for the Visual Basic projects. The SVR Project had not used any code generators at all and so the assumption of Dinesh was flawed.
4. Since SVR was using an Internet explorer as a container for displaying the state reports. However, no agreement, (to his knowledge), had been reached between RES and the client as to which container was to be used. He wanted this clarified.
5 Since RES did not have the source code for the main transaction screen the same might have to be re-written completely.
6 He did not see the wisdom of RES committing to deliver on the 1-800 Project and the SVR Project simultaneously. It would stretch the Mumbai boys beyond their limit.

Sudhir was low profile, mild mannered, and hardworking, no-nonsense gentleman who knew his work inside out. He spent a lot of time on action research, which would help RES. He liked structure and form in everything he did. Everyone respected him and he wielded a lot of power but seldom made a show of it. His word was enough to swing the balance in case of technological dispute. Being a man of few words he hardly ever offended anyone.

Dinesh was a flamboyant salesman, known for his cavalier attitude to work and an utter disdain for documentation, which he considered a clerical activity. Hence, records of transactions between him and the client were not there and one had to take his word for every query raised. He worked by his wits and delivered almost by magic. He did not believe in systems since he was a great individualist.

As expected, Dinesh did not reply to the memo but telephonically told Sudhir that though he was a very good technocrat he knew little about Marketing. So he should not worry too much about the project and leave things to those who knew the job better. Dinesh wanted to take the matter up with the Marketing Director to inform him about Sudhir's unsolicited advice but at the last minute decided against it. Hence, the Marketing Director was unaware of the potential problems that this project could give the company. Sudhir too did not take the matter up further although he felt strongly about it.

Suddenly, the RES were caught in a bind. Frederick the brain behind both project deliveries for SVR and 1-800 died in a car accident and a replacement had to be found since the future of the project and the company was at stake. A new Project Leader was hastily appointed and his name was Viraf. He had only six months experience in Visual Basic though he was proficient in SQL but had no experience in working on Design projects. Acting logically, according to the book, he divided his team of six persons into groups of two: 2 for development, 2 for quality control and 2 for maintenance. Viraf was frustrated by the utter lack of documentation both at his end and at the OSC's end. There seemed to be no clarity about what the client wanted.

Dinesh too had his share of frustrations. The client had altered his requirements several times and left Dinesh to explain matters to Mumbai. After several set backs, several exchanges of fax messages between the OSC and Mumbai the 1-800 project actually started in June 1997.

The SVR Project, which had started 6 months prior to the 1-800 project, was in full swing and Viraf's attention was divided between the two projects. He had not taken a weekend off in three months and nor had his next in command. Everyone was working his/her butt off. There was no time for him to have project meetings and appraise the teams of what was going on. With the result the maintenance people knew little about what the development people did and they in turn were unsure of what the quality people did. Anything they knew was through unofficial channels and everyone was guarding their turf. Similarly, the 1-800 team and the SVR hardly ever communicated officially with one another. What they knew about the other's work was the stray bits picked up during meal times or while having a smoke in the cafeteria.

In comparison the Directors exchanged information between themselves freely so each knew what was going on down the line. The Director (Technology and Research) called Sudhir and asked him to oversee the projects discretely which he began to do. Viraf was unaware of this development and Sudhir did not see it fit to tell him.

The culture of RES was such that OSC was the buffer rather than the facilitator between the Mumbai team and the client abroad. The client would communicate with the OSC who in turn would relay the message to Mumbai. Neither Viraf nor anyone from his team ever communicated with the client directly. When specifications were changed mid-course, things became choppier and frustrations grew.

Yet, working night and day, Viraf's team completed the first deliverable in the 1-800 system in January 1998. Dinesh took the deliverables back to the Client and was told that there were too many bugs, which had to be removed first. GUI changes as well as development of new screens were involved and top management on the personal intervention of Sudhir sanctioned a 41 man-days enhancement.

One Master Screen (Account Profile Maintenance) had to be re-developed since the functionality needed by the client was different from that provided for by the RES crew. A new master screen (Country Master) had to be developed and this would have an impact on all master screens. Viraf tore his hair in anguish since he had not been properly informed about the client requirements. He went to Sudhir who knew what was going on, stopped his research work and plunged into the project to lend Viraf a hand. Dinesh sent them a sample form in Visual Basic and a document on screen layouts without any explanation or functionality description to accompany it. Both Sudhir and Viraf wanted an extra resource for the 1-800 project and sent their requirement to Personnel Department. An internal advertisement was circulated and Peter volunteered since he stated that he wanted to work on Visual Basic and this was a chance he would not miss.

Peter was pulled out of the SVR Project and given to the 1-800 Project. His work at the SVR project had to be completed by someone else. Viraf had objected to it but the Personnel department prevailed on him in the interest of employee development. Viraf agreed hesitatingly to Peter's transfer. But within a short while Peter wanted to go back to the SVR Project since he found out that the project was using controllers for programming, which was something he had not known. On further inquiry it was found that he was not interested in working on the Visual Basic Project after all, since the libraries available in RES were not as user friendly as he had expected. Also, it was found out that Peter had opted for the transfer since he felt that Visual Basic skills were highly marketable in the USA where he wished to migrate to.

The Personnel Department cut a sorry figure since they bolstered Peter's case. Viraf was feeling let down and somewhat cheated by Peter. And everyone seemed to be non-plused by what happened. The Directors maintained a stoic silence in all this.

To add to this, the hardware provided to the team involved in the 1-800 project were very slow and they were not updated on time, despite several requests by Viraf to the Chief Project Manager. Sometimes the project files would take up to 45 minutes to load. Sudhir himself took up the matter and at last things began to improve. The Accounts Department had objected to all purchases of hardware unless complete justification for their use was not put up and proved. This took time and often the hardware was procured well after the project had begun.

The senior most member of the 1-800 team, Kulkarni, directly reporting to Viraf was very good at development work but liked to work alone, did not share information and did not treat his team members as equals. He thought of himself as the cat's whiskers and looked down on all others including Viraf. He saw himself as a research man doing a project job and that hurt his ego. He had asked for a transfer to work under Sudhir but that request went un-answered. The result of his behaviour was that when he wanted help to meet deadlines no one would volunteer to help. He had the bad habit of finding fault with and ridiculing his junior colleagues openly. The team respected his knowledge but not his person. The Personnel Department had agreed to transfer him to Sudhir's department after the project was over but neither Viraf nor Kulkarni was aware of this.

After a lot of hard work Sudhir and Viraf managed to put the almost derailed 1-800 project back on the path. They acted proactively and got a new girl named Anita from another Software Company to supplement the team effort on 1-800 project. Anita had a very positive approach and assisted in the integration of State Reports. The client came back with further queries and further corrections and these were made. But things were not easy since uncertainty about client needs hung in the air. Team members did not officially share information nor did they find time to review the progress periodically. So everyone knew just about what he or she was doing. Clarity of roles seemed non-existent and there was a noticeable lack of synergy. They were a group of people working on a project but far from becoming a real dedicated project team. The development team was working with half information and made several blunders. The maintenance team felt that they were the dog's body and their morale was low.

It was common knowledge that the team members were looking out for other jobs. The quality team was perpetually in a state of alienation and appeared to care a damn for anything and everything. All of them had one common complaint: the OSC never told them the whole story and they were fed up with the ego-related behaviour of Kulkarni.

Amongst themselves at a personal level everyone was friendly but officially they could just not work as a team. Somehow in September 1998 the project was delivered and the company was happy about the fact that Viraf had delivered in spite of odds albeit six months late. A letter from the client was sent expressing their gratitude but people were not sure that the client would come to RES again. Frustration with the situation was at an all time high and yet none seemed to take the bull by the horns and make things change. Rather they either stood by or watched with an air of indifference or waited for a nice time to quit. Everyone was job hunting and everyone knew it.

The Directors decided to declare the bonus and the kudos to the team to synchronize with the New Year Party. With this at the back of the mind, the top management issued congratulatory letters to all team members in October for Divali but withheld the remunerative hikes until January of the following year.

To everyone's shock, in late October, Sudhir applied for long leave to complete his long pending Ph.D. Shortly thereafter Viraf quit RES to join a competitor for the same salary, and so did three other senior members of his team. Kulkarni and Dinesh were not very happy but stayed behind to reap the laurels. This came as a shock to top management that was planning to promote Viraf and reward the team for the splendid performance.

What really went wrong? Where did the problem begin? Who is to blame?

HINT:

Probable Flaw:

This is by no means a unique situation because almost every software company in India has faced a comparable situation at one time or another.

It is a clear case where there was little cogency and clarity of vision, mission, role and goal. Target directed behaviour was clearly wanted as was mid-course evaluation during the project.

This is an ideal situation where the 5-D Methodology ought to have been used and this is what can happen if it is not followed.

HR presence was conspicuously absent and technocrats tried their hand at man management and failed.

Ideal Solution:

'Go back to the drawing board and re-evaluate the entire project. Then start afresh so that in future the lessons learnt here prove useful.

HR involvement in the strategy formulation and implementation team would have made a lot of positive difference and this was clearly absent.

❑❑❑

CASE 35

NATIONAL RESEARCH BUREAU OF INDIA

As India began to liberalize its markets, privatise its means of production and globalisation its competition, new imperatives dawned on industry. Firms were increasingly expected to convert their core competence into competitive advantage and thrive on the cutting edge of technology. All this needed free availability and flow of technical expertise and up to date research facilities to keep one step ahead of the competition. In 1995, some big industrial houses got together and set up six research centres, each of which would be located at the chosen six metropolitan cities. These six research centres would be controlled by a firm called National Research Bureau of India Limited and capital for the initial setting up of operations would be shared equally from public (governmental) and private (industry) sources. Each centre would be the reservoir of data required by industries to compete globally and state of the art quality assurance systems so that processes and products could be more competitively placed. Data would be shared between the centres and any firm that was a subscribing member of this bureau could (a) access data, (b) test the quality of their products and (c) share technological know-how for common gain. Accordingly, one centre for each was opened in Kolkata, Chennai, Bangalore, Mumbai, Delhi and Chandigarh. A contingent of research staff was to be also employed to man each of these six centres. By 1998 these centres would be equipped to keep track of R and D on various products meant for export and produced in the geo-physical region near the centre. However, since data could be accessed from any part of India, complete Systems Integration was called for in each centre.

Since the Government of India was a principal partner, a lot of red tape and bureaucracy came along with its involvement. The contract to install the hardware as well as the software at each centre was signed in Delhi under the watchful eyes of the Ministry of Telecommunication as well as the Ministry of Industrial Development. Based on L1 bids, a number of firms were given the contract to install the systems. Naturally, proximity of the contracting firm to the research centre was a major consideration in awarding the contract. However, no presence of the contracting firm near the other six centres was needed and most often did not exist. Hence all inquiries, complaints and amendments needed by the client (subscribing firm) would have to be routed through the Government of India, which had set up an Administrative Cell in Delhi for managing the technical requirements of all six centres.

The private industries that had contributed, the remainder 50% of the capital appointed the manpower for running the centres and meeting client needs. This was looked after by a hand-picked team of technocrats called the Projects Cell. It was located at each centre and all the six Project Cells worked as a cohesive team. Each Project Cell had a team of Logistics Support Staff who would eventually approve what software and hardware were to be acquired and for what purpose. The Projects Cell and the Logistics Staff both had regular meetings within themselves and amongst each other wherein they freely exchanged data. There was a symbiotic relationship among the Project Cells, which assisted the subscribing members greatly. However, the needs of the subscribing members varied and perfect systems integration held the key to success.

However, the Project Cell did not document their work adequately and when new recruits arrived they had a lot of catching up to do just to be in sync. Attrition in the software industry is known to be high and there were always new faces around in the National Research Bureau of India.

There seemed to be something terribly wrong as the National Research Bureau even with the best intentions was not being able to deliver the service expected of it by industry. Customer complaints reached a fever pitch in September 1998. Uncertainty about what went wrong prolonged through the last few months of 1998. Blaming the Administrative Cell, unfortunately, for just about everything became almost a ritual at these regular meetings of the Project Cell.

In January 1999 the Projects Cell gave a confidential report to all the industries that has helped to set up the National Research Bureau stating the following. (a) Free flow of data was impinged because of major operating difficulties. (b) In spite of their best effort systems, breakdowns were recurrent. (c) Testing for quality was not nationally consistent as the software was not supportive enough.

A high power team of industrialists met to deliberate on the report. Indian industry was beginning to doubt its own wisdom in setting up these six centres. At the meeting, the subscribing members had one major complaint, and that was this. Nobody had bothered to train them (the final end user) on the software supplied to them by the Centre for Quality Control. Hence, they had to learn many things themselves and were still not completely proficient. This, they felt, was grossly unfair. The Project Team retorted that their task was implementation and facilitation, not training end users. Representatives from Industry were not amused and insisted that if they had invested so heavily in the National Research Bureau, they had a right to expect customer friendly conduct.

The Administrative Cell and the Projects Cell were very soon developing unfriendly relations with each other. It appeared the crores of Rupees pumped into the six centres would be wasted away. The Administrative Cell was blaming the Projects Cell of intransigence and intellectual arrogance. On its part, the Projects Cell was blaming the Administrative Cell of indulging in counter-productive bureaucracy. For three full months prolonged discussions continued with no result. A dead-end seemed to be in sight.

Then an exasperated CII interfered and arranged for awkward questions to be raised in Parliament. The Prime Minister's Office was forced to intervene and a select team of experts from various vocations was formed. It was called the Technological Think Tank and its task was to study the situation and submit its report to the PMO by 31st August 1999. One thing, however, was clear to all and that was the fact that contract verification had been taken very lightly by all concerned. The following were the highlights of the report of the Technical Think Tank.

- The L1 bids were accepted based on geographical proximity to the Centre. The PC/ Server/HW Set at each Centre was only about 80% compatible at best. In Chennai the compatibility was lowest as 50%.
- Similarly, the MIS/ERP/Software and Data Migration systems at each centre were only 70% compatible at best. At Mumbai the compatibility was the lowest at 45%.
- The subscribing members had all along insisted on and were promised that they would get a system with 266 MHRZ while the centres were actually supplied systems with a capacity of 166 MHRZ. On scrutiny, it was found that the initial tender document had specified a requirement of 166 MHRZ. Nobody from the industry had verified the contract.
- The PCs used had the same configuration at each centre no doubt but the motherboards used were different, so the RAMs varied greatly. This was because the proximity of the hardware supplier to the centre had been the chief consideration for allocating the contract.
- Since the PCs bought were as per specifications but based on L1 quotes they were mostly the lesser known brands that did not have a national presence and servicing during breakdowns was a major problem. Also scavenging was not easy as the motherboards varied.
- It was rumoured that the suppliers of the hardware were "close" to certain bureaucrats in the government and the bids may well have been doctored. Suspicions ran high and there seemed to be some truth in them. There was, however, no conclusive proof of impropriety.
- The Antiviral Software used in Chennai and Bangalore was P-Cellin, in Chandigarh and Delhi it was Norton, in Mumbai and Kolkata it was McCaffe. There were several viruses that went undetected in each location and when data was transferred, there were major glitches.
- The Support Services, which were set up to assist each centre and to liase with the other centres, was not measuring up to expectations. They reported to the Administrative Cell whereas the management of each centre reported to the Project Cell.
- The software in Chennai and Bangalore did not work well on the hardware platform in Delhi and Chandigarh. Mumbai and Kolkata too had problems but they did not seem to be as severe. The crux of the matter was that although the RDBMS platform was universally Oracle based and the Operating System was UnixWare, the versions were incompatible. Hence, a national database was not entirely possible and there were several bugs in the system that prevented easy retrieval of information. It was clear that nobody had bothered with the Compatibility Matrix during installation.
- The cabling for the entire system in all six locations was not at all conducive to the technology used. This was because the Administrative Cell had used firms specializing in electrical cabling rather than network cabling. Again, the villain of the piece was the L1 tender.
- Lack of synergy between the Project Cell and the Administrative Cell had placed a big question mark on this national level systems integration project.
- There did not appear to be a master plan according to which the national level systems integration project would be installed.

The Project Cell of each centre collectively met in Delhi and jointly gave a memorandum to the PMO and to the subscribing members. It stated that:

1. Developing software at each location to keep track of R and D activities for export products was a pipe dream until the entire system was put into shape.
2. Why did the Administrative Cell without getting the approval of the end user, i.e. the Project Cell, release the payments in full to the various suppliers?
3. How were the contracts awarded to parties that did not have a presence in each centre location?
4. Why should all queries be routed to the supplier through the Administrative Cell, which was bureaucratic, commercial and non-technical?
5. If the contract was signed specifying 166 MHRZ when the requirement and expectation was 266 MHRZ why was there no back-to-back contract?
6. Why was there no system that would vet the contract and ensure the realistic dates and schedules for the deliverables at both ends?

A copy of the same was sent by the PMO to the Administrative Cell for its comments. The latter was miffed that the Project Cell chose to send the report to PMO with a copy to all subscribing members but overlooked to send them a copy.

The Administrative Cell met, deliberated at length and similarly raised a few queries that it sent them to the PMO with copies to the subscribing members (but not to the Project Cell). It stated that:

1. Why did the Project Cell, which claimed to be technologically well informed, not bother to verify the contract a copy of which was available at each centre from the first day?
2. Every supplier complied with the Broad Specifications given in the tender bid. Why did the industrialists not specify the intricate details if they mattered so much?
3. The Project Cell was washing its hands off from a deal that had gone sour because they had not bothered to insure compliance all along.
4. Lip service was being paid all along to Total Quality Management and to Corporate Governance. This should be replaced by action.

You are a senior member of the Technological Think Tank. How would you react and why? Do you agree with the four issues raised above? Do you have anything more to add?

HINT:

- Three imperatives for every project manager are detailed contract verification, close supervision of installation/execution, and absolute compatibility of systems.
- The project manager has to supervise, monitor and take remedial action all through the project life cycle. There are no short cuts to ensuring deliverables.
- Ego is every manager's greatest enemy. It has to be controlled and the objective must never be lost sight of. Just because he may not have been consulted does not imply that he is not accountable.

- Reporting and Operating systems are both important and must be streamlined and made known to all. Then they must be complied with.
- Training the customer is the project manager's duty. He cannot shirk away from it.
- The project manager cannot simply own off his responsibility just because the rules were not followed in awarding contracts. Pointing fingers is always counter-productive.
- Those who are not entrusted with deliverables nor are accountable for results should never release funds. If the project manager is to deliver then the marketing manager or the commercial manager should never approve payment to contractors/suppliers. At least the approval in writing from the project manager should be obtained before funds are released.
- The project manager must ensure compliance before signing on the dotted line to approve payment and here the verification of the contract is of paramount importance.
- Insist on absolute clarity and always read the fine print with great care. Seek amendments and have caveats written down in the contract with escalation clauses.
- The supplier's effective presence near the project site must be a major consideration in awarding contracts. There is no excuse for failing to closely verify a contract. There is no use crying over spilt milk if the project manager did not act when the time was ripe.
- It is the task of the logistics cell to approve systems installation, (hardware, software and networking). It must ensure that it plays its role. It too must take charge. When things go wrong the project manager must take charge and start the process of damage control without any hesitation. Delays have a cost attached to them.
- It is a very bad practice to go for L1 bids without ensuring that there is a presence at the project site and that rectification of anomalies is expedited.
- Even with the best system there is going to be some glitch or bug. Responsibility cannot be shrugged off and blame ascribed to the absent party.
- When the systems configuration is given to the marketing/commercial section, details for their compatibility must be ensured. On line checking must be a part of the project manager's repertoire when a system is being installed or when a project is being executed.
- Under no conditions can documentation be overlooked and the price for delay in projects can run to lakhs of Rupees.
- When many locations are involved, communication lines must be open all the time and networking must be perfect. This means cabling must be given top priority and quality must be ensured. L1 bids often lead to long-term troubles unless contract verification and initial compliance checks are carried out meticulously. The project manager must insist on doing so himself or get someone technically competent and responsible (from his company) to do so.
- Commercial and Marketing Managers should keep a watchful eye on long run opportunity costs and not be swayed by short run actual cost considerations. It is always better to get a second (technical) opinion before signing the final contract and (written) approval by the project manager before releasing funds to the supplier.
- There is absolutely no replacement for good working systems and there is a cost attached to having them.
- Many project managers shy away from training end users and assisting in administrative and commercial functions on the lame excuse of having "no time". If this is their attitude then clearly they are in the wrong job.

Whatever the class says the first thing to do for the Project Manager is to take charge and begin damage control operations. Setting up better systems can always follow and indeed must follow to prevent recurrence of this fracas.

The estimated delay in implementation of contract and execution of the project has no thumb rule. It is contingent upon the executive acumen of the project manager.

Even with the best of systems there will be glitches, bugs and delays. The trick is to reduce the ambit of uncertainty so that decision-making and decision executing become less onerous and the speculative-risk factor is reduced.

Whenever a systems integration project is involved the utmost care should be taken that the various software and hardware are compatible, that the supplier has a presence in the region of the project site and contract verification is taken very seriously.

A trade off between perfection and costs is always a bone of contention between project managers and marketing managers. An equilibrium saddle point must be mutually agreed upon.

The project manager must always have a contingency plan available and executable at short notice should either the marketing manager, the commercial manager and/or the supplier default on any deliverables.

Manpower on the project is prone to attrition in the infotech industry. Hence, documentation must be insisted upon and complied with. This will help to keep track of progress, detect what went wrong and update new comers on what has so far been done. If there is a culture in a firm of taking project documentation seriously, the contract will also be studied as a matter of routine. Verification and compliance of contract become relatively simple.

Remember that the project manager and the marketing manager are like two sides of a coin. One cannot subsist without the other. Hence open communication, transparency, teamwork and trust is of the essence. Both have a stake in the contract verification and compliance.

SUGGESTIONS:

The facilitator could leave the discussion open in class. This would need close monitoring and there is a chance that the argument may veer away from the desired aim. Continuous intervention by the facilitator is called for if this option were to be taken up.

The facilitator could divide the class into three groups: the Technological Think Tank, the Project Cell and the Administrative Cell. Then ask the groups to argue from their specified positions only. This is easy to manage.

The facilitator could convert this into a role-play and have the class look on and then critically comment. This is very good but difficult to manage.

❑❑❑

CASE 36

CHANDMAL SOFTWARE LIMITED

The Yakamura Insurance Company in Osaka, Japan had given a contract to Toshiba Nippon Electronics to computerize its systems so that it would become very customer friendly. This meant that accurate, on line data base management was called for, and Toshiba Nippon Electronics framed out the entire work to a number of smaller Software Companies in the Third World. One such was an Indian Company named Chandmal Software Limited (CIL).

It was expected that CIL would undertake to develop software that would work on Windows NT. It was also expected that the entire database, which was now on a RDBMS Mainframe platform, would have to be ported on to a Windows NT platform. CIL already had gained some expertise in porting contracts and it had a few software engineers who were proficient in working on RDBMS packages. On the strength of this, a bid was made and on the basis of the lowest quote CIL got the contract. It was assumed all along that an existing package could be implemented with marginal alterations to suit the Japanese client. This was why Marketing had quoted so low and bagged the contract which entailed developing an automatic conversion tool and ensuring systems integration on client site.

The Japanese client, Toshiba Nippon Electronics, had all along believed that CIL would develop an automatic conversion tool so that program conversion would be facilitated. On its part CIL had assured the Japanese client that it could deliver the automatic conversion tool. This was again based on the premise than an existing porting tool could be adapted with some small modifications. Accordingly, a contract was entered into and in January 1998 work began on the project. The Project Manager was Mr. Kulkarni who was and introvert but who could easily be ranked high on the technological competence scale. Kulkarni hated putting pen to paper and documenting his work. He somehow believed that documentation was beneath his status and may even expose his (presumed) weaknesses. It was generally believed that if Kulkarni could not do this, then that few others in CIL could.

The Project Manager had a team of fifteen persons dedicated to the project. Of these, there were six persons in development, five in quality control and four in maintenance. By February 1998, a team of five persons from the Project Team along with Kulkarni flew down to Osaka to see the client site and understand client requirements on the spot. It was then that they realized that CIL had bitten off more than it could chew. Language was a major problem and the translator picked by CIL was not computer savvy and had great difficulty converting client expectations in an understandable fashion to these five persons. In addition, the Japanese were very secretive and were prone to change specifications quite often. The lack of technical expertise on the part of the translator made things worse. This put Kulkarni in soup. He however put up a brave face and continued to develop the porting tool. In July 1998 the team returned for a few days to India, ostensibly for a holiday.

The first thing Kulkarni asked for was to change the translator. But the translator was well known to the MD so that was not possible.

In India, the Project Team held a meeting and briefed the SBU Head about the extent of the problem. Kulkarni and his team would write a porting program, physically remove the glitches after manual testing and send it across to Japan only to learn that the client did not approve of the quality. What was happening was that the conversion tool was not even semi-automatic and the conversion was actually being done by a number of young engineers manually. The data size was large and this took a lot of time.

Every time CIL converted a set of data and sent it across, it was told that the data was full of glitches, was unreliable and the Japanese end client, the insurance company would never find it acceptable. Yakamura Insurance Company had started to put the pressure on the Japanese client of CIL and the client in turn was turning on the heat on CIL. Six sets of data were sent across to Japan and all six sets were rejected on the grounds of quality.

By January 1999 the Japanese client was getting very upset and showed it unmistakably. In February 1998 the Japanese client had sent four Japanese experts to India and they parked themselves at the Project Office. They reported that there was no conversion tool in sight and that the conversion was being done manually. They also stated in their report that the quality control team was only comparing data against certain benchmarks on paper and not actually testing the data for quality. CIL insisted that the automatic conversion tool was almost developed. The client insisted that this was not so. The client office in Osaka sent CIL an ultimatum and threatened to revoke the contract as well as sue the firm for damages. There was a state of panic in CIL. At this point the SBU Head decided to intervene personally. He asked for the details of the progress made from the time the project began and was aghast to find that there was virtually no documentation made. He called in everyone who was involved in the project and had a full day closed door meeting. He let everyone speak first and then gave them a sermon on quality, procedures, teamwork and documentation. The following facts emerged:

1. Marketing had entered into the contract to deliver the automatic conversion tool but had not paid much heed to the reliability clauses.
2. Project Manager stated that the manpower he had was relatively young and unexperienced and therefore he was sending the data as well as the conversion output without testing completely.
3. The project specifications were being changed very frequently and this put too much pressure on the CIL team. In addition, of the original team members only Kulkarni and two others remained with CIL. Others had left the company for better pastures. During the exit interview each of the leavers had pointed out that Kulkarni was a competent

man but a very poor boss. They had all left out of sheer frustration especially when word spread that the exit interviews were a farce as nothing came out of them.

4. The Maintenance team did not know what the Quality team was doing and they, in turn, did not know what the Development team was doing. Only Kulkarni knew what was going on in all the three teams. And Kulkarni would not document anything so there was no way anyone could challenge his word that all was well.
5. There had been not a single Project Meeting in which everyone was present nor had the SBU Head gone to the team members to find out for himself. He would ask Kulkarni who would assure him that all was fine. He in turn would assure the MD that all was fine.

The SBU Head realized his error in depending too much on Kulkani's words of assurance and vowed never to make that mistake again. But the periodic rejections by the Japanese client worried him. He knew that Kulkarni was technically very competent.

The SBU Head then called on the Group Marketing Head and together they went through the history of the project. Three things emerged that would explain why the Japanese client was unhappy.

1. The client insisted that a quality check be done on the client site in Osaka before the deliverables were accepted and the funds released.
2. The Project Manager insisted that the testing he did in India was good enough and the client was just being awkward.
3. The emphasis was placed on developing an automatic conversion tool and not much thought was placed on systems integration.

The original contract was called for and scrutinized. The actual requirements of Yakamura Insurance Company were spelt out in fine print but nobody had bothered to study them since they were in Japanese and the translator did not "think" they were important. There they found that in fine print the client had maintained that the automatic conversion tool would have to be tested on site and there would have to be perfect integration of systems between the RDBMS platform and the Windows NT outlet. Also, the client had reserved the right to alter specifications as the need arose. CIL had tamely accepted these in the zeal to bag the account.

The Project Manager had assumed this testing was to be on Project Site while the Japanese Firm has all along implied that it mean Client Site. The contract also was silent on how the automatic conversion tool was to be developed, against benchmark what it would be tested and what would be the criteria along which quality tests would be measured.

Toshiba Nippon Electronics was all along dealing with the Insurance Company directly and as per the principal client needs the specifications were altered. This had become so frequent that the CIL team was at loss as to what was expected of them.

A high level CIL Management meeting was called. The MD himself flew down to Osaka and met the MD of Toshiba Nippon Electronics and somehow managed to pacify the irate client and buy more time. The MD flew back to India and recruited six high-level software professionals on a specific contract to complete this project. At an enormous delay, heartburn and anxiety, the project was completed. The automatic conversion tool had somehow been developed and accepted by the client. The image of CIL was saved and everyone breathed a sigh of relief.

What do you think had gone wrong and what could be done to have avoided this kind of an occurance in the future?

HINT:

- Whenever a contract is entered into the quality specifications must be clearly specified. Nothing can be assumed away. More particularly three things need to be spelt out. (a) The Testing Plan (b) The Testing Criteria and (c) The Testing Methodology. And having been spelt out they must be scrupulously followed.
- Whenever a firm is working for a client who is himself working for a principal party, care must be taken to know what the nature of the requirement of the principal client is. This is to ensure that software firms are not too dependent on the whims and fancies of some persons in the client firm in the middle of the transaction. This is not always easy but worth trying for, nevertheless.
- Quality must be built into the Project no doubt but the quality checks should objectively be made and the findings must be acted upon with an aim to improve rather than with an aim to find scapegoats.
- The contract must always contain a clause which client can freeze specifications at some point in time and the client cannot forever continue to change the same.
- When hiring a translator two things must be ensured. First that the translator is knowledgeable about software engineering and the technical requirements of the project team. Second, everything written in the foreign language must be translated for the benefit of the Project Manager. This is a problem faced when dealing with Korean, Chinese, Malaysian, Indonesian and Arab clients especially.
- There is no way in which attrition can be avoided so Project Managers must insist that complete documentation of progress is truthfully maintained on line. This will facilitate the progress of the project even when new entrants arrive. This culture of documenting progress must be built into the system.
- It is better not to have an exit interview than to have one and not act on the findings thereof. The SBU Head should insist on seeing the exit interview reports and take the criticisms positively. The SBU Head moreover must never depend entirely on the Project Manager for feedback. He must call a general and open house meeting for all members of a project at regular intervals. This is a great bonding device and acts as a safety value to let off pent up frustrations which can then be systematically addressed.

❑❑❑

CASE 37

CHOPRA AND COMPANY

Chopra and Co., is a Kolkata based plastic manufacturing firm that services the needs of local industry by making the required ancillaries for them. High-grade plastic is used as casings for electronic gadgets, for making electric kitchen equipment and household items, moulded furniture and sheets for conversion into specific use. Having been set up in 1970 the firm celebrated its silver jubilee in 1995. The top management is closely held within the family, which hails from Agra, and as a conscious policy they have given employment to persons who hail from the North, to occupy most important positions.

The firm's relationship with the Government of West Bengal has been excellent and despite a strong presence of left wing unionism in the vicinity of the factory, there has been no strike since 1983. In fact, 10,582 man-days were lost due to management fault: non-availability of raw materials between 1991 and 1993. Wages were always about the average of what the industries paid and most labour law compliance was met. The annual turnover of the firm was Rs.75 crore in 1992 and had risen to Rs. 150 crore in 1997. The firm employs 1500 workmen, of whom only 50 are executives, 200 are managers, while the foremen and supervisors account for 250 men on rolls. There are 700 workmen in various categories like skilled, semi-skilled and unskilled of whom 25% are women. There are about 300 staff working in offices of whom 75% are women. The average age of workers in the offices is 35 years and in the shop floor, it is 40 years. Attrition levels are low since the poor economic conditions in the region do not permit job-hopping.

The Managerial Style is one that can be called benevolent despotism and as a conscious strategy the firm employed neither highly qualified persons nor graduates from premier colleges. Creativity and ingenuity are unknown in the firm and all employees are content to tow the line. Bureaucrats are bought over with cash or kind regularly and with impunity. So there is no trouble from the civil services.

In 1997, Chopra and Co. called in B. S. Billimoria and Co. to help prepare the firm for an ISO 9000 series certification. Among the glaring gaps in the systems and procedures identified by the consulting firm, the most startling from a structural-functional viewpoint was the dichotomy within the Human Resources function. In response to the preliminary report of the consulting firm, Chopra and Co., grudgingly appointed a well-qualified person as Vice President (Human Resources) in the person of Dr. Dilip Bhatia. The new VP will functionally report to the Managing Director Mr. Chandrakant Chopra and operationally to his wife Mrs. Rubina Chopra who was the Joint Managing Director. Between the couple they took all major decisions and passed them down to be executed.

You are Dr. Dilip Bhatia and although you come from Delhi, you are extremely cosmopolitan in outlook and very liberal in your views. You are a kind man but a hard taskmaster. It came as a surprise to you to find that there were so few Bengalis in the organization except at the worker level. You found that there were job descriptions for everyone in the executive cadre but none for those at the lower levels. That struck you as odd.

You discover that communication was invariably from the top downwards and it took the form of individual memos and public circulars. The company had a few old timers scattered across the organization, doing unimportant jobs, and no one was sure what they actually did. Rumour had it that they were the informants of top management. When you went deep into analysing the situation at hand, you have discovered that there was a Dy. G.M. (HRD) Mr. Sanjay Misra, who was an industrial psychologist and who reported to the Joint Managing Director. He looked after training, increments and promotions, appraisals and exit interviews. There was also a Dy. G. M. (Personnel) Mr. Peter Vase who looked after security, appointment, and labour law compliance, termination and general administration. He reported to the Managing Director and there was little or no communication between the two departments.

Unlike Peter, Sanjay was very ambitious and a past master at apple polishing and politicking. However, unlike Sanjay, Peter knew his limitations and was viewed as a trusted old timer. Peter's department was bureaucratic, insular in its approach but very effective in traditional management techniques. Sanjay's department was proactive but directionless. It was also riddled wit one-up-man-ship.

The firm also had a history of having a set of HRD consultants on specific projects on an almost ongoing basis. One conducted climate surveys and compensation surveys. The other conducted specific training programs like women in industry and employee health. They reported to the Joint Managing Director. One was involved in setting up the HRIS function and one was involved in payroll and taxation. These two reported to the Managing Director. None of the consultants reported to you. There is a consultant's cabin and each comes in for work one day in a week so that none of them meet each other or exchange notes officially. All four consultants are middle-aged women who have a personal equation with top management, are well known socialites and there seems to be a lot of ambiguity about what actually they do. You also discover that at least one of them has nothing original to offer and all of them hail from the Agra-Delhi area. Senior management meetings were conducted in Hindi and Punjabi. There were at least two non-Hindi-speaking Bengalis who attended these meeting and who had to take private Hindi lessons to keep up with what went on in the office. Very often senior managers and executives would fight openly with one another and it appeared that top management revelled in the policy of divide and rule. As VP (HR) you decide to grab the bull by the horns. Your task is made difficult since there is no clear direction coming from either the MD or the JMD and yet both seem to wish to interfere with your work. Top management, moreover, gives more importance to line managers than to staff managers and HR is looked upon as one of those unavoidable costs of modernity. Besides, the Chopras believed that having a good HRD facility and a hand full of consultants enhanced the chances of getting an ISO 9000 certification and that would ultimately help the business.

Clearly there is something to be said for their organizational structure and reporting systems. How will you go about planning and executing a strategy for change, using all the techniques of Strategic HR intervention you have learnt over the years?

HINT:

Desired Discussion:

There is no way that HR Administration and HR Development cannot report to the same person. In addition, there is no way that they can be allowed to operate independently of each other. Hence, HR Planning, HR Development and HR Administration should work as three wings of one major function. It is a fallacy for some so called specialists of HRD to talk of teamwork in organizations and then insist that there is one head of the function. Is it not conceivable to have the Heads of HR Administration, HR Planning, and HR Development work as a three-person team? Also, functionally they must report to the same person as they report operationally to. If not, any disagreement between the MD and JMD will throw the HRD intervention out of gear. The absence of goal and role clarity at the very top seems to be the root cause of this malaise and it is up to the HRD facilitator to sort it out slowly. A bull in a China shop type intervention is bound to ruffle feathers and founder.

Desired Strategy:

Once again the issue here is changing the mindset of top management. Once this has been achieved then the standard practice of defining vision, mission, goal and role must be entered into. At every step the question should be asked: Are we adding value by doing this or that? If not why should we do it ? Is it because some author said so or that our professor (who may be out of date and out of context) taught us so? Why can the HR professional not blaze a trail for himself? And the key to doing that lies in promoting a value based management which is strongly grounded in business ethics and which creates a climate of trust and faith such that creativity is given a chance to blossom and ingenuity to succeed. This is a climate where insecure Business Heads, when they see a subordinate proffer a brilliant solution, are quick to say I know this will not work, but the self-same Business Heads are at a loss when the subordinate says what is it that you feel will work?

❑❑❑

CASE 38

ABDULLAH CONSULTING AND TRAINING INSTITUTE

Freddy Mathias was up in Mangalore. He came from a conservative Christian family and his father even considered himself some sort of an authority on Catholic Christian scriptures. His mother Francisca was suffering from psychiatric ailments and their domestic life was far from peaceful. Freddy grabbed every opportunity he could to stay away from home. He studied Engineering at R. E. C. Calicut and came home only once a year and that too for Christmas. On graduation, he became a Research Assistant at his alma mater and eventually obtained a scholarship to go and study Management Sciences at the University of Santa Clara in the USA. While studying for his MBA Freddy fell in love with a Malaysian girl named Noor who was studying for a Masters Degree in Mass Communications and Public Relations and lived in a small flat near his hostel. She had excellent Public Relations and Secretarial skills, which were evident when she landed a very comfortable job with a multinational firm based in Santa Clara as soon as she obtained her Masters Degree. When he completed his MBA Freddy had originally considered coming back home but his girl friend was not prepared to follow him home to India. Therefore, he stayed on and studied for a Doctoral Degree in Management Sciences again on a scholarship given by the Church for Christian students coming from the developing world. During the time he was working on his Doctoral Thesis, his parents died in a freak car-accident on their way to do Sunday shopping. Freddy at once rushed to Mangalore performed the funeral rites and was back in USA within a month. Noor financed that trip and helped Freddy with money matters when his funds were low.

Freddy was in love with Noor. There was nobody in India who Freddy cared enough about to return home for good so he had even decided to apply for US immigration. However, just as he had obtained his Ph.D., news came that Noor's father had passed away leaving her a bountiful legacy. Noor decided to return to Kuala Lumpur, persuaded Freddy to give up his plans for obtaining a US citizenship and come along with her. He followed her without much ado. Together they set up a Consulting Company named after Noor's late father, Aslam Abdullah who had left her a villa and lots of money. It was getting difficult for Freddy to obtain a permanent Malaysian visa so he decided to marry Noor and to do so even agreed to be converted to Islam. He then assumed the new name of Freddy Mathias bin Abdullah and became a Malaysian citizen.

Between the husband and wife, they made quite an effective team. Starting in a small way, the firm named Abdullah Consulting and Training Institute (ACTI) set up an office in Central Kuala Lumpur at Bukit Bintang. Within three years, they had expanded their operations to Penang and Johor Baharu. Within Malaysia, their firm was well respected and sought after by corporate houses especially for conducting organisational diagnosis. As days became months and months became years the firm grew in stature and size. By 2000 the firm had 76 employees most of who were well qualified and located in Kuala Lumpur from where they controlled operations all over Malaysia. The Penang office controlled operations and serviced clients to the north of Malaysia whereas the Johor Baharu office controlled operations and serviced clients to the south of Malaysia. Business was growing steadily as was their brand image. Two excellent professionals Dr. Henry Yip and Dr. Muhatir Yakub were handpicked from the USA and appointed Chief Consultant and Chief Trainer respectively. The rest of the organisation reported to them but they regularly reported to the partners.

The performance of Dr. Yip and Dr. Yakub was beyond reproof. Dr. Yip in addition to being a Chief Consultant was Branch Head for Penang while Dr. Yakub in addition to being the Chief Trainer was also the Branch Head of Johor Baharu. Their loyalty to the partners was unquestioned and many a time they had bailed out the firm when things had got sticky with the clients owing to contradictory instructions received by their consultants and trainers from Noor and Freddy.

Any employee could "informally" speak to either Noor or Freddy in confidence and inform them about what was happening and what their boss was doing. This informal channel of communication allowed the partners to keep their fingers on the button at all times and small things like which boss went home early and who took an extra half hour for lunch was known to them on a regular basis. The end result was that group dynamics suffered and employees vied with one another to play favourites of the partners.

However, as a matter of practice all inquiries had to be routed through Kuala Lumpur and all client relations came under the scanner of Noor whereas all technical matters had to be vetted by Freddy. The firm was doing reasonably well but the personal finances of the couple were multiplying at a higher rate than the growth of the firm. The firm was able to proudly list a galaxy of clients and the bank manager at HSBC was very pleased with the firm's account. However, the employees at ACTI were not a very contented lot. Noor and Freddy were aware of this but did not care too much since the pay scales at ACTI were higher than anyone else's and they sincerely believed that working in ACTI would add to a person's professional bio data and so nobody would quit the firm easily. There was a general perception among the employees that Noor knew little about organisational diagnosis and other technical matters, and yet interfered in these matters. She was a smooth talker, knew what was to be said to whom and when and being a Malaysian by birth she had excellent contacts in the corporate sector as well as in the political cicles. On the other hand, Freddy was excellent in diagnosis and taking on turnkey projects but could be very abrupt and abrasive in his dealing with people. He was not a bad person at heart but had the ability of offending people quite easily and often unintentionally. The advantage of being Muslims in an Islamic country could therefore be better exploited by the couple if there was some clear understanding about role demarcation between them.

There were plans to open an office in Hong Kong and space in the hub of Shim Sha Chui was earmarked and purchased for that purpose. Eventually the firm planned to tap Indian corporate houses as well, but that would be after 2005. It was common knowledge that Noor did the envisioning and planning while Freddy looked after matters of detail and education. Since the couple were issueless they could concentrate on the business front without worrying about normal domestic chores.

With a lot of fanfare a meeting was organised in October 2002 at P. J. Hilton where future plans were announced to all. The Press carried details about the company growth and its client list. Every thing was going well up until January 2003 when Noor discovered that three of ACTI's senior men from the Johar Baharu branch and three senior men from the Penang branch had resigned from ACTI in quick succession and teamed up to start their own consulting and training business which was identical to ACTI. In addition they registered it as a Private Limited Company rather than a Partnership Firm which ACTI was. A small but significantly placed news item in the New Straits Times signalled the formation of the new company and its objectives. They had even influenced Noor's trusted lieutenant Miss Ma Chi to quit ACTI and join the new firm to handle their customer relations, on the same salary but with fewer perquisites.

To add to their woes Freddy and Noor discovered that several clients of ACTI had gone over to the new company and that the new company was called Malaysia Consulting and Training Institute (MCTI). In May 2003 the new company took a small office in Bukit Bintang, Kuala Lumpur not far from the head office of ACTI. This is when alarm bells started clanging loud and clear.

In a hastily summoned meeting with Dr. Yakub and Dr. Yip, Noor and Freddy took the decision that expert intervention was called for. Consequently, they took a rare consensus decision and employed the services of Dr. Peter Shepard a renowned professor and an internationally known consultant with an impeccable academic record to find out why the new company was formed and why people had quit ACTI even when they were paid handsomely.

After six months of painstaking research the learned professor Peter Shepard had summarised his findings thus:

- Although the recruitment of consultants and trainers was flawless and the incumbents of high quality they were not given the professional respect by the partners. In addition, there was no role clarity and often Noor and Freddy both gave separate orders to the same consultant or trainer leaving the person quite confused and often frustrated.
- The chain of reporting was clear when it came to communicating from the bottom up but when it came to a top down positivist command and control, these official hierarchies were overlooked. Often the boss did not know what the subordinate was told by Noor or by Freddy and this added to the fuzziness about what was expected of these consultants.
- In the attempt to keep client relations in tact many times orders were countermanded by the two partners and ACTI's consultants were told to turn the Nelson's eye to certain irregularities in the client's organisation.
- What bothered the consultants working for ACTI was the statement of Freddy at the October meeting: "We promote creativity and innovation in ACTI but be sure that I personally am kept informed and approve everything that the consultants take on and do."
- Consultants resented the fact that although the clients accepted them as experts, Freddy and Noor were constantly looking over their shoulder and often interfered with what they were doing.

- Even when the Chief Consultant and the Chief Trainer procured a client it was always either Noor or Freddy who would write to the client and many times the terms of agreement were changed without informing the Chief Consultant and the Chief Trainer.
- The role ambiguity between Noor and Freddy stemmed from the fact that as Partners to the firm they assumed that they could look into every aspect of its operations and guide people who (obviously) knew more about the work in hand than they did.
- Noor and Freddy ran ACTI as their personal fiefdom and it was standard practice that on their respective birthdays a lavish party would be thrown and though everyone was invited to it, they had to contribute towards the purchase of the birthday present.
- When an employee had to overstay at office or come to work on a holiday the firm never compensated them either by way of overtime or compensatory off. The refrain then was "this is your company and your commitment should come from within your self". However, when the same person came more than 45 minutes late to work due to any reason whatsoever the person lost half a day's salary. The refrain then was "we believe in discipline". This incongruence led to resentment on the part of the consultants and trainers.
- Noor and Freddy forgot that they were dealing with knowledge workers and this is a species that needs to be treated with a great deal of respect. If such persons were to be asked to be creative then they should be given some degree of freedom at work.

Going through the consultant's forty page report, summarised above, Freddy and Noor thought it wise not to take Dr. Yip and Dr. Yakub into confidence. Instead they called Dr. Shepard for a private meeting over dinner and asked him to facilitate the culture change at ACTI so that employee satisfaction improved.

- ***If you were Dr. Peter Shepard what would you have done and why?***

HINT:

This is a typical case where the owners of a firm do not walk their talk and unwittingly create a culture of opportunists and yes men. Trust relations are low and when transparency is most called for it is found to be wanting. This is the climate under which the mediocrity usually thrives and the fact that ACTI was doing well so long may have more to do with lack of competition than anything else.

A program of change management through value based OD intervention is called for. And since the bottleneck is always at the top of the bottle, change must be started at the top. Noor and Freddy should be firmly but politely told that trust, respect and belief in colleagues are reciprocal. They must start earning the respect of their knowledge workers before demanding obedience. This is more so with the knowledge workers than with any other species of the proletariat since the knowledge workers have a high self-esteem and a brittle ego which once damaged can put and end to creativity, innovation and competitiveness. Positive group dynamics is vital for such an organisation and the corporate culture must create conditions that effectively promote it.

Only after Noor and Freddy are fully convinced of and committed to the above should Dr. Shepard start the intervention. Dr. Yip and Dr. Yakub should be taken into confidence at once, since they are the de facto CEOs while Noor and Freddy are the owners (partners). This role clarity must be candidly addressed as soon as possible. If not, the partner's insecurity may prevent change from taking place and the good professor may earn a bad name for no fault of his.

CASE 39

AMBADEVI COMMUNICATIONS

This is the story of a company started by Mr. Manubhai Gujjar, an entrepreneur, way back in 1946, when he returned home to Kutch after gallantly serving the country in the World War. He brought back with him the idea of having a courier service that would be quicker and more personalised that than the Indian Postal Service. He employed angharias, or local carriers who would take parcels from one remote location to another at a price and ensure safe delivery of goods. His firm was registered under the name of Ambadevi Communications since being from a staunch Gandhian family he did not like to attribute his or his family's name to the business. He chose the name of the Great Deity instead. In his initial years, he was alone but in 1953, his maternal first cousin Mr. Mansukhbhai Panchamia joined him and the ambit of his business grew. In 1955, they obtained a licence and Ambadevi Communications became accredited freight and cargo handling agents. In 1968, they started importing telephone instruments and set up telephone systems for many business houses in Kutch and Gujarat. In 1975, they expanded the business to provide tele-printer machines and obtained several Annual Maintenance Contracts (AMCs) from the business houses to who they supplied telephones and tele-printers. By 1977, they had set up a chain of photocopying kiosks that also served as sales outlets and points from which the angharias could collect the goods for door-to-door delivery.

Mansukhbhai was a confirmed bachelor while Manubhai had a son named Kantibhai from his second wife and who having completed his Bachelors in Commerce joined the father's business. Manubhai also had two daughters from his first wife and they were named Shantiben and Jyotiben and who had completed their Bachelor's Degrees in Arts. While Mansukhbhai and Manubhai treasured tradition, custom and Gandhian values, Kantibhai was a carpetbagger and quite bohemian in his values. In 1990, Ambadevi Communications bagged a contract to import British Fax Machines.

In 1989, there had been a major family fall out and Ambadevi Communications split up into two divisions in 1991. Mansukhbhai and Manubhai took charge of the Telephone Freight and Cargo Division under which came the local courier service and tele-printers as well. Jyotiben and Shantiben stayed on to help the old men as Directors of the Company at Rajkot. Kantibhai took charge of the new fax machine imports and sales and formed a new division as the Director taking it to Bhuj. While Manubhai remained Chairman of the Company and Mansukhbhai remained the Joint Chairman, it was clear the Ambadevi Communications (Rajkot) had little say in the affairs of Ambadevi Communications, Bhuj Division. The work culture, managerial values and people relations at both divisions was markedly different. Most of the old clients remained with the Rajkot Division (even those in Bhuj) and were doing quite well, whereas the Bhuj Division was forced to look for new clients, markets and venues. The Rajkot Division was content with a steady pace of growth and profits. They were benevolent employers with a strong social conscience. Employees of the Rajkot Division were content and though not paid high salaries were reasonably well taken care of, had secure jobs and put in their best and even willingly rose to the occasion when called for. New corporate customers were soon converted into loyal clients when they saw the honesty with which they were treated by the Rajkot Division of Ambadevi Communications and the company's brand equity soared. Top management's word could be blindly trusted.

Kantibhai who had a king size ego was desperate to see that the Bhuj Division faired better than the Rajkot Division. He seemed to have made it a personal prestige issue. Consequently, he was scouting for both people who could help him as well as new lines of business. Three ne'er-do-well drifters named Dutta, Bannerjee and Sirkar had been driven out from Bengal for reasons that nobody was sure of. However, they were wily, possessed the gift of the gab and were qualified engineers. They met Kantibhai who spotting an opportunity hired them at once for his Bhuj Division. The trio convinced Kantibhai to go into computers and he bit the bait. By 1995, they were the sole agents for reputed MNC selling computers in Gujarat and Kutch and providing AMCs from which they made quite a big profit. They realised that Kantibhai adored sycophants and by showering him with praise and doing his odd jobs as if it was a privilege to do so, slowly but surely won Kantibhai's trust. The trio were in full command of the new projects undertaken by the Bhuj Branch, before long. Indeed, it was their idea to go in for the setting up of systems that could enable their clients in bugging telephones, hacking into personal e-mails and tape recording employee conversations.

When one entered the portals of Ambadevi Communications one could not but help admire the statue of the Deity so decoratively kept in a small temple outside the office. One could see that on top of the gate, Ambadevi Communications was written in big letters that were illuminated at night and below that the words Rajkot Division appeared in much smaller lettering. In contrast, display of any religious symbol was banned in the Bhuj Division and even the lettering on the entrance were reversed. Ambadevi Communications appeared in smaller size letters whereas the words Bhuj Division written bellow were considerably larger. Whereas Mansukhbhai, Manubhai and his daughters remained Gandhian to the core, Kantibhai switched political party allegiances as and when it suited his business interests. Hence, people generally felt that he was ideologically unprincipled and could not easily be trusted.

Top management at Rajkot Division saw the organisation as a coalition of contending forces and interests. Consequently, it adopted the role of a mediator between these forces such that organisational objectives were met. They saw trade unions as legitimate representatives of employee interests and gave them due recognition and respect. They believed that stability in the industrial relations scenario was a product of concessions and compromises between management and trade unions. After all, the needs and aspirations of the angarias, freight and cargo handlers, telephone engineers and tele-printer salesmen were different. These needs and aspirations were handled differently such that satisficing behaviour, (to quote Cyert and March), was achieved at all levels. Promoting group dynamics featured high on the corporate agenda.

Top management at the Bhuj Division assumed that employees who were paid high salaries should co-operate with management on all counts as a rule. Furthermore, the management's right to manage was insuperable and inalienable. Management prerogatives were not to be questioned. All conflict was endemic and must be avoided at any cost. Statements like: this is your company so you should not ask for overtime were commonplace. Also heard were homilies like since if I (Kantibhai), as the CEO, can put in a 12-hour workday why should young men like you not do so? Do you not consider this to be your company? Consequently, employee burnout was high and medical ailments due to hypertension and overwork were commonplace. Many engineers suffered from an identity crisis since Kantibhai was not a great decision maker and vacillated a lot before he came to any conclusion. Invariably it was his close confidants who indicated the direction he should take in company affairs.

The total number of employees in the Rajkot Division was 1700 including managers. Everyone was given a full time employment, wages were paid in time and although net profits after tax did not soar the division certainly kept increasing its profits that they shared willingly each year with its employees over and above the provisions of the Payment of Bonus Act.

The official union was affiliated to the Hind Mazdoor Sabha and except for token strikes and sympathy strikes called by HMS, workers in the Rajkot Division were peaceful on the industrial relations front. As and when the trade union took up a cause they were listened to with dignity and an amicable solution was negotiated such that a win-win situation emerged. This was not always easy but it was zealously pursued. The trade union was accepted as a legitimate countervailing tendency and even encouraged to support projects that improved the common good of all. However, the company never interfered with the internal affairs of the union nor did it proffer any advice on what the union ought to do. The line demarcating the ambit of concern of both the management and the union was cleanly drawn and respected.

Attrition levels at the Rajkot Division remained between 5% and 8% per annum and the Division's credibility as a good employer increased steadily along with its corporate bank balance. Every employee had to undergo a Hindi and an English certification course conducted by the Ministry of Labour of the Government of India. Periodic worker training programs were mooted and in 1995, the concept of quality circles was introduced. Any body could speak his mind openly and all criticism was welcome even when it was not constructive. The lowest level of qualification of an employee in the Rajkot Division was a Class XIII pass while the highest level of qualification was a Bachelor's Degree. The average salary of an employee of Rs. 7,000 per month while the average salary of a manager was Rs. 15,000 per month. Nobody was paid below the stipulated minimum wage.

The total number of employees in the Bhuj Division was 2500 of which only 50 were in full time employment while the rest were on contracts. The lowest level of employee qualification was a Bachelor's Degree while the highest was a Doctorate Degree. Most of the middle level employees were engineers and by 1999, the Division had started setting up Intranet systems for corporate clients and started enabling individuals and corporate houses to float their Websites on the Internet. Attrition levels fluctuated between 20% to 35% per annum even when the lowest salary paid was Rs. 25,000 per month and the highest salary was Rs. 55,000 per month. There was no trade union since it was generally known that any attempt to unionise would attract a termination notice and officially, knowledge workers were supposed to be above unionising. In 2003, the attrition level shot up to 45% and ESOPs was introduced. However, since employees were on contracts this did not have the desired attraction.

Whereas employee training was seen in Rajkot as a corporate social responsibility, in Bhuj it was viewed as an avoidable cost that was to be reduced. This was especially so since the management philosophy was "why train someone who is bound to leave sooner or later?" Whereas trade unionism was treated with respect in Rajkot, it was scoffed at in Bhuj. In the last Chairman's speech to employees, Manubhai had stated that it was the social obligation of Ambadevi Communications to set up schools, contribute towards developing the local hospitals and taking up environmental concerns throughout the areas surrounding Rajkot and Bhuj.

However, a fortnight later when a local newspaper interviewed Kantibhai he said that the sole business of a businessman was to do business and make profits. That was his dharma and the end justified the means. He portrayed himself as a modern manager who had scant regard for custom and tradition and whose mission in life was to make profits so that his Division would grow. Whether the means adopted were fair or foul did not matter to him as long as corporate goals were met. It was common knowledge that corporate philosophy and the resultant organisational culture at Rajkot and Bhuj were very different.

Among the specialist tasks undertaken by Rajkot Division was setting up cargo freight, telephone connectivity in remote parts of the country, training the purchasers in its regular maintenance, and effective use of these facilities. Many foreign institutions and bodies honoured both Manubhai and Mansukhbhai, for their social work and the Government of India bestowed upon each of them the title of Padmashree. Every charitable cause that was laid at their doorstep was championed and every company policy was targeted towards improving the quality of life of the common man.

Among the specialist tasks undertaken by the Bhuj Division for corporate clients was bugging of employee telephones to facilitate tape recording of conversations, the facility to hack employee e-mails to see who was applying where and for what job. Many of the smaller and profit minded corporate houses sought their services and their clients were situated as far away as in Nasik and Jaipur. Even some Management Institutes clandestinely sought and obtained this expertise from the Bhuj Division to keep a tab on their faculty. Before long the Buj Division has a list of clientele that wanted to cut corners, exploit their employees, break laws with impunity and still keep a respectable face in public. Dutta, Bannerjee and Sirkar were the usual interlocutors for all such contracts.

Attrition levels in Rajkot Division rose from 5% to 7% per annum during 2003-04, whereas in the Bhuj Division it increased from 35% to 53%. When in 2004 at Divali the salary of every employee was increased by Rs. 3,000 per month across the board in the Rajkot Division, the Bhuj Division increased their total wage bill by 10% and reduced their manpower by 5% simultaneously. Hence, the average employee stood to gain substantially in monetary terms. Yet, in October 2004 the attrition at Bhuj had shot up to 53%. Kantibhai knew it was time to seek expert advice from a consultant,.

This caused Kantibhai to employ a marketing professor cum consultant and friend from Pune named Mr. Mathew Venkoba Rao who came into Human Resources via the Industrial Engineering route. With strong corporate connections in Aurangabad and Nasik Mr. Rao seemed to be an ideal expert to come and see what was going wrong. Moreover, he was an old friend who could be trusted to not rock the boat. He was accordingly invited to study both Divisions and the Rajkot Division saw nothing wrong with the idea. In fact, Manubhai and Mansukhbhai welcomed the idea of getting expert help. They had always had an open mind and were not afraid to learn new things.

After spending four full months in Bhuj and Rajkot and charging a whopping Rs. 5 Lakhs in consultancy fees, the report was submitted and it highlighted four points on a scale of 1 – 10 rising from low to high. His main contention was that the Bhuj Division did not conduct its people-management in a correct manner and that the problems rose from poor handling of industrial relations.

Consequently, the consultant short-listed the names of three industrial relations men who could be considered for the position of Corporate Head of Human Resources and who would oversee the operations in both Divisions. All three contenders were well qualified, had law degrees and impressive bio-datas.

- The industrial relations climate in Bhuj Division stood at 2, whereas that in Rajkot Division it was 10.
- The level of employee motivation on the same scale in Bhuj Division was 4, whereas in Rajkot Division it stood at 9.
- Trust relations and loyalty in Bhuj Division stood at 3, whereas in Rajkot Division it stood at 8.
- Rajkot Division paid its employees 2% above the industrial mean in the city, whereas Bhuj Division paid its employees 15% above the industrial mean in the city.

While Manubhai and Mansukhbhai read the consultant's report nonchalantly, it had ruffled many feathers in Kantibhai's camp. This was obvious by the way in which the two Divisions responded to the report.

1. ***What do you think went wrong at Bhuj Division and why?***
2. ***Which of the two Divisions of Ambadevi Communications was more professional and why?***
3. ***Do you think the consultant missed the point when he identified industrial relations to be the problem area? Explain your position.***

HINT:

This is a fit case where the company's culture can be studied using the OCTAPACE instrument developed by Professor Udai Pareek. Kantibhai obviously got away with a lot of impropriety because Masukhbhai and Manubhai had "abdicated" their control over a company they had founded and helped to grow. This was unfair on their part.

Bhuj Division failed to create a sense of belonging among its employees and since many of the projects undertaken by the company were plainly unethical, trust relations on top management deteriorated. People work for money but they also want stability, which an employment on contact does not give. Stability leads to comfort and this lays the foundation for being innovative and creative. This was absent in Bhuj Divison so although its profits grew, the division failed to develop as an organisation. Corporate culture was based on low social values with the result that both the internal customer and the external customer did not see the Division in a good light.

Kantibhai sadly missed the point when he expected the employees employed on contract to work with the same zeal as he did, since he owned the company and they did not. People work for money no doubt but they also have a life outside the employer's zone of control. This fact must be respected and employees cannot be taken for granted. Even signals as increasing cases of employee burnout and medical ailments did not seem to wake him up from his self-imposed intellectual slumber.

A professional is a person who promises to deliver and delivers as promised without giving up his/her own values. Under the leadership of Kantibhai it was clear that the Bhuj Division was less professional than the Rajkot Division. Kantibhai was seen as an opportunist sans conscience whereas Manubhai and Mansukhbhai by contrast were viewed as social responsibility, business ethics and good corporate governance personified.

This case concerns corporate culture rather than industrial relations so Mathew Venkoba Rao had clearly missed the wood for the trees. Whereas the managerial style at Rajkot Division was Pluralistic, the managerial style at Bhuj Division was Unitarist. While free will and open dialogue was promoted at Rajkot it was sycophancy that was rewarded at Bhuj. The former style and emanating policy paid rich dividends, whereas the latter created frustration among employees. This moot point seemed to be lost on the consultant.

All public utterances by top management contribute towards building or breaking a company's brand image and therefore statements made to the Press should be tempered with caution. What endeared Rajkot Division to the public eye was their social responsibility of business and how they treated their employees with dignity. What gave Bhuj Division a poor image was their relentless pursuit of profit at any cost.

Remedy:

What is called for is to revive the corporate culture so that both Rajkot and Bhuj Divisions share common values. Employees in Bhuj moreover needed the stability seen at Rajkot and a corporate culture that was people centred. One cannot expect someone to be committed to long-term growth of the company unless (a) values are in place and (b) employees' future was assured. Hence, a culture building exercise through HR intervention should feature high on the agenda of Kantibhai. The Bhuj Division lacked a social conscience and its value system left a lot to be desired.

The time has come for deep introspection and a sea change in the work culture that exists in the Bhuj division. When Kantibhai was desperate, he had chosen to go along with the trio of Dutta, Bannerjee and Sirkar who took him down the garden path. Why did Kantibhai not go into a thorough antecedent check of these three before hiring them? What was the hurry in employing them? Kantibhai should get rid of them as soon as possible since it seems it was their idea that he start and if he cannot do so, he must at least marginalize them. Instead, Kantibhai should re-examine his priorities and learn a lesson or two from the manner in which the Rajkot Division is managed.

Ego is man's worst enemy. Kantibhai should shed his ego as well as his carpet-bagging instincts and start learning how to manage a Division professionally and ethically. If not the corporate culture will remain in its present retrograde state and things could get worse in the end.

Kantibhai should start looking inward and contemplate a lot. He should use his head more often than using his heart that he seems to be doing. For instance, even his choice of consultant was questionable. What was needed was an organisational analyst with sociology or psychology as the core disciplinary competence rather than industrial engineering. Friendship must be separated from professionalism and business. A consultant is employed to help find faults and fearing that such a person may rock the boat shows a low sense of self-confidence and the tendency to hear what he likes to hear. Sycophancy is another enemy of managers and so must never be either indulged in or encouraged. Professionalism and sycophancy do not go together. The time has come to wipe the board clean, get a competent H R facilitator, stop taking on dubious contracts in the name of making profit and start afresh. If not, corporate culture will never improve and instead of seeing a light at the end of a dark tunnel, Kantibhai may well be looking at the headlights of an oncoming train.

As Chairman and Joint Chairman of Ambadevi Communications, it is neither clear nor logical for both patriarchs Manubhai and Mansukhbhai to give Kantibhai such a long rope. They too should now intervene and improve the public perception of the Bhuj Division, since eventually this negativity could rub off on the image of the Rajkot Division as well. To begin with, employees needed to be given some job security and a sense of belongingness through people-friendly HR interventions. The corporate culture needed to be revamped at Bhuj on a priority. What however could be a potential HR problem was the wage disparity between Rajkot and Bhuj employees and this issue could be addressed in the next stage of HR intervention.

CASE 40

DESAI MACHINE TOOLS LIMITED

Desai Machine Tools Limited was a well-established company in the outskirts of Aurangabad. The company had been started by a mechanical engineer who had studied for his Masters Degree at the Imperial College of Science and Technology in London. Desai had worked in a Machine Tools Company in Slough for five years thereafter. Then in 1956 he returned home to set up his own plant just when the Government of India had brought out the Industrial Policy Resolution. He handpicked a team of engineers who had specialised in different aspects of the manufacture of machine tools. The Company's products catered to small and medium scale industries in Western India and very often these products were custom made for the consumer. Over the years the company had grown in almost every direction but the corporate culture remained pretty much unchanged. The top management style was benevolently paternalistic and the mindset of the Board of Directors was of the feudal-mercantilist-trader variety. This company knew how to take care of the old and faithful employees even though their per capita productivity was below the industry par.

In 1990 a sea change in the economic and business environment of Indian business and industry appeared imminent. They invited a team of four HR experts selected from B-Schools in Pune to study the company and submit a report to management on what could be done to make the firm more competitive. A cursory study convinced the team that there was ambiguity regarding what the company expected of the employee and what the employee thought was expected of him. Obviously there was a lack of clarity between the average employee's perception of his goal and role. So as a first step, the team conducted the Role Efficacy study based on the well-known scale developed by Udai Pareek, worked on by T V Rao and implemented by Sadri and Jayashree. The following results were thrown up by the study, which had used the 10 dimensions for measuring the role efficacy following the Pareek - Rao model. The crux of the lengthy report thus stated:

On taking the arithmetic mean it was found that on a scale of -2 to +4 for each dimension the average scores ranged from 2.39 to 3.84, which shows that on an average the executives rated themselves to be effective along the ten dimensions. The coefficient of variance was less than 0.3 in 8 dimensions except in the case of super-ordination (0.42) and influence (0.53). Hence, on the whole, we see that there is not much variation in the responses of the executives for each of the ten dimensions between the various organizations studied. Some generalization of the findings is therefore permissible given the rigor used by these social scientists.

Centrality: The average score (2.91) indicates that the senior executive perceives herself/himself to be playing a central role in the organization. She/he considers her work to be quite important.

Integration: The average score (3.42) indicates that the executives perceive their training and knowledge to be utilized to a great extent in their present role. They are seen to be enjoying most of the parts of their role. This has to be studied in light of the organization surveyed; a majority fell in the slow moving public sector or tradition based category.

Productivity: The average score (2.94) indicates that the executives perceive themselves as having a goód amount of freedom to take initiative and act on their own in their role.

Creativity: The average score (3.48) indicates that the executives are able to use their creativity effectively in their roles.

Inter-role Linkage: The average score (3.48) indicates that the executives perceive themselves as working in close collaboration with their significant others in their organizations. They also perceive that their significant others see their role (the executives') as significant to their own role.

Helping: The average score (3.39) indicates that the executives perceive their environment as being helpful and conducive to their work. They are also seen to be experiencing mutual help in their role. The coefficient of variance in this case is 0.42, which indicates that there is a fair amount of variance on this dimension.

Super-ordination: The average score (2.39) indicates that the executives perceive themselves as not being able to contribute to society to an extent that they would like to do. The coefficient of variance in this case is 0.53, which indicates that on an average the senior executives are not able to relate his role to the society at large. There is a lot of hype and false consciousness

Influence: The average score (2.82) indicates that the executives perceive themselves as being able to influence important decisions and also be consulted frequently.

Growth: The average score (3.18) indicates that the executives perceive themselves to be growing within their roles. Their role is seen to be contributing to their learning.

Confrontation: The average score (3.85) indicates that the executives perceive themselves as effectively confronting problems through mutual aids.

The Board of Directors of Desai Machine Tools Limited wanted to make trust, transparency and teamwork as the watchwords of the new corporate culture. Armed with this report, how would you as the Chief OD Facilitator of this company go about changing the corporate culture?

DEFINITIONAL UNDERPINNING TO AID ANALYSIS

- Role is defined as the position a person occupies as determined by expectations from significant persons, including the person himself.
- Behaviour of individuals in relation to their role expectations is called role behaviour. We adopted this working definition.

- The concept of role efficacy or role making, it may be argued, is not a new concept in India. It has its roots in the Bhagwat Geeta, which preaches the individual to feel pleasure in each and every process of work (karma) and not bother about results. But role efficacy is born out of a sense of self worth.
- Role space can be defined as the dynamic interrelationship both between the self and the various roles an individual occupies, and amongst these roles.
- The role set is the pattern of relationship between the role and other roles in the organizational context as well as in the general environmental context.
    1. Inter-role distance is the difference between the organizational and non-organizational roles.
    2. Role stagnation is a result of the gap between the demand to outgrow a previous role and to occupy a new role effectively.
    3. Role expectation conflict is a type of stress generated by different expectations by different significant persons about the same role, and the role occupant's ambivalence as to whom to please.
    4. Role erosion is a function of the role occupant's feeling that some functions, which should properly belong to her/his role, are transferred to or performed by some other role. This can also happen when the role occupant performs the functions but the credit for them goes to someone else.
    5. Role overload occurs when the role occupant feels that there are too many expectations from the significant roles in this role set, she/he experiences role overload.
    6. Role isolation refers to the psychological distance between the occupant's role and other roles that in the same role set.

Personal inadequacy is a type of feeling arises when the role occupant feels that she/he does not have the necessary skills and training for effectively performing the functions expected from her role.

Self-role distance occurs when the role a person occupies goes against her self concept then she/he feels self-role distance type of stress. This is essentially a conflict arising out of mismatch between the person and the job.

Role ambiguity refers to the lack of clarity about the expectations of role which may arise out of lack of information or understanding.

HINT:

First talk through and find out what kind of corporate culture top management wishes the company to have and is it prepared to go the whole hog in backing you if there is resistance to change, which is very likely. Use the 5 D methodology before mooting an HR intervention to change corporate culture. But do not attempt to do so unless top management as well as the line and staff management is completely with you in mooting this exercise. So first convince them and only then begin. Change is not easy to implement and sabotage cannot be ruled out. Most importantly, change for the sake of change is foolhardy and so be sure that change in this case is actually needed. It is at such times that the true mettle of the HR Head is discovered. This is when the men stand apart from the boys!

❑❑❑

SECTION FIVE

SHORT CASE STUDIES IN INDUSTRIAL RELATIONS

CASE 41

MANDAL AUTO PARTS LIMITED

Mandal Auto Parts Limited is a part of a large business group, which operates with its headquarters in Bhubaneshwar, and the plant is located at about 100 kilometres from Cuttack. The plant had manpower strength of 20,000 employees in 1996 but in 2002 it was reduced to 13,000 as a part of an overall policy to develop a lean and mean organization. However, the total production of Auto Parts in the plant increased raising the annual profit from Rs. 20 crore to Rs. 30 crore during the same period. In addition, the plant expanded its capacity to produce spare parts for two wheelers, auto rickshaws and six seater vans. This streamlining of manpower was made possible more due to a consistent policy of attrition rather than one of retrenchment. Large-scale unemployment and poverty levels brought home to the Unions a change of attitude, from one of confrontation with the Management to one of co-operation, in the 2000s.

The Personnel Department had always been manipulative and administered through a management of divide and rule. The labour collectivity was pampered and a labour aristocracy mushroomed. This led to the production, maintenance, materials, and construction divisions having to endure the most of labour unrest and being unable to give the kind of productivity it was capable of giving. The hallmark of the industrial relations environment was the emphasis on 'institutional relationship' as against a 'people-centred relationship', which was looked down upon as nurturing individualism and being occidental.

In the mid 1990s, Mandal Auto Parts Limited turned a new leaf with a new Chief Executive Officer (CEO) at the helm of affairs. Four functional directors assisted him. It became easy to inculcate a corporate culture in the direction of professionalism. This was more so as the Director of Personnel, who had been responsible for pampering the Union leadership, had just retired. He was replaced by a handpicked dynamic and secular-minded person, recently transferred from its sister organisation, to inject a new and progressive perspective in industrial relations. The Deputy Director, Personnel, was not promoted. He was re-designated as Director of Administration with reduced managerial powers and made in-charge of housing and canteen. This raised the number of Directors to four. Management then initiated the process by which to treat the Union as an equal, inspired a sense of maturity in their conduct and held them accountable for production, since they were now partners in progress.

The market for its products was sufficiently good and the inflow of funds was positively progressive. Hence, human resource management (still called personnel management) was not a major concern for the top management. Besides shop floor industrial relations, Personnel Management in the early stages of the company's growth had concerned itself with traditional functions of welfare management on the shop floor. Slowly its welfare activities grew outside the plant; and schools, hospitals, crèches, and housing came within the ambit of its authority.

As an offshoot of the politics outside the plant, workers became divided on the basis of caste and creed. This process was assisted in by the policies of the Personnel Department, especially up until the 1980s. Many of the middle ranking managers were so divided even today. However, it has been seen in the 60 year history of the company, that any time a Manager who was perceived as being principled, he automatically gained respect from all sections of the workforce.

The Personnel Management was a highly efficient department, which worked in tandem with the desires of the top management as its appendage. Consequently, it was not alienated from top management at any point and any policy pursued by the Personnel Department had the tacit support from the top.

An HR Consultant from XIMB had been commissioned to study the phenomenon of inter-group rivalry at various levels of the organisation, since there were some adverse reports about this in the national press. The report stated unequivocally that whereas Mandal Auto Parts had declared in its policy to be secular, reality indicated that the reverse was the case. This report was unceremoniously shelved.

During the 1980s and 1990s, Mandal Auto Parts Limited employed a lot of contract labour. Slowly, the more skilled labour got absorbed into the plant on a permanent basis. Contract labour figures fell from 10,000 in 1986 to 5,000 in 1999. However, there were four groups among the workers, which were brought to surface, based essentially on caste affiliations, in the 1990s and early 2000s possibly due to the general environment in the Converted-Christian community after the Graham Stains tragedy. To this was added a fifth group in the late 1990s, which called itself the Converted-Christian group.

On a day-to-day basis, the groups worked as a team on the production line, irrespective of their caste affiliations. These caste affiliations would, however, surface only when some people with high personal stakes began to play favourites.

Each group canvassed for the intake of casual labour on a permanent basis, based on caste affiliations. The Converted Christians felt that they were not given a fair share and a protest movement developed within the working class. This protest movement had the support of political parties who were out to fetch votes, but remained covert. An easy target to voice their dissent was the canteen facilities, which were managed by a contractor, Biseshwar Thakur.

There are two main canteens located at different places within the 105 square kilometre plant. In addition, tea trolleys with snacks are being sent to the shop floor three times a day. During lunch and dinner breaks, workers can either order a packed meal or go to the main canteens to eat. The meals are heavily subsidised.

Two Unions, based on caste grounds, but on paper shown to be affiliated to the INTUC and AITUC, had a lot of influence on the management of the canteen. The Converted Christians automatically saw the canteen as a target to vent their anger. In the meanwhile, the canteen contractor found out that his manager and some of his supervisors were making money on the sly and he dismissed them after a domestic enquiry. A new manager and six supervisors were appointed. Three of the dismissed supervisors were Converted Christians and this added fuel to fire.

In July 1999, an important local politician gave an inflammatory speech in the city of Cuttack and fanned the fires of discontent among the Converted Christians. One of the concessions given in 1989 was the absorption of three Personnel Officers from the newly vocal Converted Christian category. Yet, the workers in that camp continued to feel persecuted and un-represented. The corporate policy of Mandal Auto Parts Limited did not distinguish on grounds of caste, religion or political ideology between one employee and another. Nevertheless, it was the divide and rule policy of a small section of top management that created such a perception in the minds of the employees. With time, this perception grew stronger.

In 1999, a series of incidents revolving around the canteen took place and are sequentially chronicled below:

1. Some canteen vendors suddenly stopped service in the canteen. They were unsympathetic to the Converted Christians on grounds that they needlessly interfered with their work.
2. The Contractor's Manager was forcibly removed from the premises and beaten up by the Converted Christians on grounds that the food supplied was sub-standard.
3. Twenty two incidents were reported when the canteen staff had misbehaved with members of the various unions.
4. It was then reported by Thakur that this misbehaviour was caused by sympathy for those employees who had been dismissed. However, the canteen staff counter claimed that it was they who were insulted and framed by persons loyal to Thakur, who had allegedly married a Converted Christian nurse. According to rumours, he had also converted to Christianity and had plans to change the entire canteen staff and replace them by his own clansmen.
5. The new uniform which were of better quality and supplied before Durga Puja, on the same pattern and colour, as the old uniform, were rejected by the canteen staff on grounds that the tailoring was sub-standard. A Converted Christian firm did the tailoring of new uniforms.
6. Thakur claimed that he was being victimised by members of other groups (especially the Muslims) who are putting pieces of string, biddis and insects in the food thalis. Then these same workers were, he says, making an issue of the unhygienic food and creating chaos.
7. Thakur requested the Personnel Department to permit him to get a new set of canteen workers so that such chaos was avoided in future. The names of canteen workers, Thakur had submitted, were after all contract labour and not company employees.
8. The Personnel Department concluded its investigation and replied to Thakur that he could not do so. However, they gave him permission to hire more supervisors to keep a check on the unruly elements.

The CEO was not satisfied with the spate of events. He ordered an inter-functional group to conduct a total management and social audit and asked an outside agency once again the XIMB to help that group in the investigation, to get an unbiased report. The new investigative committee came up with the following findings, annexed to the main report:

- That Thakur had been giving kick-backs to the Materials and Personnel Departments up until 1990. This was stopped when the new CEO had cracked down on inefficiency, corruption in an attempt to promote a healthy work ethic.
- That older members of the Personnel Department, although Muslims, were instrumental in fomenting unrest among the Converted Christians.
- The Director of Production, who belonged to the old school of thought, wanted to become the CEO. Nevertheless, since the Board did not appoint him, he had collaborated with some managers to destabilise the industrial relations scene, using the canteen as a pivotal point of concern. He had been having an extra-marital affair with a Converted Christian school teacher.
- The new Director of Administration, under whose control the canteen services directly fell, was a good friend of the Director of Production. They both belonged to the same political party and the same exclusive clubs. They also had a soft corner for enjoying wine and women.
- There is a great divide between the Union leadership and the rank and file.
- The Management and Social Audit Report, minus the annexure, were circulated among all the members of the top management to solicit a feedback. Copies of the report by the executive officer of the Personnel Department, which had earlier been shelved, was also retrieved and circulated selectively among the top management.

Soon thereafter, there was a minor argument between two canteen workers and the canteen supervisors loyal to Thakur. The canteen supervisors allegedly used foul language and the Converted Christian group took up the case of the canteen workers, demanding a public apology from them by Thakur, who refused to oblige. The canteen workers went on strike. Production workers consequently suffered and there was every chance that the situation could escalate into a major work derailment if the situation was not quickly resolved. A high level meeting was called by the CEO to decide whether a new contractor would be appointed in the canteen or to ask the Personnel Division to take over the job of the contractor. This would mean that the 100-contract labour in the canteen would have to be made permanent. The Director of Administration and the Director of Production wanted the company to take on the task of managing the canteen. The Director of Finance said that this was not a feasible solution cost wise. The Director of Personnel wanted a new contractor appointed for the canteen.

The CEO now had the casting vote, as opinion was equally divided among his four senior Directors on the issue. The leaders of Converted Christians had made it amply clear that their sympathies lie with the CEO, who was generally seen by all employees, as an ethical and fair-minded person. The other Union leaders have taken a position in support of Thakur while the State Government favoured the Converted Christians.

It may be worthy to note that in the last "Quarterly Open Forum Dialogue" between the employees and the CEO, flanked by his four Directors, in August, there had been overwhelming support by the employees for an organisational culture founded on business ethics and free of caste and creed biases. The CEO has sufficient reason to believe that the Union leadership, which supported Thakur, may not be able to carry the regular members along with them. Furthermore, the CEO felt that if a new contractor were to be appointed to manage the canteen, it would take a minimum of 9 months for the new contractor to get established and accepted. During this period, vital production time might be adversely affected, a situation that any Management would have liked to avoid getting into.

You are an experienced executive who has had considerable exposure in this company and elsewhere in industrial relations matters. Due to your seniority and record of accomplishment, the Top Management has chosen you to objectively examine the matter and submit an Action Plan within a week, addressing the issues raised below. Your report will form the basis of Management Policy. Detail your plan and show how you will activate it.

ISSUES:

- ***Why do persons at the helm of affairs seek to compartmentalise employees on the grounds of religion, caste and creed and then control them?***
- ***When the mistake is detected or when the problem is defined, why do successive Managements traverse the same route of divide and rule on the basis of religion, caste and creed?***
- ***Granted that compartmentalising subordinates on ground of religion, caste and creed pays dividends in the short term, is it a good policy to adopt in the end?***
- ***Assuming that division on religion, caste and creed is a social fact, how can fairness and meritocracy be introduced into the system so that trust, legitimacy and commitment can be nurtured and manifested?***
- ***In this case, what would be your Action Plan for the CEO?***

HINT:

Always proceed to act upon policies and practices based on promoting the three Ts of trust, transparency and teamwork. Simultaneously, work harder to keep the three Ss of scheming, swindling and (back) stabbing out of the industrial relations scenario.

❑❑❑

CASE 42

DECADE TEXTILE MILLS

Decade Textile Mills is located in Western India. It has grown from a small enterprise and today is a major exporter of cotton yarn and cotton textiles. The Management of Decade Mills is very orthodox, clan controlled and traditional. The Board of Directors is a mixture of old timers and fresh blood. The Quality Control Manager, Gopi Haricharan, looks after the HRD function and those employees who have secured an MBA from local colleges while in employment often question his knowledge of the subject; "yes men" as well as his "clansmen" who are different from the "clansmen" of the owners surround him. Anyone with new ideas is welcomed so long as the new ideas fall in line with Haricharan's thinking. He is a trusted officer of the top management, but to the workers, he is a person to be kept at an arms length and given due respect mainly in the light of his position in the company. Decade Textiles does not employ MBAs as a matter of policy because the Management feels that such a "Johnny come lately" might rock the boat. Management students are permitted to go there for summer training but kept under very strict supervision and if a student begins to ask too many questions, they write an adverse report to the Institute about that student. However, Haricharan is a very persuasive speaker, can convince many a recalcitrant employee and is held in high esteem by the older managers as well as certain academics, whom he obliges from time to time by arranging consultancies for them.

The informal reporting system in the company is very efficient and top management has a finger on every pulse that beats in the organisation. Leaders whose election is supervised by the Management man the Union. Anyone not following the Management dictate is summarily dismissed. The Consultant on Personnel matters to the company is a self styled OB specialist, Dr. Shanker Iyer, who works at a local institute and lends some credibility to many of Haricharan's training plans by virtue of his support. The "style" of management could be described as "benevolent despotism". The wage structure as well as the organisation chart is considered confidential; documents and job descriptions are a classified document. The span of control is not well laid out, nor is the hierarchy clearly demarcated. Personal equations between certain managers and the top brass are in charge, prevail.

The level of technology used in the Mills ranges from the ultra modern to the ultra archaic. The plant has grown with time and the expansion has not been planned in any orderly fashion as any visitor to the premises will notice. However, this does not present a major "movement of goods" problem. Some parts of the plant are labour intensive, whereas some other plants are capital intensive. The erstwhile policy of advertising all vacancies throughout the plant has run into rough waters since the union contends that only those from within the section are being promoted and the company wide advertisement is a wash out. Now with the possible change in leadership of the union looming on the horizon, this is one of the issues on the union agenda.

Every day, at 1:30 pm sharp, the Works Manager has a spot meeting in the portico outside his office, where senior officers come and keep him up-to-date with the progress of the day. He maintains that he wants to have the meeting outside, as he does not wish to waste time and let the managers get on with their tasks. Some managers "jokingly" remark that he does so in order to prevent their shoes from soiling his office carpet. But there is no denying the fact that outwardly, everyone appears to be one big happy family. The premises are kept very clean and the shop floors are very tidy. Environmental pollution is at a minimum. The gardens surrounding the offices and the canteens are excellently maintained. The canteen food is subsidised, nutritious, vegetarian and generally good value for money. On every festive occasion, workers get discount coupons to buy cloth from the retail outlets determined by Decade Textiles for their products: good quality cotton dhotis and cotton saris. The demand for cotton yarn and textiles universally is high and the Decade Mills enjoy a privileged position as a supplier, because of the contacts that the top brass has with the Central Government. Export orders are bountiful and the company is cash rich. For the fifth year in succession, Decade Textile Mills has made super profits, when their sister company, Decade Rayon, has registered a loss and faces closure.

Decade Textile Mills, through subsidiary holdings, owns cotton plantations. Due to interference from anti-social elements (thugs) and the bad weather conditions, Decade Mills is inclined to sub-contract the growing of cotton, since this is the fourth year in a row that production has been more than actual realisation of the crop.

The shares of the sister company, Decade Rayons, located in another district of the same state, have been doing particularly poorly due to financial mismanagement and labour unrest. Haricharan has publicly vowed that history will not repeat itself in his company.

While all this is going on, a scheme has been floated by which retainable staff from Decade Rayon will be transferred to Decade Textiles and instead of filling up vacancies caused by death or superannuating, these will be filled up by transfers from Decade Rayon. This has compounded the problem of labour transfers and resentment is running high on this score.

The union membership is faced with a dilemma. Should it ask for in-company transfers and remain in the condition wherein only in-section transfers take place or should it close up completely and allow transfers from Decade Rayons to go ahead. One group in the Union Committee wants to stop the transfers from Decade Rayons, while the other group wants it to remain untouched, as more important issues are at stake at the moment. This could form the agenda of further action at a later date, they argue.

The Management does not believe in hiring female employees and the highest position a woman can aspire for is an Assistant Telephone Operator. Recently a top level "lady professor" who is an expert in communication, was slated to take a Management Development Programme on behalf of the Institute that had the contract for in-house Management Training. Haricharan and Dr. Shanker Iyer sidelined the proposal to invite the lady as this invitation; they felt, "might" go against top management's wishes. Although very good friends, the lady professor was seen as an intellectual threat to Dr. Shanker Iyer, whose knowledge of his subject lacked both rigour and depth.

Professor Prem Hegde, the other Management Trainer from the same Institute as Dr. Shanker Iyer (who was present at the meeting when the lady was dropped from the programme unceremoniously), objected on the grounds that such discrimination was against the Fundamental Rights guaranteed by the Constitution and amounted to a violation of the ILO Charter to which India is a signatory.

When Professor Prem Hegde took up the matter with the Director of his Institute, he was brushed aside. The argument tabled was that the institute was starved of funds and the Director did not think that discrimination against women was something important enough to lose a Training Consultancy on. Professor Prem Hegde is on the Western India Committee on Discrimination in Employment set up by the Government of India and is very active on morchas and dharnas organised by the body. His report to the ILO on the exploitation of women and children in Indian industry was hailed as a landmark study. Some committee members feel that the discrimination against women is archaic and must be done away with, but they do not know what to do about it. They have confided their feeling to Professor Hegde.

Dinesh Joshi is the General Secretary of the union, which is affiliated to the INTUC. Dinesh has occupied the position since 1984, when he won the election and every third year he has been re-elected to the post. Joshi's reputation is without blemish and the elections were fair. But, because he is not hard headed, workers assume that he is a "management stooge". To be fair, Joshi himself has done little to dispel that image.

The manpower strength is 3,000 workers, of whom about 60% are contract labour and 300 are officers/supervisors. Of those, 40% of the total workforce are permanent, about 60% are card carrying members of the official house union and the rest 40% join the union cause on a case by case basis. Labour turnover would have been high if the labour market could accomodate the frictional unemployment.

At the last Annual General Meeting of Decade Mills, two old timers retired from the Board of Directors. They were replaced by a Finance Expert and a Marketing Expert, both of whom had MBA Degrees from IIM (Kolkata) and IIM (Ahmedabad), respectively. In addition, the post of Vice President (HRD) was created, and although he was not on the Board, he was given wide ranging powers. He reported directly to the Managing Director, who occupied the highest position in the company's hierarchy.

The Board observed that changes were called for. Wage rates at the plant in Mumbai and in the plantations are poor, as is the quality of skill of those employed. The HRD function is non-existent.

The Board also agreed that professionally qualified Managers must be recruited, but without creating a panic amongst the "old guard". There was no real countervailing tendency within the organisation, which could take on the "old guard" and bring about change. So "new blood" at the highest level was scouted for and found.

The new Vice President of Decade Mills, Dr. Yashvir Sinha, has a Doctorate from Harvard Business School. He is shocked at the lack or absence of an HRD function in Decade Mills. He believes that forming an Human Resources Management Department would be the start of a new era and many of the inherited ills of the past orthodoxy will soon disappear, if the Department is successfully set up and made operative.

Both, Dinesh Joshi and Prem Hegde, now agree with Sinha and have volunteered help in setting up such an HRM department at Decade Mills. Haricharan and the old guards feel threatened and are planning to sabbotage the move. Joshi is well connected with the Government of Maharashtra and the Press although he does not belong to any political party. Haricharan is distantly related to the Director of the Institute, which has the contract for Management Training, and the Director has friends in "high places". Haricharan, on his own has no clout.

Both, Dinesh Joshi and Prem Hegde, also support Yashvir Sinha's idea of recruiting MBA's and PM specialists from the top institutes of India from May 1994 and of not rushing things this year for fear of rocking the boat too much.

The Management at the Annual Meeting on 31.12.1992 has declared a dividend of 22% on equity shares and the share prices are rising at an average rate of 35% per annum consistently since 1987.

The inflation rate in Greater Bombay, according to official Government figures for 1991-92, was 8% per annum but the Bombay University Economists have calculated it at 14% per annum during the same period. The unemployment rate for Greater Bombay, according to Government figures for 1991-92, was 25% per annum (for the category employable in Decade Mills) but the Economists calculated it to be in the region of 40% per annum.

Relationship between Dinesh Joshi and his team with the leaders of the "contract labour" is cordial. The leadership of the "contract labour" has promised not to take up the issue of regularisation until the position of both Dinesh Joshi and Yashvir Sinha are secured in Decade Mills. No one is sure whether the leaders can carry the contract labour with them when the crunch comes. Traditionally, the behaviour of contract labour has been "mercurial". Traditionally, the union leadership has been known to be "reactive" and lacks an ideological base. Hence, any change must be initiated by socially conscious members of the management.

The Problem:

1. The workers want a pay increase to keep up with the rise in the cost of living. Dinesh is under pressure from the rank and file to pursue their demand. Dinesh is assured of support by 85% of the workers. When the union action begins in Mumbai, the plantation workers will join the struggle. If Dinesh does not agree to their demand, he will lose all credibility, support and respect.
2. But Dinesh has taken a company loan of Rs. 1.5 lakh to buy a flat in Thane. Haricharan has quietly sent word to him that if he leads the strike, Haricharan will have him sacked and demand that the loan be paid back at once. Dinesh has paid up only Rs. 50,000 so far.
3. Militancy among the workers is well known but their real strength has not been tested. They are quite vociferous in their demands, but they are not unreasonable men.
4. The workers who follow Dinesh Joshi are highly skilled. They man a vital section of the Mills and can bring the production to a grinding halt despite being few in number.

5. One group of militant workers who are faithful to Haricharan has united and wants Dinesh removed and are pressing for fresh elections to be held. If that happens, Dinesh is sure to lose, unless he takes up the case of the workers within the week. One other group of militant workers want to tie up with Dr. Datta Samant and disassociate with the INTUC totally, if the workers' case is not taken up. They have no dealings with either Haricharan or with Dinesh.
6. Women's Rights activists from Baroda, Nagpur, Pune and Greater Bombay are putting pressure on Professor Prem Hegde to expose the discriminatory practices of Decade Mills. In fact, he first brought this discriminatory practice to the knowledge of the Women's Rights activists.
7. Hegde, however, knows that if this is done Dr. Shanker Iyer and the Director of the Institute, will gang-up on him and put his employment in jeopardy. Professor Prem Hegde is a family man but also has a conscience.
8. Two union committee members who hail from eastern India see nothing wrong in the indiscrimination against women, but agree to go along with the band wagon if the majority so decide. With their support thus secured, the committee could be used to take up the question of discrimination.
9. Dr. Yashvir Sinha has got wind of the situation and has called a secret meeting over dinner at his residence to decide what is to be done. Invited to that dinner are Dinesh Joshi, Prem Hegde, a top-notch politician whose reputation is impeccable and the Regional Editor of a respectable national newspaper who is a common friend of all and can respect a confidence.
10. Prem Hegde and Dinesh Joshi have often felt that Yashvir Sinha is a little too cautious, although his heart is in the right place.

ISSUES:

- ***This is the month of September 1992 and if production stops a large foreign contract may be lost. This would adversely affect all parties.***
- ***How will the problem of manpower allocation be handled? Can it be kept on the back burner? If so why?***
- ***What will Dinesh's strategy be in the light of the above scenario? Plan the strategy and justify each move.***
- ***Should Prem go against the Director of the Institute that employs him? How should he go about doing it?***
- ***How can Yashvir help the union leader, the conscientious professor and begin to form a Department for Human Resources Management as soon as possible?***

HINT:

This case shows four things that are commonly found in many shop floor IR situations. (a) Delayed action is detrimental to everybody. This is called analysis paralysis. (b) When clans, castes and tribes enter the IR calculus invariably there is discontent and strife. The HR chief must avoid this from occurring. (c) When one is being blackmailed the best thing is to go public and keep all the cards open for all to see. This takes the sting out of the blackmailer's proverbial tail. (d) The attitude of the institute director shows that many a time pecuniary considerations overtake ethical actions. In such cases bringing in external pressure from women's groups or the press is the best possible thing to be done. This kind of networking is necessary for every HR Manager to develop.

The author developed this case in 1992 from a consultancy experience, when he was in NITIE. This case was first written, in this present collection, and was completed in 1993. It was subsequently published in Sadri, Sinha and Bonnerjee (1998): Business Ethics, Concepts and Cases.

❑❑❑

CASE 43

BHAGWAN STEEL STRIPS (PVT.) LIMITED

Bhagwan Steel Strips (Pvt.) Limited was a private company, set up in 1945 by a Sindhi entrepreneur named Bhagwan Shivdesani whose family had settled in Mumbai since 1857. The private company grew from a small concern to major steel strips manufacturing concern located in Khandala, in Maharashtra. In 1957, it was taken over by the Government as per the provisions of the Industrial Policy Resolution 1956 and consciously no attempt to disrupt custom and tradition, in so far as labour policies were concerned, was made after the takeover. Consequently, one of the policies inherited was that of giving employment to at least one dependant of an employee who had put in 15 years of service or to a member of a household that was located in the community for over 15 years. This was not a problem because the company recorded a steady profitability from 1955 up until 1990, owing to the fact that the Government was the sole buyer and there was little competition in the market. The Management did not attempt to find greener pastures and was content with preserving the status quo. The only difference now was that the company had a Board of Directors consisting among others, of an eminent banker, a well-known lawyer, a retired Professor of Metallurgical Engineering. The Chairman was invariably an IAS Officer on a five-year deputation. Bhagwan Shivdesani's grandson Vasant Shivdesani was appointed the company's Managing Director. Vasant was a postgraduate in mechanical engineering from University of Brunnel in the UK and had worked with US Steel for five years before returning to India in 1988.

Thereafter, the management policy towards capital and labour continued unchanged, due to the cushion provided by Government subsidy and aided by the fact that the high rate of attrition permitted the steady in-take of young persons. Changes in technological requirements of the buyers and the inability of Bhagwan Steel Strips (Pvt.) Ltd. to modernise, led to stagnation of output and capacity.

In 1990, this policy of providing automatic employment ran into rough weather, as the company did not grow any further nor was the subsidy forthcoming. Other players had entered the market and the size of the clientele had depleted. Profitability fell between 1970 and 1990 by 65 per cent on output and total market share fell from 82 per cent to 43 per cent during the period.

In addition, the demand for steel products needed by the manufacturing sector had changed, as the technology demanded greater precision parts and the company had not modernised since the Government takeover. However, labour turnover was minimal and the workforce was committed to Management policies, which were rewarding without insisting on either performance or accountability.

There was another shift in the Industrial Policy of the State in 1986. According to this, the subsidy given to Bhagwan Steel Strips (Pvt.) Ltd. was reduced and the automatic sale of steel strips to larger public sector concerns was no longer valid. The State Government believed in enforcing self-reliance and self-sustenance, but did not provide the means by way of capital investment for such concerns to grow any further. Rather, some people in the Government preferred to start new ventures since the political kickbacks in these were higher. The management also made no effort to change its corporate strategy in view of the changed environment. Incidentally, by 1989, the top management team changed considerably. Old hands retired and newer men, selected by the Government, came to replace them. It may have been a coincidence but the new top management team were all Congress supporters. The perspective of the newer managers at the top was one of opportunism, since they were IAS officers who had little technical background or interest. They were simply careerists.

Bhagwan Steel Workers' Union (BSSWU) was affiliated to the INTUC and was led by a graduate engineer named Sailesh Masal. In fact, Sailesh was politically motivated and had more than one portfolio. He was local Secretary of the INTUC, as well as the right hand man of the MLA from NCP. He saw himself as somewhat of a power broker in labour related matters and his proximity to the politicians in the Ahmednagar-Loni-Shirdi area made this possible. On a personal front, he was not at all principled nor did he follow a strict code of personal discipline. He was a prolific womaniser.

The tribal population respected him and he had a considerable following even outside the company. Sailesh had all along supported the Management of Bhagwan Steel Strips (Pvt.) Ltd. because many members of the earlier Top Management team shared his ideological persuasion. Also being somewhat of a opportunist-careerist himself, he found it easy to work with the new Management as well.

Members of the rival union, CITU, on the other hand, were less opportunistic and really believed that they could make an improvement in the quality of life of workers by their intervention. For instance, in a recent meeting, they took the stand that: had the profits of Bhagwan Steel Strips (Pvt.) Ltd. been gainfully re-invested, (as the Government now claimed it should have been done), the company still had a chance to modernise its operations and meet the market situation.

The Congress Government at Mumbai made it known that Bhagwan Steel Strips (Pvt.) Ltd. could be privatised in order to ensure growth and profitability. CITU, as well as, INTUC objected to this on ideological grounds. However, since Sailesh saw that privatising Bhagwan Steel Strips Ltd. was in the larger interest of the working class, he readily agreed to play along with the management. Sailesh was approached to help in the temporary closure of the company, so that it could be easily privatised after it was declared sick and the matter referred to BIFR.

Accordingly, Sailesh who was well schooled in sugar co-operative politics manipulated some of his supporters to stage an agitation and put forward a ten-point charter of demands. The management retaliated by declaring a lockout. The company was declared sick and referred to BIFR. An investigative team from the Parliament exposed the collaboration between Sailesh and the management. The Board of Directors of Bhagwan Steel Strips Ltd. reacted sharply to the report.

The radical faction within the Bhagwan Steel Workers' Union managed to remove Sailesh from his position as General Secretary despite opposition and pressures being brought by politicians from the Ahmednagar-Loni-Shirdi area. However, they did not cancel his membership of either BSSWU or the INTUC. The politicians made conciliatory noises in support of Sailesh Masal but did nothing concrete to assist him. Sailesh was not happy with the treatment meted out to him by his own Union as well as his political patrons in the Congress and NCP. The plan to privatise the company was kept on the back burner on his advice.

Arising out of the changing Government policy and the lack of subsidy received, there was a ban, imposed by the State Government, on further recruitment of personnel, and made effective from 1987. The General Manager in the light of a reduced profitability in the company justified this. From 1989, however, Bhagwan Steel Strips (Pvt.) Ltd. adopted a dual policy on labour recruitment. It had not given jobs to the dependants of long serving employees and yet had recruited apprentices, each year, in accordance with the Apprentices Act 1961. Since there were few colleges coming up in and around Khandala, and since Pune was not very far away, many of the wards had acquired university degrees, but failed to gain employment in Bhawan Steel Strips (Pvt.) Ltd., which was the largest industrial concern in the area. Over and above this, the management recruited some Graduate Engineers who had come with weak credentials but strong political recommendation during the same period.

Being dissatisfied with the position taken by the economic situation and fearing the mala fide intention of the General Manager, the local youth formed an Action Committee supported by some of the conscious workers. The parents of the unemployed wards had their sympathy for the Action Committee and silently supported the cause. However, they feared for their jobs and so did not take active part in the agitation. Many of them were old, uneducated and could not hope to obtain alternative employment. Hence, they went along with the management dictat on the surface.

Sailesh, incensed by the treatment meted out to him by his Union and in order to redeem his image, joined the fray and championed the cause of the Action Committee. Very soon, Sailesh emerged as the new leader of the disgruntled youth and joined the Shiv Sena. He now played his union politics as an outsider.

By 1991, manpower was being re-deployed to fill the vacancies caused by superannuating and management sought the support of the recognised collectivity (BSSWU) for doing so. The recognised collectivity agreed with the management in their long-term interest, because they knew that the financial situation of the company was in poor shape and they might be unemployed if the company closed down. The parents of the unemployed wards did not support the position taken by the Union, but they had no choice but to keep silent. Sailesh used his influence in sugar belt to find out that the Government ban on recruitment had been lifted, albeit without fanfare, on 1.4.1990, but the General Manager of Bhagwan Steel Strips (Pvt.) Ltd. had not made this fact known to the workers.

Sailesh informed the Action Committee of this lapse on the part of the General Manager and used it as a weapon to organise the youth against the company. The Action Committee then began to take subscriptions from members of the BSSWU, who gladly obliged. Some senior officers were known to be openly supportive of the Action Committee. A small office was constructed outside the main gate of the factory and this became the focal point of agitation: with the recognised Union on the one hand, and the officers supporting the General Manager on the other. Gate meetings, pamphleteering and statements to the press were used to pressurise the General Manager. On 30.10.1992, the Action Committee gheraoed the General Manager and blackened his face as he was about to enter the Works premises. The local police was called in and the Action Committee members were dispersed.

The following week, (alleged) members of the Action Committee entered the premises and gheraoed the General Manager in his office. Furniture was broken and several computers were destroyed. To break the deadlock, the General Manager agreed to meet the Action Committee to discuss matters further, shortly. The gherao was removed and the Action Committee waited to hear from the General Manager. It was secretly believed that it was the hand of Rafique Sheikh that was behind this hooliganism. Sheikh was a smooth operator, had no scruples whatsoever and managed to have a finger in several pies. In addition he had several known and unknown links with the underworld and was even an active partner in a ladies bar, which was a cover for flesh trade. On 1.1.1993, the Action Committee petitioned the General Manager to honour his words and come to the bargaining table with the Action Committee. At this point, BSSWU called a gate meeting and the General Secretary, Rafique Sheikh, took up the case of the unemployed youth.

On 31.3.1993, the Action Committee called for a 1-day symbolic strike on 5.4.1993, stating that nobody would be allowed to enter the factory in the morning shift, which began at 6:00 am, and the general shift, which began at 8:00 am. The General Manager refused to negotiate with the Action Committee and on 14.4.1993, issued a circular instructing all officers to report to duty by 5:00 am the next day and decided to hold back the workers of the night shift of the previous day. The Government declared the strike notice as illegal and the INTUC affiliated BSSWU first sided with the Action Committee and then switch its allegiance (without notice) to the General Manager and went against the Action Committee. It was then that Shiv Sena came out openly in support of the Action Committee. There was a negotiating deadlock that had to be resolved if production was to continue.

The Board of Directors held an emergency meeting and instructed the Managing Director to appoint an HR Consultant of national repute and an impeccable record for credibility and fairness to advise the company on how to break the deadlock and get back into business. A Search Committee was appointed and they have identified you as the person who can deliver the goods. You have accepted this project based assignment on condition that you will be on a retainer as their expert HR consultant once the winds of uncertainty have been blown over. You have brought with you a team of three HR specialists one each in the areas of manpower planning, personnel administration and human resource information systems. You are the expert on Industrial Relations yourself.

You have called a meeting of your team and briefed them about the facts. You have to give the company a mutually acceptable solution to the employers and the employees and implement the same as soon as possible. What would you do?

ISSUES:

- ***Given the fact that you are not really a consultant but a facilitator what will be your role in the immediate future?***
- ***Should physical violence in industrial relations situations be condoned?***
- ***Critically evaluate the roles played by the Government, the General Manager, Sailesh Masal and the Bhagwan Steel Strips Workers' Union.***

- ***What should Sailesh's next move be?***
- ***Was the demand of the Action Committee for employment of wards justified?***

HINT:

In dealing with such issues in industrial relations, nine things must always be kept in mind.·

- The first thing in industrial relations is to allow people to speak and be a patient listener. The fact that someone listens empathetically to them often diffuses the anger of the parties involved.·
- Operate on the Pareto paradigm by isolating the trivial many issues and zeroing in on the vital few.
- Be absolutely sure you have the power to promise anything and also the ability to honour the same before you enter the collective bargaining exercise.
- Never short-change the employees or play the divide and rule game. Take the workers' collectivity into confidence and work along with them.
- When two or more unions are involved, always deal with both of them simultaneously or openly deal with only one of them. Negotiate with only those who can deliver.
- Even if the union is unrecognised always keep your communication channels open and be fair to all concerned.
- Take a principled but realistic stand and do not prevaricate.
- Always negotiate from a position of strength but also negotiate only with those who have the power to deliver.
- Maintain a healthy disrespect for middle men and lumpen petty bourgeoisie who are basically fixers and often make tall claims, not supported adequately by fact, to build a halo around them.

❑❑❑

CASE 44

THE CHURNING OF VALUES

Ganesh Pandey was a graduate in Industrial Relations from XLRI, Jamshedpur, having secured a consistently high score in all his subjects. On graduation, he joined an international firm, Tandon Forge at Pimpri, Pune, as a Personnel Officer, in the year 1991. He was bubbling with energy, but he also had an intellectual bent of mind. He was principled, polite, well mannered, and articulate. Unfortunately, for him, the legacy of the personnel department was one wherein managers were expected to have a feudal-mercantilist-trader mindset. The price placed on innovation and creativity was a lot less than that on conformity and servility. Trust, transparency and teamwork were terms that were spoken about freely but equally freely were the terms scheming, swindling and backstabbing that were practiced. Ganesh felt like a fish out of water and his idealism of student days received a severe jolt when confronted with the reality of work life.

In, 1995 Ganesh was appointed as Senior Personnel Officer of the Hammer Division, which had 2,200 men on rolls. One day, when he was in a meeting with the Union Shop Steward and the Divisional Manager, there was news of a wildcat work stoppage on the shop floor. He rushed to the shop floor to look for the Committee Member, Sheikh Akhtar, and his friend John Jacob, the local opinion leader. However, they were not on the shop floor and Ganesh's attempts to convince the workers to resume work, failed. The workers told him that they had put down their tools on the say so of Akhtar and Jacob. Since the two were not to be found, he sent for them and scheduled a meeting that very afternoon in the Divisional Manager's office.

Those who were present in the meeting, that afternoon, were the Divisional Manager, the Manager, Ganesh Pandey, the Shop Steward, the Committee Member, and the Union Vice President. The Opinion Leader was not present. The Vice President of the Union personally sent for him and Jacob came in a few minutes.

The Committee Member and the Opinion Leader both refused to talk to Ganesh because, they said, he had refused to give them special treatment as was given to them by the Divisional Manager. They complained that Ganesh had falsely implicated their names as troublemakers in his confidential reports to management on the Quarterly Status of the IR situation. However, if he did not show them preferential treatment, production would suffer and the Divisional Manager did not like that to happen under any circumstances. Therefore, he re-convened the meeting next morning. The Divisional Manager knew very well that the allegation against Ganesh about implicating them as troublemakers was false.

In the absence of every one, Ganesh got a dressing down by the Divisional Manager. Ganesh said that if the DM so wished, he would show the file to Akhtar and Jacob and make an entry in the file to that effect. This was taken as an insult by the DM. Ganesh had no choice. Either he stuck his neck out and showed a confidential report to the two Union authorities, which was against the rules, or risk a rebuke at a later date from the self-same DM, who was well known for such contradictory and opportunistic behaviour.

After introspecting all evening, the decision was made. Ganesh would not show them special treatment unless the Divisional Manager asked him to do so officially. The Divisional Manager refused to commit himself officially and the fall out was that Ganesh was not invited for the subsequent meeting with the Union. On the recommendation of the DM, acting on the advice of the Union, Ganesh was shunted out to Community Development as a Senior Welfare Officer. The plea taken was that he had failed to maintain an environment of harmonious industrial relations in the Division.

In the Community Development Division, Ganesh reported the matter to Miss Bharati Ladkat. She was single, flirtatious, hardworking and consequently in the good books of both the Management and the Union. She broke confidentiality with impunity, but was amply rewarded because she maintained a good rapport with the Union. She was a very special friend of the General Manager as well. It was rumoured that she carried a pocket tape recorder and had a lot of compromising information on many people. She was quite feared and nobody crossed swords with her. Everyone kept her happy but she had no real friends.

Ganesh soon found out what the game was. Therefore, he started to come close to the Union office bearers by leaking official data contrary to official rules, but in conformity with the organisational culture, as he understood it. He took care, however, that sensitive information was leaked without the finger of accountability being pointed squarely at him. It was all done in a very subtle way. He also went out of his way to praise Bharati and literally doted on her. This was not done in a subtle way!

Bharati, in turn, was pleased with his work, the attention and praise she received, gave a good performance review report, and recommended that he be promoted: a promotion that was long over due. Ganesh Pandey was no longer the conscientious student from XLRI. He had begun his journey to prosperity, as the capitalist world knew it. Soon, thereafter, he started having an open love affair with Bharati. He did not have enough money to take her to a plush hill resort, so they invariably rented a small room in a moderate hotel in Panvel for weekends. To her, wealth and property were not trivial pursuits. She was not content in her meagre station in life and could stoop to any level as long as she had the power to call the shots. Bharati found a good friend in Ganesh; a friend she never really had. When Ganesh started showering her with all sorts of costly gifts, she slowly moved away from her other (so called) friends including the General Manager. All now knew about her love affair with Ganesh and when she moved in to live with him, the General Manager publicly made sure that both of them knew that he was not pleased about it.

Soon, however, Ganesh was promoted to Divisional Personnel Officer in-charge of the Production Division. Simultaneously, Bharati was transferred on promotion to the General Manager's Office.

One day, while attending a meeting in the General Manager's office, Ganesh was bluntly told by the Divisional Manager that he would no longer be trusted as he was still sending confidential reports against Jacob and Akhtar the two persons who had earlier been a thorn in his career. This time, however, there was no prolonged dithering. Boldly he walked up to the office, brought the file and showed those present that he had never written any such report. That ended the debate and, to his surprise, the Divisional Manager did not even raise an eyebrow at the fact that a rule regarding company confidentiality had been broken. The General Manager realised that it would be better to have Ganesh on his side than have the Divisional Manager who was due to retire in three year's time anyway.

Ganesh was yet to get another revelation the same week. Officially, the company policy stated that there were managerial prerogatives, which were unalienable. However, the General Manager, openly stated that if a Union leader complained against any officer, and the complaint was backed by the flimsiest of evidence, that officer would be sacked. Furthermore, managerial prerogatives did not mean a 'bloody thing' to him and all he wanted was productivity.

Ganesh discussed his options with Bharati and they agreed to damn the principles of fairness and equity and grab as much power as possible. She said that power brings wealth and is a great aphrodisiac. One evening soon thereafter, Bharati told Ganesh that the General Manager was going to escort a team of governmental dignitaries through the plant next week and that a fresh contract with the firm depended on them. Bharati and Ganesh hatched a plan. Next day Ganesh took two of his henchmen cum informants Ram Shivade and Mohan Patil into confidence. They were also the top fixers upon whom the trade union leaders depended. He gave them Rs. 5000 each for creating a problem on the shop floor during the visit. Furthermore, he instructed that, he would come and quell the crisis. In addition, it was agreed that when he shouted at them they would all meekly listen to him in front of the visitors. This stage-managed plan was operationalised and went off smoothly. Ganesh was given a letter of appreciation by the General Manager and promoted to Divisional Manager (Administration).

As DM (Administration), Ganesh was in-charge of Personnel, Security and Public Relations. He invested in property and made a lot of money, doing favours and arranging contracts. Soon, the general manager took him into greater confidence, gave him more powers and called him in every time for advice when there was trouble.

The company even sent Bharati and Ganesh together as their emissaries to Singapore for negotiating a merger. There again, he used his Machiavellian instincts to amass wealth and indulged in every kind of compromise to ensure that personal aggrandisement was the result. While at Singapore, he bought Bharati a full gold and diamond set, costing US$ 25,000. That night however, over a lot of the amber nectar he had tears in his eyes, but Bharati knew not why. She.presumed, however, that the tears were of joy as they were having a great time together. When questioned next morning Ganesh confided in her that he could not do anything honourable as the Personnel Division itself has lost all credibility. Over lunch, he discussed the morning's outburst with Bharati further. She found that he had done nothing wrong since the rules of the market rewarded the winner irrespective of the means.

Ganesh stared at Bharati for a long time, lost in a haze of conflicting emotions. Bharati stated that if he could not grow up and did not have the guts to play hardball he should quit and go to some ashram. Then he too got up, took a long solitary walk in silence, and let his heart weep unrestrained. His tears brought forth deep anger, frustration, and agony and, finally, a gentle paced determination. Soon, thereafter, he began his meditative journey in search of the Ganesh Pandey that his inner self was looking for and whom he had left by the wayside so many years ago. Moreover, as he journeyed, his conscience smiled even more. He knew that his affair with Bharati would soon become history and a new Ganesh would emerge from the churning.

ISSUES:

Consider yourself to be Ganesh Pandey, your new goal is to re-instil credibility in the HRM function amidst the turbulent situation of conflicting values in Industrial Relations as mentioned above.

- ***Would you blame Bharati for your deviance?***
- ***What would be your immediate strategy?***
- ***What would be your long-term strategy?***
- ***Where would you begin? Justify yourself.***

HINT:

No amount of success is worthwhile without self-respect. If you want to regain your self-respect, you have to make a fresh start. You cannot do that in the present organisation since you will only expose yourself and nobody will trust you. You have no choice but to look for another job, make your intentions clear to Bharati and give her the option to change and come along or retain her values and hold on to her old job.

Make up your mind whether you want to be known as a consequentialist manager or a non-consequentialist leader. Then act accordingly. However, let the churning of values be free and complete before you take the final plunge. People like Bharati are a dime a dozen in the real world and history forgets them even before they are dead. People like the new Ganesh are hard to find and it is they, who make the difference. Always be loyal to your values and guard them zealously without being rigid and unbending. Always realise how you would like to be remembered and act accordingly. Ends do not justify the means used under any conditions and especially so in Industrial Relations where the HR Manager must emerge as a role model if he/she has to make a mark in his/her career. There are no other options and there are no short cuts. Next to God, if you have to fear anything then the best advice is to please fear history. When history passes judgement, it is most unforgiving and spares none.

❑❑❑

CASE 45

TOTARAM TRANSPORT COMPANY

Totaram Banarasidas of Ajmer was a shrewd businessman and an astute planner. He strategically and slowly captured the public transport business in the Indore-Bhopal belt of Madhya Pradesh. Indore stood at the crossroads since traffic from the east to the west and from the north to the south of India had to go through Indore. The Madhya Pradesh State Road Transport Corporation (MPSRTC) was a public sector monolith, which was laid back and traditional in its approach to business. Consequently, a number of smaller companies mushroomed and ate into its market. Totaram, who was a highly successful stockbroker, observed this and floated a company that had the financial muscle to buy out a number of these smaller companies under the umbrella of Totaram Transport Company (TTC). For this he took a whopping Rs. 10 crore loan from the State Bank of Indore and added an equal amount from his own funds to make a corpus to run the business. Totaram had one daughter and one son who were given the charge of the company as Directors. Strategic planning, finance and investment were functions that he retained with him.

Under the able guidance of Totaram, TTC managed its business interests professionally and treated its workers with dignity. His daughter Jaya was a postgraduate scholar who had specialised Logistics and Operations at IIM (Kolkata) and thereafter in Organisational Behaviour for her Fellowship at IIM (Bangalore). She was the Director who was in charge on the public relations and human resources fronts. The son Pyarelal who had an M.Tech. in Mechanical Engineering from IIT (Powai) looked after the maintenance and operational fronts, while it was Totaram who as the Chairman and Managing Director laid down the strategy and overall work values.

There was a team of engineers who ran a maintenance shop off Rajender Naka in Indore, which was also bought out, and Totaram's son took over as its Director. The engineers immediately received a monthly pay rise of Rs. 3,000 each, were fitted in a proper scale of pay and assured certain benefits such as Mediclaim Insurance up to a limit of Rs. 2 lakhs and a Life Insurance of Rs. 5 lakhs each. The work environment was both physically and sociologically improved and a good canteen was added to the premises. Caterers from Pune were given the contract to run the canteen professionally as well as manage small food outlets at every major point of the bus route throughout Madhya Pradesh. Leave rules were introduced and a sense of belongingness was inculcated in every employee. To begin with, every bus that was bought out when Totaram Transport bought out the smaller companies was given an overhaul, refurbished and repainted. Every bus would, as a rule, come to the now named Totaram Maintenance Shop for monthly servicing and for all major breakdowns. Pyarelal tied up with all Indian Oil outlets so that the buses could be refuelled en route. Jaya did the same with all major hospitals en route so that both employees and passengers could get immediate aid in case of accidents. In both cases the bills could be settled by the company on a monthly basis.

Every bus had a driver, a conductor and a helper who all possessed driving licences and basic knowledge of bus repairs. They were all covered by a Mediclaim Insurance of Rs. 1 lakh and a Life Insurance of Rs. 2 lakhs. It also had a mobile phone, a first aid box and a fully equipped tool kit. In addition every bus had a contingency kitty of Rs. 3000 which could be used only during an emergency. Pay scales for each category were:

Driver	: Rs. 4500 - 100 - 6500
Conductor	: Rs. 3500 - 50 - 5500
Helper	: Rs. 2500 - 50 - 4000

There was only one union for all Totaram Transport Employees controlled by the Party in power and the industrial relations climate was peaceful. Relationship with the State bureaucracy was also congenial and officialdom was never an impediment to the company. The Press also was favourable since the employees were treated professionally and received a better deal than any state or privately owned organisation could offer.

During the one-year period before the 2004 elections however, leaders from the INTUC started making trouble and started harassing the employees of Totaram Transport. The Opposition Party used its influence to get the Police to also harass the bus crews. The MPSRTC also put pressure on the Government to limit the expansion of Totaram Transport's business. Many politicians from the Opposition Party applied for and received licences to ply mini buses, which offered fares that were cheap for the passengers. Of course, the company over worked and underpaid employees operating these mini buses. Fringe benefits were virtually non-existent and everyone was on a daily or hourly wage.

This presented a threat to the business interests of Totaram Transport Company since the Indian masses were generally uncaring about safety and comfort as long as the fares were low. The employees of the mini bus companies were contract labour and non-unionised. Totaram went into action at once and contacted his friends in the trade union. He told them to make inroads into the unorganised min bus employees.

The Trade Union controlled by the Party in power slowly took over the control of these mini-bus employees and championed their cause. They went on a public awareness campaign using the press to show the difference between the benefits given to the employees of Totaram Transport Company and the employees of others. The owners of the mini buses cried foul and filed a case against both the union and owners of Totaram Transport on grounds of inciting workers and causing wilful hindrance to free trade. The Government supported the mini bus owners and the Indore Bench of the M.P. High Court placed a stay on the union propaganda. The mini bus business began afresh and the owners summarily dismissed the workers' leaders of the workers were by The Press took up the case of the dismissed workers and top leaders in all major political parties in MP distanced themselves from the issue.

ISSUES:

- ***What should Totaram Transport Company do?***
- ***What should the Trade Union do?***
- ***What can the Press do to help the cause of the contract workers?***

HINT:

The public relations department of Totaram Transport could mount an aggressive publicity campaign showing what they are doing for their employees and not draw any comparisons. This is something the company can do legitimately and nobody can object to it. The High Court stay order will not affect it. This will assist the striking workers. Totaram Transport Company could even try to buy out the mini bus owners and thereby expand their own business. This is where industrial relations and corporate strategy meet to join hands. The Trade Union Act 1926 allows any seven workers to form a union and so the option of forming a trade union and registering it could be looked into. Once the union is registered, the dispute becomes an industrial dispute and the provisions of the ID Act 1947 come into play. The union should at once proceed against the owners of mini buses in the Labour Court for unfair dismissal of an employee.

A Strike is a legitimate trade union weapon and its use in this case could be considered. However, secondary picketing is illegal so the employee of Totaram Transport Company should remember to stay afar and lend moral support in the event of a strike. The Strike must be legal in all ways e.g. a charter of demands must be submitted and due notice be served. The Press should be mobilised to help the cause of the striking workers. It is precisely because of the feudal-mercantilist-trader mindset of the owners of capital that contract labour is so wantonly exploited in India. This point, if used carefully in the Press, before the general election could tip the scales in favour of the workers.

The importance of public perception of any industrial cause is very important and industrial relations officers should never allow the Press to be antagonistic to the company. This is where maintaining proactive contact and liaison with the larger society becomes important for Strategic HR.

❑❑❑

CASE 46

INCIDENT AT CALICUT REFINERIES

Calicut Refineries Limited (CRL) is a publicly owned company set up with Saudi collaboration in Kerala. It is situated about 25 kms north of main city. It had the latest equipment when it was set up in 1960 because of a Member of Parliament honouring his electoral pledge to the people. However, since then technology was not updated adequately for a variety of reasons. However, certain amendments had been made in CRL designs and the layout of the shop floor was quite modern by Indian standards. CRL had about 12,000 men-on-rolls and the Head office of the company was located in Cochin, which is also known for its rich petroleum refining resources. About 750 persons manned the Head Office while the General Manager sat in the plant office.

CRL consists of several divisions each of which had a dedicated Personnel Officer, who reported administratively to the Divisional Manager, but functionally, reported to the Chief Personnel Manager, CRL, who sat in the head office. The same was true of functions like Finance, Materials and Maintenance.

The trade union, CRL Mazdoor Sangh (CRLMS), was not affiliated to either the CITU or the AITUC but individual workers were members of CITU and AITUC by personal choice. The union consequently enjoyed dual support and had a 3-tier organisation. The General Secretary and the President were political leaders not in the employment of CRL. Each Division had an Assistant General Secretary and a Vice President who were CRL employees, but who were relieved of their job responsibility for full time union work. The third tier consisted of Shop Stewards who were full time employees of CRL. The Assistant General Secretary and the Vice President were elected every five years and experience showed that, once in power, they were never removed. The Shop Stewards were elected every three years and there were instances when persons were not re-elected if they fell foul with the union leadership. There were other small unions, like the one affiliated to the INTUC and the HMS, which were very much on the fringes and did not have a sizeable membership.

It was, therefore, not unexpected that when Sunita Singh, a student from IIM (Calicut) who was majoring in Human Resources did her summer project at CRL, her findings showed that: (a) There was evidence of a labour aristocracy. (b) There was a degree of alienation between the regular members and the first and second tier leadership of the union. (c) There was some degree of cohesiveness between the regular members and the shop stewards. (d) During times of crisis, the shop stewards were known to invariably take an anti-management stand. (e) There were also occasions when the shop stewards openly fell out with the second tier leadership but these incidents never escalated.

According to the Personnel Officer in charge of the oil tank division an amount of lethargy and sloth had set into the first and the second tiers of the union leadership essentially because of four reasons:

(i) Some senior members of the Personnel Department had pampered the union leaders.

(ii) They were too sure of their continuation in office.

(iii) Divisional Heads had helped union leaders to become sub-contractors through firms opened up in the name of their kith and kin to which the refinery was outsourcing certain functions like transportation and canteen services.

(iv) Senior members of the trade union came to work in chauffer driven cars and although they were drawing wages as workmen, they never did a bit of work.

Consequently, a number of sweat heart deals' were struck between some members of the Personnel Department and the Trade Union for mutual benefit. To add to this some strategic changes in policy were also made in the interest of the refinery. For instance, target setting was introduced along with productivity based incentive schemes in 1994. The workers accepted these after a bit of grumbling and they were working out quite well.

Globalisation and liberalization of India's economy coupled with a rise in oil prices in 2004 to a high of US$50 per barrel of crude had placed enormous pressure on the company to perform better. This forced CRL to tighten its belt and cut costs. Since safety costs were conveniently cut, many divisions were forced to gloss over the provisions of the law in respect of industrial safety.

CRL had also traditionally guaranteed a job to one person from the family of every employee who had served 25 years in the company, and one person from the family of every person who had a fatal accident out of and in the course of employment. As a part of the cost cutting exercise, Radhakrishnan Pillai, the General Manager, had arranged with Kallu Rao, the Chief Personnel Manager, and, Srikumar Jayashanker, the Chief Finance Manager, to do away with the automatic employment clause. Every case would henceforth be decided on its individual merit. The union did not object.

On Saturday, attendance in the evening shift was unusually low because of a traditional festival the following day. The shift began at 10:00 pm and ended at 6:00 am, and the following day having been a festival, the plant had been shut down for routine maintenance giving automatic leave to a majority of employees. One man operating from the cabin and one attendant below giving directions manned the overhead crane. This was usual but what was unusual was the fact that there was no work for the crane after 3:00 am so the crane operator went to sleep in the cabin above and man working below on the shop floor went off to catch a quick 40 winks behind the huge oil container, which stored processed crude.

The crane driver had overslept. On Sunday morning the cabin operator opened his eyes to see the morning maintenance crew coming in for work and rather than being found asleep he quickly left the premises and went home. He thought that his crane attendant too may have gone home but that was not the case. Unfortunately, soon after the crane attendant had dozed off, a dumper-tipper had unloaded its waste behind the tank and unwittingly covered the sleeping man with tons of rubbish.

On the following Monday the family members of the (now) dead attendant came to the refinery to find out what had become of their man since he had failed to go home on Sunday. The police who had been alerted accompanied the family but nobody at work had a clue about his whereabouts. The same evening a strong stench came from the unloaded waste and people started searching under the pile for what the stench was from. This was about 9:00 pm and the night shift came in and found the police, the fire brigade and a mobile crane being employed to clear the waste. An hour or so later the dead body was found.

After the accident was noticed by the workers and supervisors of the Division in 'night shift, senior officers of the Division were informed and they rushed to the spot. They attempted to send the dead body to the Hospital, for an autopsy, but the workers in the department, as well as some workers of other departments, did not allow the body to be moved. They assembled near the spot. The work in the adjoining departments joined the workers and all work came to a halt. The workers demanded immediate employment to wife/son of the deceased, besides other statutory compensation.

The situation worsened in the morning, in that the dead body of the deceased employee was not allowed to be lifted from the shop floor, even as a mark of respect for the departed soul. More people gathered near the accident site and agitated for immediate employment of wife/son of the deceased. Work on the shop floor in the entire division came to a halt. In spite of several rounds of discussion with the workers, the Personnel Officer failed to make headway. There was hardly any change in the situation next morning. However, attempts for lifting the dead body and starting of work in the division continued and ultimately, work was resumed and the dead body sent to the Hospital in the late evening of Tuesday.

It was an unfortunate event that an accident of this nature took place on the day of the traditional festival. Equally, unfortunate was the fact that the workers did not permit the workman's corpse to be lifted from the spot and sent to the Hospital for well over 36 Hrs. In addition, this became the causal factor for the work stoppage in the almost entire refinery for one and half days. There was no disagreement by anybody that the said workman died in the accident due to employment injury (Injury On Works) and that compensation benefits would be given to the family of the deceased, as per the statutory provisions and other rules in force in the company. The agitation prolonged on the demand for immediate employment of wife/minor son of the deceased workman, which was not justified.

It was revealed during the several rounds of discussions/meetings with workers at various levels, spread over two days, that there was lack of awareness about legal provisions relating to injury on work, IOW. Under the existing statutory provisions and Memorandum of Settlements of the Company, in the case of death of a workman due to IOW, permanent employment of his son/son-in-law was guaranteed, subject to his being found suitable for employment, in addition to the monetary compensation payable under the Workmen's Compensation Act. The agitating workers were asking for immediate employment of the wife of the deceased workman or of the minor son, who was below 18 years of age. The workers' demand was unacceptable by the company authorities since under the Company's Standing Orders, there was no provision for employment of a person below 18 years of age, and there was genuine difficulty in placing an uneducated woman, who came from an orthodox family background, on a shop floor. Even an assurance to the effect that employment of the son will be considered when he attains the age of 18 years, could cut no ice. Since workers were demanding preparation of employment papers either of the wife or the son before permitting the dead body to be sent to the hospital, and this was not possible, there was some amount of needless acrimony. Constant counselling had to be done to convince workers about this provision, which revealed total lack of awareness of IOW provisions among Workers, Supervisors and Managers of the Division.

During the two days of volatile situation in the refinery, some of the Union Committee Members showed total indifference to the situation, while others were helpless, (because, by that time, external forces had taken over the leadership of the agitation) and some of the Committee Members joined hands with the agitating workmen. The Union Office-bearer also could not do much to improve the situation.

From the morning shift (6:00 am - 2:00 pm) of Wednesday, many external forces with stakes including the local Congress Party leader joined the issue and it was felt that leadership in the agitation had been taken over by them. These forces included forces opposed to the recognised Union, temporary workers who were expecting permanency in the company, neighbours of the deceased employee working in other divisions of the refinery, relatives of the deceased who were employees of the refinery and some other disgruntled elements, with a view to fish in troubled waters. This was the reason that whenever a group of workmen agreed to transfer the dead body to the hospital, some of these forces provoked the workmen not to do so. Some of the examples were:

- Whenever senior officers of the Division/Company were counselling the workmen, these external forces were very vocal in raising issues on behalf of workers. The issues were: 'Why the deceased person's wife cannot be given employment?', 'Why his son, who is about 18 years old, cannot be given employment and why his employment papers cannot be made right away?', 'What is the guarantee that after the dead body is lifted from the shop floor, employment of the ward will be provided ?', etc.
- When management attempted to resume work the next morning, these forces would not permit it nor would they allow the body to be lifted.
- During the 1st day of the agitation, there was no work stoppage in other divisions of the refinery but on the 2nd day, some of the workers, who either were neighbours of the deceased employee or had some axe to grind, took the lead and stopped the work throughout the refinery in the morning shift. Work could be re-started there only after the situation had become normal in the late evening of the second day.

During the whole period of turmoil and indecision, most of the middle managers and supervisors of the refinery showed an attitude of helplessness, either with regard to the issue of the dead body of the workman lying on the shop floor or with regard to the work stoppage in their departments. Investigation revealed that a few of them spoke in tune with the workers, without realising the implications. This aggravated the situation considerably.

ISSUES:

1. ***Why did it take the management so long to remove the dead body?***
2. ***Why was outside workers leadership able to come in and exploit the situation?***
3. ***Examine the role of the Divisional Management, the Supervisors, Union and the Personnel Department in the light of what transpired in the case.***

HINT:

It is always a good practice to deal with a strong union i.e. one which can commit to deliver and deliver as committed. In this case, the union on the shop floor was relatively weak and had allowed external forces to gain control of a situation and exploit it.

Lines of communication through constant dialogue between the Personnel Officers and the workmen must be kept open. In this case, the Personnel Officer failed to make any headway because he had come on the scene too late and had allowed the situation to escalate.

Safety is a major industrial concern that cannot be compromised in the name of cost cutting or competitive pressures. It is the duty of the HR Manager to insure that this never happens.

Whenever the labour aristocracy becomes powerful, mediocrity thrives and the union leaders become managers of discontent. The gulf between the leadership and the regular members widens and in times of crisis, the situation easily gets out of hand. Then the organisation suffers and so it is the duty of HR Administration (Personnel Officers) to make sure that this situation does not arise.

This case is based on an accident in a non-oil company in Northern India during the Autumn of 2002, to the facts of which the author was privy.

❑❑❑

CASE 47

WHEN LIBERTY BECOMES LICENSE

Ajay was in shock as his job was at stake. Sitting in the enquiry officer's room for the first time, in the summer of 1995, he realised how everything was suddenly so different, how vulnerable he was. All along, he had thought that he could do anything he wished. Therefore, there was a gnawing feeling that he may have been used and discarded by the very management who seemed to have empowered him in the first place. Pico Steel was a private sector company with a turnover of over Rupees 4000 crores in 1994-95. The company belonged to a well-diversified group, with the group turnover of over Rupees 25,000 crores in 1994-95. Founded way back in 1920's, the company had adopted a technology that was primarily labour intensive. Management, hitherto, felt that the company's strength lay in its ability to produce almost anything, ranging from pins to cranes, 'in-house'. This kind of an attitude on the part of the early planners led to massive investments in several related areas. Therefore, though the investments in fixed assets were substantial, the asset turnover rate was far below industry standards.

With liberalisation in the country's economy leading to de-licensing of the industry and de-control of steel, it was evident that something had to be done quickly. Import duties were being slashed and there was widespread belief that free market economy would soon take over. With prices being determined on a competitive basis, it became even more necessary for Pico Steel to cut flab as quickly as possible. Having failed to invest in the state of the art technology, it became imperative for the company to drastically improve upon labour efficiency and productivity, since the already high capital output ratio was adding weight to the sinking company's bottom line. Profitability was gradually but steadily declining over the years and especially after the recent wake of liberalisation, the dip became even more perceptible. In fact, the company was in the red for the past 2 years and had been struggling to stay afloat. The accumulated losses, as on date, were more than Rupees 1000 crores. With the creditors adding more and more strings to their lending, the company had little options but to resort to some drastic measures. The industrial relations scenario, over the years, was largely stable. Barring a few minor disturbances in 1946, 1951 and 1955, the overall relationship was congenial. A bitter experience in the past had led to a lockout of the factory for over 6 months, in 1946, leading to damages of capital equipment itself amounting to several lakhs of rupees. Therefore, to safeguard itself against such similar recurrence, the management decided to keep the union 'satisfied'. Collective bargaining was more or less a formality and the management seldom turned down any issue.

There were over 80,000 employees in the organisation, of which the workers and supervisors segment comprised of 75,000. The managerial cadre comprised of the rest. The structure was typically pyramidal, with over 14 layers between the highest and the lowest levels. Decision-making was usually top down and the large number of levels was not without its own problems of delays and distortions in communication. Initially, during the 1940's, there were over 25 unions, each vying for membership. The inter-union rivalry was so intensive that management then was at a fix as to how to put an end to it.

The management was quick to realise that with too many unions claiming majority, it would become difficult for the management to strike out a long term settlement with any source of power that could ensure long term stability. A conscious effort was put up to unite all those petty unions and thus a representative group was formed, which over the years, consolidated into a single large union with a membership of over 50,000 employees. In fact, this situation has remained for over the past 35 years and has led to the union to grow from strength to strength. Every now and then, the union would flex its muscle and the management would have no other option but to humbly submit to the charter of demands put up by the union. In fact, it became apparent that the management had created its own Frankenstein. Over the years, the company enjoyed monopoly profits and it did not mind keeping the workers satisfied, as long as industrial harmony was not adversely affected. This led to a progressive deterioration in the work culture and ever increasing demands by the union. Now, the management reckoned, the time had come when the company would not only face domestic competition with new technology, but also on the import front, things would be different. The time had come to tighten belts.

Ajay, 29, was a worker in the SMS (Steel Melting Shop) Unit. He had joined the company 5 years back at the lowest level, as a mazdoor. Somehow, things never went right for Ajay, ever since he dropped out from the school in 1980. Having been born in a good upper middle class family, Ajay was the youngest son of his parents. However, he somehow had walked into wrong company and the situation had worsened since then. Not only did he neglect his education, he started smoking pot and took to alcoholism. Even at his home, there prevailed a tense atmosphere. The family members somehow never seemed to have time for each other. Everyone always seemed too busy with his or her own affairs. The father was a strict disciplinarian, but never cared to help beyond that. Ajay used to get beaten up invariably. He was the problem child for his parents. Therefore, when he dropped out from the school in 1980, his father was so furious that he disowned him and asked him never to come back home again. With nobody to turn to, Ajay undertook odd jobs every now and then, until one day he managed to find employment in Pico Steel, through a family friend. With lack of educational qualifications, he could only gain entry at the mazdoor level. Nevertheless, he accepted the offer, because it was the most that he could get.

As if his problems were not enough, he landed himself into even greater difficulty, when one day, while travelling by the local train, he fell in love with the girl sitting opposite. It was quite an impulsive decision and he got married to her within a week. His wife was a nurse in one of the local hospitals and also a graduate. She was earning more than him. Initially, for the first few months until the glamour lasted, it was all right. However, Ajay was not the kind who could settle down. He was highly temperamental by nature and the slightest provocation was enough to ignite him. Finally, the male chauvinism in him overpowered him, and he forced his wife to quit her job. This was just the beginning of his troubles. He soon became the father of a baby girl and found it almost impossible to make both ends meet.

Though the company paid him a substantial salary, it just didn't seem enough. He did manage a couple of over time bookings every month and it barely helped him make both ends meet. One day, his friend suggested to him a way to become rich fast. "Why don't you take a loan from the company and invest it in the stock market? You could get rich overnight". Acting on this suggestion, he managed a loan of Rupees 25,000 and invested it in the stock market, on some speculative scrip.

As luck would have it, there was an immediate crash in the stock market and almost everything was sunk. This was a major blow to him and he totally lost control. At home, he even started beating his wife on the flimsiest of excuses. In his workplace, there was a marked change in his attitude. He became insincere. His job was to shift bags of raw material on the furnace floor, from the railway wagons to their respective places. Not only was his job physically labour intensive, it was perceived to be non-challenging and non-satisfying. The working environment was very dusty and noisy. Ajay did not have good relations with his colleagues and remained aloof. Although his work started at 0600 hrs, he invariably reported late to duty. Everyday he would come up with some excuse for coming late to the factory. After roaming here and there, he would go to the canteen at 8.30 and would finally be ready for work by 9.30 hours only. At 10.30, he would again visit the canteen for tea and by 11.30; he would be back at his job, knowing that his supervisor would be out for lunch by then. This way, he effectively managed to dodge work.

There were complaints from all quarters about Ajay. His boss was getting increasingly concerned everyday. Not only was Ajay not doing his job, he was setting bad examples for others. However, the boss was hesitant to take any action against Ajay, as Ajay had some connection with the underworld mafia of the city. Earlier also, when Ajay was reprimanded, he had threatened the use of external parties to settle accounts. This way, Ajay almost invariable got his way out. In view of the competitive business environment, the management decided that it would undertake the following measures with immediate effect:

1. All overtime arrangements would be stopped.
2. A card punching system would be introduced, to log in and out time of the workers.
3. Unauthorised absence from work to be strictly dealt with.

Although a settlement had to be made with the union representatives on these points, there were quite a few who were not satisfied. For Ajay, this meant a lot of restriction, something that the he was never used to all his life. Until now, overtime was taken for granted. Now, even that had come to an end. The idea of punching card was just too repulsive for him. Only for special cases, it was left to the discretion of the boss to certify late coming to work. Seeing the loopholes in the system, Ajay was confident of getting his daily attendance certified by his boss and he continued to come late everyday.

On the last day of the month, when Ajay, as expected, produced the certified attendance sheet for approval by his boss, he had a surprise in store for him: a charge sheet was forwarded to him. In addition, the boss was not alone in his office. Seeing the charge sheet, Ajay saw red. How could anyone dare to charge sheet him? The devil in him took over. He resorted to abusive and filthy language in front of everyone. When the boss reprimanded him for his language, Ajay turned on the boss, held his collar and slapped him. Then he charged out of the office. A second charge sheet, with suspension pending enquiry, was immediately typed out in the name of Ajay. It was clear that the boss had stored enough gunpowder to confront Ajay this time. In addition, he was working to a plan.

ISSUES:

What could have been done to avoid this ugly scene? Should a stitch in time not have saved the proverbial nine stitches?

In industrial relations situations should special concessions be allowed to certain individuals by the HR Officer, whatever be the reason?

HINT:

There is no doubt that a sinner has to be condemned. In this case, it is Ajay. However, what of those who encouraged and pampered Ajay by ignoring his earlier misdemeanours? And what of those who brought Ajay to this world and considered status building in the society to be a far greater priority than nurturing a responsible citizenship?

Is freedom not the ultimate goal of Man and Civil Society? When does individual freedom become the bane of society? This can be insured only when industrial relations practices are based on trust and transparency and when industrial relations policies are based on business ethics and corporate governance.

This case study is born out of a personal experience of a former work colleague of the author's father, late Mr. Georgy Sorabji of Jamshedpur. The colleague in question had left TISCO to join another steel company. This case study was first included in the book Business Ethics: Concepts and Cases 1998.

❑❑❑

CASE 48

KALIMATI FOUNDRY AND FORGE SHOP

Located 15 Kms north of Jamshedpur on the highway to Ranchi, Kalimati Foundry and Forge Shop came into existence in 1980 when industrial giants like Tata Steel, Tata Motors, Indian Tube Co. and Indian Steel & Wire Products started outsourcing their requirements of spares and small machine parts that were not economical to manufacture in their own factories. In spite of being a privately owned Medium Scale firm, Kalimati Foundry and Forge Shop (KFFS) was managed professionally. Total Quality Management (TQM) was a byword for their operational processes, and by 1992 it had already applied for the ISO 9002 certification and obtained it the following year.

The General Manager, Mr. Shashi Bhushan Tiwari one very early morning in May 1999 while on a surprise check of the plant found a group of workers playing cards behind an empty ladle. When he asked them why they were not at work, they replied that the night shift target had been met and since it was only 4:00 am they were relaxing before the end of shift (i.e. at 6:00 am). The same evening Mr. Tiwari called a meeting of the senior officers and did two things. First, he formed a committee of four persons (the Head of Production, the Head of Maintenance, the Head of Quality and Inspection and the Head of Human Resources to devise a new productivity linked incentive scheme that would motivate employees to continue working even after the targets were met. Second, he issued instructions to every Senior Officer above the rank of Manager to pay at least two surprise checks on the entire shop floor during each month. All irregularities were to be reported to Mr. Tiwari personally next day. The HR Officer was, in addition, asked to liase with the trade union to secure their cooperation in this exercise.

Exactly one month later to the date Mr. Ashutosh Dubey, the Manager of the Heat Treatment Section was on a surprise check at 1:00 am. He found Mr. Ram Khelawan, the Supervisor of that Section, sleeping on a bench away from the heat of the 30 ton Mains Frequency Induction Furnace. Waking him up rudely, Mr. Dubey demanded an explanation from Mr. Ram Khelawan. It was well known that Mr. Ram Khelawan was popular with his workers and although he had an M. Tech. Degree from IIT Kharagpur he never flaunted his qualification or his knowledge. Mr. Ram Khelawan responded by stating that since it was an unusually warm night he was exhausted by the high furnace temperature and was merely resting while the heat of the furnace was getting ready to be tapped and he was not asleep. Mr. Ashutosh issued him a warning letter next morning and left it at that. Three weeks later when Mr. Ram Khelawan was in the night shift again, Mr. Dubey went for a surprise check at 2:30 am. Once again he saw Mr. Ram Khelawan sleeping and once again he woke him up rudely. When asked for an explanation, Mr. Ram Khelawan repeated exactly what he had said on the previous occasion. This time however, Mr. Ram Khelawan added that his statement about the furnace heat waiting to be tapped was correct, as was the case earlier. Mr. Dubey found this to be true but to hide his humiliation he issued Mr. Ram Khelawan a second written warning.

This time Mr. Ram Khelawan replied in writing. He stated that Mr. Dubey was a Brahamin and was needlessly picking on Mr. Ram Khelawan who was a Bhumihar. He added that Mr. Dubey had an inferiority complex since all he had was a Diploma in Engineering from a Polytechnic and everybody knew that Mr. Ram Khelawan was more qualified and skilled than he was. He pooh poohed the issue and went to the extent of accusing Mr. Dubey of playing caste based politics on the shop floor.

You also know that Mr. Dubey is an upright man who would never indulge in playing workplace politics. Although he was a Brahamin, Mr. Dubey had never displayed a caste bias. He was surely less qualified academically than Mr. Ram Khelawan but on the work front his knowledge was insuperable. He was generally an amiable person but was known to have a short temper, which would cool down as soon as it had shot up. He bore no grudges and yet took no nonsense from anyone. During his 8 years career with the company his record was spotless. He was a disciplinarian but was always ruled by his conscience. Such an accusation by Mr. Ram Khelawan has both angered Mr. Dubey and rendered him distraught.

You are the HR Officer in charge of the Heat Treatment Section. Maintaining shop floor discipline is one of your KRAs. Mr. Dubey approached you the next morning with the complaint and asked you to advise whether a charge sheet for gross insubordination could be issued. You made independent inquiries and found that Mr. Ram Khelawan was indeed in the habit of sleeping during the night shift since he also ran tuition classes and was usually very tired at the end of the day.

What would you, as the HR Officer, advise Mr. Dubey the Manager of the Heat Treatment Section? Explain why would you take the stand.

HINT:

Such acts of indiscipline are not uncommon on the shop floor. Ideally Mr. Ram Khelawan should be counselled first. But that option is no longer available to you as two warnings have been issued.

As the HR Officer it is your duty to give legally correct advice under the law of the land. In this case it is an offence under the Industrial Employment Standing Orders Act 1951 and a domestic inquiry under the Industrial Disputes Act, 1947 can be conducted. As HR Officer you must first enlighten Mr. Dubey regarding the law and then advise him how to deal with smart offenders. This is perfectly ethical since sleeping while on duty is hazardous as well as improper.

A caution is not a punishment but a warning is. Hence, it is always better to issue a verbal caution, record it and then issue a written caution the next time. A warning can be issued on the third occasion either with or without an inquiry. But it is better to have witnesses on Mr. Dubey's side while recording the evidence on the scene of the offence.

Hence, if Mr. Ram Khelawan was indeed in the habit of sleeping on the night shift, Mr. Dubey should pay another surprise visit to the shop floor at night in a month or two. Then if he found Mr. Ram Khelawan sleeping he should get a supervisor (even from another department like maintenance or stores or inspection) to come as a witness and to confirm the fact and then only wake him up in the presence of the witness. Thereafter a charge sheet can be issued to Mr. Ram Khelawan for dereliction of duty. The statement of the supervisor must be taken in writing before issuing the charge sheet to avoid retraction at the inquiry.The fact that previous warnings were issued to Mr. Ram Khelawan would help to strengthen the position of Mr. Dubey at the domestic inquiry.

The fact that the furnace was not yet ready to be tapped while he was resting is no defence. Furthermore if it could be established that Mr. Ram Khelawan was taking private tuitions could be treated as either double employment or moon lighting and another charge could be added to the charge sheet.

It is your task to help Mr. Dubey to draft the charge sheet but as an Inquiry Officer you cannot sign the charge sheet. That has to be signed by Mr. Dubey as the Departmental Head. It matters not that he is also the main complainant. That supervisor who witnessed the act would confirm the charge.

❑❑❑

CASE 49

TAKING ON THE OWNERS

Dr. Deepak Mehta was a microbiologist by training who had secured a Doctorate in Management Studies as well. The family to which he belonged was very feudal in its outlook and had their own (substantial) investments in the agriculture, wine making and transport businesses. However, Deepak looked upon himself as a modern manager who had always been interested in starting his own business. The Mehta family came from a small village some 200 kilometres away from Baroda off the Ahmedabad Highway from where all operations were conducted by remote control. The patriarch of the family was into big time politics and he wielded enormous clout in the rural-industrial sector. His power base came from the Muslim population in his electoral district whom he pampered and even gave special allowances to pilgrims going on Haj every year.

Deepak had married a German lady and lived in India only about ten days in a month spending the rest of the time abroad. Nobody was quite sure what he actually did but he had contacts with several middle order educational institutions abroad. From time to time some foreign academicians would accompany him to India and the good offices of the family patriarch were used to arrange visits of these foreigners to Indian universities. Deepak started a company dealing with engineering parts, based it in Pune but within three years it failed miserably and was wound up in 1995. Deepak decided that his next venture must be in Gujarat where his family had political clout. Two years later he started a drug manufacturing company with Scandinavian collaboration on the Surat-Ahmedabad road. The company was called Mehta Pharmaceutical Drugs and was managed by Deepak's nephew (elder brother's son) Jitendra Mehta. Having a Masters Degree in Management gave Jitendra a kind of false consciousness wherein he saw himself as an industrial magnate. Unfortunately, Jitendra was a little dim witted and very much of a Casanova whose indiscriminate drinking and womanising record was public knowledge. At heart he was a nice person but was unable to take any decisions on his own and had to rely on Deepak to tele-guide him at every step. Deepak believed in the policy of hire and fire, expected his managers to be transparent although he never was so himself, and except for a handful of persons nobody was employed on a long-term basis. The employment in these cases was contractual and renewable. The company was not a very good paymaster but did not enforce targets, standards and quality rigidly giving the supervisors a very long rope. Since the company did not pay well, many of its employees were of mediocre quality and many of these were persons who could not get a job elsewhere.

By 1998 the US - Arab relations had soured and its effect on the import of pharmaceutical drugs had been telling. Deepak grabbed the opportunity and took a few influential Mullahs along with him for a tour of Arab countries in the December of 1998. This is when Mehta Pharmaceutical Drugs got their first export order and slowly this gambit paid off. Then in 2000 Mehta Pharmaceutical Drugs entered the export market with a bang and by the May of 2003 they became a recognisable player in the export market of pharmaceutical drugs to Arab countries. In order to make profits the company was cutting corners at every step and when George Bush invaded Iraq their profit levels soared.

The Quality Control Manager, Dr. Debashish Govind, who was very popular with the employees for his honesty, spoke to the HR Manager about the possible problems of chasing profits blindly. The HR Manager replied that this was a policy issue over which he had no control. In frustration Dr. Govind wrote a strongly worded confidential letter to Jitendra Mehta pointing out the hazards of some of the drugs supplied to Arab countries by the company and requested management to take a fresh look at things. Instead of appreciating this social concern, Jitendra on the orders of Dr. Deepak Mehta tape recorded his telephonic conversations, hacked into his personal e-mail account and on some trumped up charges dismissed Dr. Govind in August 2004. It was no wonder that a competitive pharmaceutical drugs firm in Gujarat employed Dr. Govind at once, gave him a higher salary and made him in charge of its three plants scattered across the state.

Dr. Deepak Mehta then called an impromptu meeting, addressed the other executives and told them that if anyone dared to question company policy, they could look out for other pastures. Soon thereafter three top-level executives known for their knowledge of drug manufacturing quit the company. Mr. Jitendra Mehta suddenly became more aggressive and autocratic than before and in the process even antagonised an otherwise conciliatory local trade union leadership.

One day in November 2004 a computer operator accidentally found the letter written by Dr. Govind to Jitendra Mehta, took a print out of the same and gave it to the local Trade Union leaders. They in turn passed in its contents on to the workers in a public rally. The Union demanded an explanation from Mr. Jitendra Mehta and when this was not forthcoming, they called for an indefinite strike. Mr. Jitendra Mehta responded by ordering a lockout and stated that everyone who took part in the spontaneous strike would be covered by the no work, no pay dictum. Workers abstained from work en masse. The Union passed on the letter to the Chief Labour Commissioner and he, in turn, asked the State Government to ask the CBI and the Anti Corruption Bureau to institute a judicial inquiry. A question was raised during the Zero Hour debate and next morning the newspapers carried the story in gory detail. Mr. Jitendra Mehta sent a lawyer's notice to Dr. Govind charging him with breach of professional confidence. Mr. Govind calmly passed the letter on to the Press that published it next morning. The Union simultaneously circulated Dr. Govind's letter to the workers and gave copies of it to the Press. Along with it came a summary of the well known report on banned and banable drugs by Dr. Mira Shiva and Dr. Wishwas Rane that was freely distributed. Public outcry against the company followed and civil society in general started supporting the striking workers giving them food, money etc. The local schools also waved the tuition fees for the children of the striking workmen.

When the company saw that things were getting rough, they lifted the lockout and invited anyone willing to work to come to duty. The HR Manager sought police protection for the workers who elected to return to work while secondary picketing outside the factory gates escalated.

The points which Dr. Govind had raised questions are summarised below.

1. Using industrial rather than medicinal glycerol is dangerous and can lead to deaths. In May 2003 there were 15 such deaths in Iran and 31 such deaths in Iraq as the hospitals were supplied glycerol by us. The finger of suspicion was pointed towards us but we managed to escape getting blamed. We cannot expect to be the lucky next time around.
2. In UAE we have supplied Rofocoxib regularly. This popular painkiller is known to trigger heart attacks and since the State Policy there is not to report drug related deaths, we once again escaped negative PR and possible conviction in 2003.
3. Severe blood disorders among troops in Iraq were associated with the intake of Analgin, which we supplied to them. The International Red Cross reported this but for want of conclusive evidence we once again escaped the dragnet in early 2004.
4. The Company and especially Mr. Jitendra Mehta was specifically requested by Dr. Govind to go slow on chasing profits at the cost of overlooking social responsibility of business. He also cautioned against the continued policy of exporting dangerous drugs especially without the correct expiry date printed on the boxes and sachets, as had been the company practice.

ISSUES:

- ***Did the computer operator do the right thing by blowing the whistle when the letter was discovered?***
- ***Did the HR Manager act professionally by absolving himself from the issue when Dr. Govind sought his counsel?***
- ***Did the trade union do the right thing by taking up a matter that was directly related to industrial relations?***
- ***What kind of management under Dr. Deepak Mehta and Jitendra Mehta did the company have and what are the possible HR fallouts in such instances?***

HINT:

When a larger issue is at stake and especially one which effects the well being of mankind, blowing the whistle on any irregularity is a social compulsion. In this case the irregularity was criminal in nature.

Strategic HR implies that the HR Manager is a part of the decision-making and decision executing team. In addition, organisational culture building, business ethics and corporate governance fall within the ambit of his professional concern.

There is no hard and fast rule that says that trade unions should take up only those causes that arise out of and in the course of employment.

The feudal-mercantilist-trader mentality of the Mehta duo is not unknown. In fact such attitudes prevail in many privately managed educational institutions as well. Since the HR Manager failed to be the conscience keeper of the organisation this task fell to the lot of the employee collectivity. Care however should, in such cases be taken to insure that the law of the land is not violated because this would arm the trader, (especially with political connections), with a weapon to attack the union.

❑❑❑

CASE 50

WHEN KNOWLEDGE WORKERS UNIONISE

The software engineers at Hyderabad Infotech were very upset. For once, the project leaders, software developers, team members, quality assurors and maintenance engineers spoke in a united voice. The owners of the company were two twin brothers from Kolkata who had studied for their undergraduate degrees at BIT Mesra, hailed from a very rich family background and who had started the company with Rs. 180 lakhs of borrowed capitai and Rs. 80 lakhs of personal investment. One of them, Dr. Lakshmipati Das was an expert in software engineering having earned his Ph.D. from IIT Delhi. The other was Dr. Durgacharan Das was an expert in Marketing having completed his Fellowship in International Business from IIM. Bangalore. When the software boom shifted from Mumbai towards Bangalore and Hyderabad they decided to set up their organisation in the south. Owing to poor electrical power supply situation in Bangalore they chose Hyderabad, bought a plot of land and started their company. From modest beginnings in 1990, they had made a name for themselves by 2003. Their size of market had quadrupled and their profits had risen six times over the period. The company was known for sticking to schedules and for ensuring quality deliverables. In 2000 the two brothers took a decision, which was perhaps the reason for their own undoing. Lakshmipati Das decided to concentrate on research and development activities and Durgacharan Das decided to build international contacts so as to take full advantage of the post 2005 WTO regime. For day-to-day operations they appointed a CEO and his name was Mr. Manoj Gande. He had an MCM Degree, and although a hard worker, was not very well acquainted with the latest technology but was a past master at networking and getting things done. Above all, Manoj gave the picture of being straightforward and honest. In reality he was just the reverse in character. Leaving the responsibility of day-to-day operations to Manoj and introducing a policy of monthly reporting, both the brothers went about creating fresh opportunities of growth for the company.

In order to show him in good light with the Das brothers, Manoj wanted to demonstrate that he was seriously into cost cutting and generating profits. To him the ends justified the means. Consequently, Manoj became parsimonious with his handouts and started short changing the employees and making promises that he had no intention of keeping. In this he was assisted by two yes men one of who was a marketing officer and the other was a handyman who doubled up as the in charge of a computer laboratory and the executive assistant to Manoj. The employees had derisively nicknamed them as Twiddle Dum and Twiddle Dee. The third person who lent support to Manoj was a person from his village who had an Australian wife and could be conveniently described as a comprador bourgeois with rural roots. He kept Manoj happy with a stead supply of wine and ostentatious other creature comforts. He was known as the Kangaroo. Over a three-year period Manoj lost touch with the grassroots of the company and was doing exactly what his three relatively dim witted but capricious henchmen told him to do. Uncertainty and frustration started taking its toll as productivity levels fell. This spurred Manoj into declaring that since profit levels were below expectations there would be no annual increments given until the financial situation improved. Many old timers left the organisation and new recruits were given a lower starting pay than that was given to their equals when they had joined three years ago. This created a little more resentment and employees began to speak openly of things like having a proper grievance handling system, transparent promotion and transfer policies, and proper wage scales for everyone implying an end to the consolidated salary system along with a proper leave policy. There were several spokesmen but no leader in this fomentation of employee discontent. In fact nobody had even mentioned the fact that a union should be formed. All they were speaking of institutionalising systems and processes. What appeared to be a promising business proposition had become sour by May 2004.

Both Lakshmipati and Durgacharan realised that while they were operating in a rarefied business atmosphere and planning along international standards, ground realities in Hyderabad Infotech were steadily regressing both in form and content. They asked Manoj Gande to find an H R Specialist who could help set things right. To begin with he stipulated that all decisions made by Project Managers must be approved by him and that no expenditure (including travel bills) could be settled without his approval. This took days as a strong office bureaucracy prevailed. This added to everyone's frustration uniting knowledge workers at all levels in the hierarchy.

Manoj left this task to his three henchmen who went about looking for someone who could crush the aspirations of the knowledge workers with an iron fist and prevent them from forming a union. In their quest they found one Dr. Ms. Shubhada Kumar to be the right person for this job. She was a socialite, had several contacts in high places across the country but was not quite a person who would roll up the sleeves and get on to doing the task. Moreover, although she was a good human being, she was a little too confident of her abilities. To her credit lay the fact that she was a persuasive speaker and the ability to charm male members into listening to what she spoke and act accordingly. She assured Manoj that she would keep the situation under control and not allow the knowledge workers to unionise. Accordingly, Manoj assured Lakshmipati and Durgacharan that all would soon be well on the people management front.

Next morning (Friday) she issued the following circular.

Dear Colleagues 21.05.2004

It has come to my notice that some of you are not too happy with the state of affairs here. Management has taken some very necessary measures with which you are not in agreement. That is natural given the turbulent market situation and our need to keep the company afloat. However, I would like to remind you that unions are for blue collared workers and you as intelligent people should not unite against management for any cause whatsoever. Please remember that nothing is gained without some sacrifice and I am concerned that the level of belongingness towards the company on your part is so low.

I am sure you will not take the rash step of forming a union. To demonstrate the goodwill of management all annual increments that were due and kept in abeyance as from June 2002 will be released for all employees with effect from June 2004. However, if anyone is not satisfied with the arrangement he/she can meet the undersigned in her office and provision for a full and final settlement on existing terms will be made at once.

Looking forward to working with you in the future and assuring you of management's kind consideration at all times.

Yours truly,

Dr. Ms. Shubhada Kumar
General Manager Human Resources.
Hyderabad Infotech

On Monday 24.05.2004 Manoj read the notice and was very happy about her stern stand. He caused the notice to be placed on the bulletin board and issued orders to prepare salary cheques according to the circular giving everyone one increment from 01.06.2004. Everybody seemed to be pleased about it but the pleasure was subdued.

One copy of the circular was also sent to both Durgacharan Das and Lakshmipati Das who were visibly upset at the curt language used. They sent a perfunctory reply acknowledging the work and asking the Managing Director to carry on with genuine people management policies.

On 01.06.2004 everybody received their new pay cheques and there was even a small picnic organised the following Sunday. But nevertheless the knowledge workers went ahead and registered a trade union with the authorities naming the union Knowledge Workers' Welfare Association. Its charter read that the Association would work towards ensuring better standards of treatment to the members and a more transparent and fair culture where a learning organisation could flourish. Dr. Kumar and Mr. Manoj were shocked at what happened and did not hide their feelings.

What went wrong and detail what could have been done step wise to avoid the formation of a trade union.

HINT:

- When any employee unionises it is a good thing for the organisation since the employee collectivity acts as a safety valve for releasing tensions and airing grievances, which, if allowed to go un-addressed, would fester and become cancerous.
- A trade union is not necessarily a bad thing to have. In fact it is good for the employees to have a forum that would take up their grievances. It is a fallacy that trade unions are meant only for blue collared workers. It is equally wrong for management to attempt to break any movement by employees to form a union.
- Empowerment without accountability breeds tyrants and arbitrariness flourishes as was the case with Manoj.
- Accountability without empowerment breeds slaves as was the case with the Project Managers.
- Knowledge workers are by temperament very sensitive and must be handled with care. This was not done by Shubhada Kumar.
- The Das brothers trusted the wrong man (Manoj) who had no capacity to deliver results due to his tradition bound mindset. Manoj, in turn, isolated himself from the ground realities by depending excessively on his three favourite henchmen.

- In any organisation where the mediocrat-bureaucrat is all powerful, real time development does not take place. Power must be placed at the point of production or marketing or any function where results can be benchmarked against set targets.
- On the part of the leaders of the employee collectivity, care should always be taken not to become either labour aristocrats or mere managers of discontent.

❑❑❑